Practical Smoothing

This is a practical guide to P-splines, a simple, flexible, and powerful tool for smoothing. P-splines combine regression on B-splines with simple, discrete, roughness penalties. They were introduced by the authors in 1996 and have been used in many diverse applications. The regression basis makes it straightforward to handle non-normal data, like in generalized linear models. The authors demonstrate optimal smoothing, using mixed model technology and Bayesian estimation, in addition to classical tools like cross-validation and AIC, covering theory and applications with code in R. Going far beyond simple smoothing, they also show how to use P-splines for regression on signals, varying-coefficient models, quantile and expectile smoothing, and composite links for grouped data. Penalties are the crucial elements P-splines; with proper modifications they can handle periodic and circular data as w as shape constraints. Combining penalties with tensor products of B-splines extend these attractive properties to multiple dimensions. The appendices offer a systema comparison to other smoothers.

PAUL H. C. EILERS is Professor Emeritus of Genetical Statistics at the Er University Medical Center, Rotterdam, The Netherlands. He received his PhD biostatistics. His research interests include high-throughput genomic data anal chemometrics, smoothing, longitudinal data analysis, survival analysis, and st computing. He has published extensively on these subjects.

BRIAN D. MARX is Professor in the Department of Experimental Statis Louisiana State University. He received his PhD in statistics. His main rese interests include smoothing, ill-conditioned regression problems, and high-chemometric applications, and he has numerous publications on these top currently serving as coordinating editor for the journal *Statistical Modell* coauthor of two books and is a Fellow of the American Statistical Assoc

Practical Smoothing

The Joys of P-splines

Paul H. C. Eilers
Erasmus University Medical Center

Brian D. Marx
Louisiana State University

CAMBRIDGE
UNIVERSITY PRESS

University Printing House, Cambridge CB2 8BS, United Kingdom

One Liberty Plaza, 20th Floor, New York, NY 10006, USA

477 Williamstown Road, Port Melbourne, VIC 3207, Australia

314–321, 3rd Floor, Plot 3, Splendor Forum, Jasola District Centre,
New Delhi – 110025, India

79 Anson Road, #06–04/06, Singapore 079906

Cambridge University Press is part of the University of Cambridge.

It furthers the University's mission by disseminating knowledge in the pursuit of
education, learning, and research at the highest international levels of excellence.

www.cambridge.org
Information on this title: www.cambridge.org/9781108482950
DOI: 10.1017/9781108610247

© Paul H. C. Eilers and Brian D. Marx 2021

First published 2021

Printed in the United Kingdom by TJ Books Ltd., Padstow Cornwall

A catalogue record for this publication is available from the British Library.

Library of Congress Cataloging-in-Publication Data
Names: Eilers, Paul H. C., 1948– author. | Marx, Brian D., 1960– author.
Title: Practical smoothing : the joys of P-splines / Paul H. C. Eilers,
Erasmus University Medical Center, Brian D. Marx, Louisiana State University.
Description: Cambridge, UK ; New York, NY : Cambridge University Press,
2021. | Includes bibliographical references and index.
Identifiers: LCCN 2020016638 (print) | LCCN 2020016639 (ebook) |
ISBN 9781108482950 (hardback) | ISBN 9781108610247 (epub)
Subjects: LCSH: Smoothing (Statistics) | Spline theory.
Classification: LCC QA278 .E397 2021 (print) | LCC QA278 (ebook) |
DDC 511/.4223–dc23
LC record available at https://lccn.loc.gov/2020016638
LC ebook record available at https://lccn.loc.gov/2020016639

ISBN 978-1-108-48295-0 Hardback

To my family (PE)
For Arnold; to Leopold (BDM)

Contents

Preface

It is rare to see the word *joy* in the title of a statistics book. The only example we know is *The Joy of Statistics* by Selvin (2019). We will do our best to be a worthy runner-up.

Our first goal is to present a practical, consistent, and versatile tool. We are not modest: our claim is that P-splines are the best smoother on the planet. Our motto is "show, don't tell," so we present many applications, illustrating the power of this tool. For the skeptics, we provide an appendix with a tabular comparison to the competition. However, our confidence stems from external validation: the many citations that our original paper received in the past quarter century or so. Many of them appeared among the work of other statisticians, yet the majority came from applications in a wide variety of fields of science. Our tool is being used and appreciated.

The plan to write this book is over a decade old; the delay is due to a variety of reasons. Fortunately, over the last few years progress toward this book project changed, and the writing wheel starting spinning. Such a long incubation period can have its drawbacks, but we now have the benefit of writing a much riper book, one that reflects our own distilled understanding of the subject, in combination with a much more mature literature base.

In the chapters to come, we present theory and applications in an easygoing way. We show many graphs to illustrate concepts and applications. The R code for every graph is available as a set of independent short programs on the website https://psplines.bitbucket.io. Not only does this make our results reproducible, but it also gives the reader an accessible and smooth start to analyze their own data. A small R package (JOPS) provides supporting functions.

We have aimed to keep the programs small and self-contained. We make little use of large packages like mgcv and gamlss. Of course, these packages are excellent, and we do not want to compete with them. We believe that our approach provides better insight in the simplicity and power of P-splines. We have done our best to make our programs easy to read.

We have been working together with many colleagues in a number of countries, many of whom we have met at many editions of the International Workshop on Statistical Modelling. Our first contact was at the Workshop in Trento in 1989. Over the years, an active band has formed, of sisters and brothers who enjoy getting together each year, especially in Spain, and discussing developments in theory and practice of P-splines, which indeed has brought joy to our work together.

We thank (in alphabetical order): Martin Boer, Giancarlo Camarda, Iain Currie, Maria Durbán, Gianluca Frasso, Jutta Gampe, Oswaldo Gressani, Philippe Lambert, Dae-Jin Lee, and Maria-Xosé Rodríguez Alvarez.

Iain Currie and Jutta Gampe reviewed a late version of the manuscript. This was a mixed blessing. They are excellent editors, and it was sobering to read their many comments. But they led to an improved book.

We also thank Lauren Cowles, our main contact with Cambridge University Press. She was patient, consistent, and supportive for well over a decade, and sometimes it looked as if she was more confident about the final result than we were ourselves.

Over the years, when we presented several courses on P-splines and B-splines, people asked where their names came from. The prosaic explanation is that the *P* stands for penalties and B-splines is the name de Boor gave to his invention. Jokingly we said that *P* stands for Paul and *B* for Brian. Now that the book is ready, reflecting our long experience, we are confident to say that *B* stands for *best* and *P* for *practical*.

We wish you an enjoyable and very useful journey in the land of P-splines. Don't forget to take a look at the website `https://psplines` `.bitbucket.io`, where you will find a package with data and useful functions, as well as the scripts for all graphs in this book. Play with them to improve your understanding, and adapt them to analyze your own data. Please acknowledge us in a fair way.

1

Introduction

This is a book about P-splines, our favorite smoother, and the best one you can find. We may be a bit biased, because we invented them, but we will try to convince you by showing many applications. We also provide the necessary theoretical details that are needed for a complete understanding. We have practical data analysts in mind, who want to extend their statistical toolbox in new directions, and we rely on many illustrations to stimulate an intuitive understanding of P-splines.

Why are P-splines so good? They start from (generalized linear) regression, the strongest workhorse of statistics. The estimation of curves or surfaces is our goal, so the building blocks of the regression are B-splines. We combine them with a less-familiar ingredient, a penalty, giving P-splines their name. A penalty is a device that, more or less gently, forces the fit of a statistical model in a desired direction, in our case smoothness. Figure 1.1 illustrates the core idea behind P-splines: (i) the smooth fit is the sum of many B-spline basis functions, each having local support and scaled by its own coefficient, and (ii) the penalty enforces further smoothness by discouraging adjacent B-spline coefficients from having values that are too different from each other.

Neither B-splines nor penalties are new ideas, and each has found many applications. B-splines are smoothly joining polynomial segments (of a chosen degree), and they are completely defined by the "knots," the places where the segments meet. You can try to optimize the number and the positions of the knots when fitting a curve to data, but this is a tricky nonlinear problem.

A step forward is to use evenly spaced knots, leaving only the number of B-splines as a design parameter. New problems now arise, especially when the locations of the data points are not evenly distributed. In such a case, some of the splines may have little or no support, meaning that coefficient estimates will be unstable or even impossible to obtain.

1

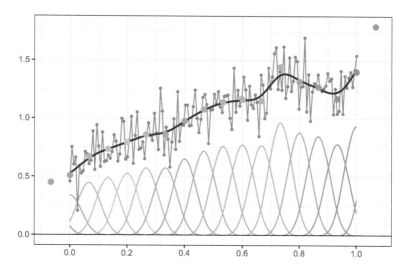

Figure 1.1 The core idea of P-splines: a sum of B-spline basis functions, with gradually changing heights. The small connected gray dots show simulated data. The blue curve shows the P-spline fit, and the large dots the B-spline coefficients (they have the same colors as the splines). R code in f-ps-show.R

O'Sullivan (1986) eliminated the instability problem by combining a relatively large number of B-splines with a roughness penalty. He was inspired by the classical smoothing spline that uses the integral of the squared second derivative of the fitted curve. Exploiting the fact that the curve consists of polynomial segments, he derived a matrix that forms the core of the penalty.

Let B be a regression matrix that contains the B-spline basis functions, and denote α as the corresponding vector of coefficients. The fitted values are $\mu = B\alpha$, and the objective function to be minimized is

$$S = ||y - B\alpha||^2 + \lambda\alpha' P\alpha. \tag{1.1}$$

In the first term we recognize the sum of squares of residuals, familiar from linear regression. The second term measures the roughness of the fitted curve, expressed in the B-spline coefficients. O'Sullivan derived the analytic form of the matrix P; we do not need it in this book, so we skip the details. The parameter λ sets the balance between the deviations from the data and the roughness of the fit. Increasing λ gives the penalty more influence, resulting in a smoother result.

The only innovation of P-splines is a small modification of the penalty: it is based directly on (higher-order) differences of the coefficient vector α, avoiding integrals of squared derivatives. This has several advantages. It is almost trivial to compute the penalty term in (1.1), as P is replaced by $D'D$, where D is a matrix such that $D\alpha$ forms dth-order differences of α. The matrix D can be obtained with one line of code in R or Matlab, for any value of d. One is free to choose any order of the differences, without complications. In principle, O'Sullivan's approach allows higher-order derivatives, but the degree of the B-splines must be high enough, or the derivatives disappear (and with them the penalty). In P-splines, the degree of the B-splines and the order of the penalty can both be chosen freely and independent of each other. In some applications it makes perfect sense to combine, say, piecewise-constant B-splines with third-order differences in the penalty.

We do not pay a price for these attractive simplifications. A look at the Contents should convince you that there are many and diverse applications of P-splines. You will also learn that they are easy to implement. Along the way, you will discover some surprising results and the amazing power of penalties.

The Road Ahead. We lay the groundwork in Chapter 2, presenting (B-spline) regression bases and penalties while illustrating our first applications. In this chapter we also explore responses with non-normal distributions, like counts and binary data, adapting the setting of generalized linear models. We explore interpolation and extrapolation and limits of heavy smoothing. We also present the Whittaker smoother, which can be viewed as a bare-bones form of P-splines. It is suitable for data on a uniform grid when we only are interested in smoothed values on that grid. The B-spline basis matrix is now simplified to the identity matrix. The Whittaker smoother is ideal for studying essential properties of penalties, avoiding details of a B-spline basis. We will employ it several times.

We introduce an important theoretical and practical tool: the effective (model) dimension. It tells us how complex a model is; it will appear frequently in many chapters, especially when we estimate variances.

Next, in Chapter 3, we investigate how to obtain a reasonable value for the penalty tuning parameter λ in (1.1); one option is to minimize data-driven criteria, e.g., cross-validation or AIC. Density estimation by smoothing of histograms gets much attention here. It is a problem of great practical relevance and a good vehicle for showcasing various approaches to optimal smoothing. We also introduce automatic tuning of P-splines with mixed models, showing how penalty parameters can be interpreted as ratios of variances. The same is true for Bayesian P-splines.

We have the tools for automatic selection of smoothing parameter, but we should not use them blindly. Autocorrelation, overdispersion, and digit preference can do serious harm, and we discuss how to handle them properly.

In Chapter 4, we take our first steps into the field of multidimensional smoothing, starting with the generalized additive model. As the name suggests, it neglects interactions and models a response (or its linear predictor) as a sum of smooth functions. B-spline bases are very attractive, as they can simply be chained into one large design matrix, while the penalties can be neatly placed into an appropriate block-diagonal matrix. With this construction, the strong properties of P-splines for simple models automatically become available for additive models. Next, we develop varying coefficient models, which allow standard regression coefficients to vary over another variable, e.g., time, depth, or age.

To fully allow for nonadditive features, like interactions between the explanatory variables, we use tensor products of B-splines in conjunction with proper multidimensional difference penalties.

In the first four chapters, when smoothing a cloud of (x, y) pairs, our interest is only in the expected value of y, conditional on x. Chapter 5 sets a more ambitious goal: estimating sets of curves that characterize the conditional distribution of y. An example are quantile curves, corresponding to a chosen set of probabilities. Although less familiar, expectile curves look better, are easier to compute, and are more efficient than quantile curves. We also pay attention to the GAMLSS framework (Rigby and Stasinopoulos, 2005). It fits models where the distribution of the response variable can be non-normal, and the parameters for variance and skewness of that distribution are modeled as smooth functions of explanatory variables.

Chapter 6 is devoted to the penalized composite link model (PCLM) for counts. This model has received little attention in the literature, but it is a natural candidate when observations are generated by distortions of underlying smooth distributions. Examples include grouping in coarse intervals, digit preference, and overdispersed discrete distributions.

In Chapter 7, P-splines are used for regression on signals, such as spectra and time series. The number of coefficients is large, but they are ordered. This allows the use of a roughness penalty on the coefficients for regularization. Modeling these coefficients by B-splines gives a strong reduction of the system of equations to be solved. Multidimensional signal regression, single-index models, and other extensions are also presented.

The final Chapter 8 presents special applications, like circular B-spline bases, and the separation of signals into components. We also discuss specialized penalties for shape constraints, piece-wise constant smoothing, and adaptive smoothing. Survival and mortality smoothing are also given proper attention here.

The appendices fill in a variety of details, starting with *P-splines for the impatient*, followed by a detailed comparison of P-splines to other popular smoothers (Appendices A and B, respectively). Computational details for the construction of B-splines and efficient computation of (sparse) B-spline bases and stable penalized regression are presented in Appendix C. For large data sets, a straightforward implementation of tensor product P-splines puts very high demands on memory use and computation time. Appendix D presents a very efficient alternative, the so-called array algorithm. P-splines can be written as a mixed model, and variance estimation can be used for optimal smoothing. Appendix E discusses the mixed model equations in detail and shows how they can be simplified. A short Appendix F also discusses standard errors.

The final Appendix G outlines our website. Here we provide documentation – with descriptions and scripts – for every figure in the book. In this way, readers can reproduce our graphs and investigate details of the calculations. We hope that they will explore variations by modifying our code, and applying it in their own work. Our R package (JOPS), with support functions and help files, is available on the website – hopefully, it will find its way into the CRAN repository. It provides core functions for working with P-splines and also contains all data sets that occur in the book. As a teaching tool, a special section of the website provides programs for playing with P-splines interactively.

We have a remark about terminology. When we coined the name P-splines in our 1996 paper (Eilers and Marx, 1996), we thought it was clear what it stood for: many evenly spaced B-splines, combined with a difference penalty. We did not own a trademark, but we hoped to establish a clear name for a clear product. Surprisingly, many workers in the field called various types of penalized splines "P-splines." For example, Yu and Ruppert (2002), Ruppert et al. (2003), and Jarrow et al. (2004) referred to truncated power functions (TPF) with unequally spaced knots as P-splines. This is unfortunate, as we have exposed the disadvantages of penalized TPF in several places in our publications. We hope this book will set the record straight. Historical overviews of P-splines can be found in Eilers and Marx (2010) and Eilers et al. (2015), while our very first writings on the subject go back to Eilers and Marx (1992).

A final remark, about notation. We have not tried to achieve strict uniformity between chapters. That would demand too many symbols with too many decorations like tildes, subscripts, and superscripts. We take a more relaxed approach: notation is consistent within, but not always across, chapters.

2

Bases, Penalties, and Likelihoods

P-splines combine two simple ideas: regression on (many) B-splines and a difference penalty on their coefficients. The B-splines are local functions, each of them covering only a small part of the x-axis. They can give a very flexible fit to data. To keep a fitted curve from getting too flexible, the penalty comes in. It lets adjacent coefficients "hold hands," encouraging a smooth fit. Once the number of B-splines has been set, a single parameter, λ, tunes smoothness.

P-splines have many interesting and useful properties. Interpolation and extrapolation of the fitted curve are automatic. Standard errors and derivatives of the fitted curve are easy to compute.

With a heavy penalty a polynomial curve fit is obtained, creating a bridge between semi-parametric and classic parametric models. But in essence, P-splines are parametric models. The coefficients have a very clear interpretation and can be presented graphically as the skeleton of the fitted curve.

P-splines are grounded in linear regression. Extensions to generalized linear regression are straightforward through penalized likelihood. Counts and binomial data can be handled in an elegant way.

The penalty makes the number of B-splines irrelevant, as long as it is large enough. With many of them, say 10 to 50, the number of coefficients in the model is moderately large. Yet, as will be shown, the effective dimension of the model will be (much) smaller than this number, depending on the amount of smoothing.

2.1 Linear and Polynomial Regression

Consider a scatterplot of data pairs (x_i, y_i), $i = 1 : m$. Figure 2.1 displays $m = 111$ daily readings of wind speed (mph) (x-axis) and the maximum of daily ozone (ppm) (y-axis) in New York City (data set airquality in R).

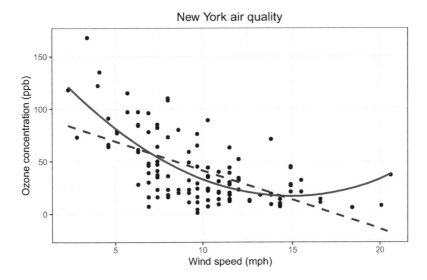

Figure 2.1 Air pollution in New York: scatterplot of daily maximum ozone concentrations and wind speed. Least squares linear (blue broken line) and quadratic (solid red curve) fits. R code in f-air-wind.R

The straight blue broken line shows the linear least squares fit, while the solid red line shows the quadratic fit.

The formula for a quadratic curve is $\mu_i = \alpha_0 + \alpha_1 x_i + \alpha_2 x_i^2$. The vector $\alpha = [\alpha_0 \; \alpha_1 \; \alpha_2]'$ that gives the "best" fit to the data is found by minimizing the least squares objective

$$S = \sum_{i=1}^{m}(y_i - \mu_i)^2 = \sum_{i=1}^{m}(y_i - \alpha_0 - \alpha_1 x_i - \alpha_2 x_i^2)^2.$$

It is easier to work in matrix notation. For the above quadratic curve, we express the m by 3 regressor matrix B, the 3 by 1 unknown parameter vector α, and the m by 1 mean vector μ as

$$B = \begin{bmatrix} 1 & x_1 & x_1^2 \\ 1 & x_2 & x_2^2 \\ \vdots & \vdots & \vdots \\ 1 & x_m & x_m^2 \end{bmatrix} \qquad \alpha = \begin{bmatrix} \alpha_0 \\ \alpha_1 \\ \alpha_2 \end{bmatrix} \qquad \mu = B\alpha, \qquad (2.1)$$

respectively. Now the least squares solution minimizes the objective

$$S = ||y - B\alpha||^2, \qquad (2.2)$$

defined as the squared-norm $(y - B\alpha)'(y - B\alpha)$. This leads to the normal equations $B'B\alpha = B'y$ or $\hat{\alpha} = (B'B)^{-1}B'y$.

A more general setting introduces a vector of weights, w. They can reflect known precisions of the data, or w can contain zeros and ones, where a zero indicates a missing y. Using such weights, missingness can be introduced deliberately, e.g., to (temporarily) exclude selected observations. It is more convenient than excluding rows of B and y. With $W = \text{diag}(w)$, we get

$$S = (y - B\alpha)'W(y - B\alpha), \qquad (2.3)$$

and the normal equations $B'WB\hat{\alpha} = B'Wy$, with solution $\hat{\alpha} = (B'WB)^{-1}$ $B'Wy$.

The regression scheme can be extended to higher powers of x by adding columns in B with third, fourth, or higher powers. In theory, the computation of $\hat{\alpha}$ does not change, but in practice one has to center and scale x to avoid numerical instabilities. Modern regression software overcomes this issue by using specialized algorithms, like the QR decomposition (Wood, 2017). We will not get into the details of the QR decomposition here. After showing that high-degree polynomial curve fits have serious and fundamental problems, we will discard them as a general smoothing tool.

More generally, the nth degree polynomial model is

$$\mu_i = \alpha_0 + \alpha_1 x_i + \alpha_2 x_i^2 + \alpha_3 x_i^3 + \cdots + \alpha_n x_i^n,$$

resulting in $n + 1$ columns in the matrix B, augmenting (2.1) to powers of n. This again gives $\mu = B\alpha$ in matrix notation. We call B a basis matrix and the powers of x the basis functions.

Figure 2.2 shows data from a simulated motorcycle crash, with a complicated trend: it is a time series of the acceleration of a helmet (Härdle, 1992). These data have become a workbench data set and a rite of passage for many smoothing techniques. A polynomial of low degree has no chance to fit these data well, so we try degree 9 (an arbitrary choice). Two fits are provided: one where all data were used (solid blue curve) and another where all data less than 5 ms were dropped (broken red curve). This small change has rather large consequences. The two curves differ strongly at the left (near 5 ms), which is expected, as we have changed the data there. But we also find large differences at the very right end (near 50 ms), which is unsettling.

Polynomial basis functions are global: they have a nonzero value for almost every x. The net effect is that any change in one of the coefficients in α results in a change in the curve over the entire domain of x. Worse, the higher the degree of the polynomial, the stronger this effect becomes.

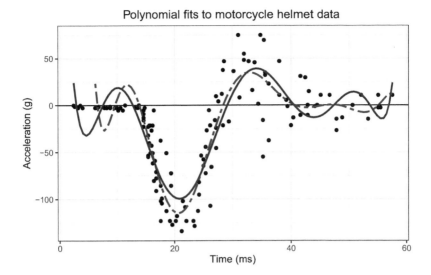

Figure 2.2 The acceleration of a motorcycle helmet in a simulated crash. Two polynomial (degree 9) fits are displayed. Blue line: based on all data; red broken line: after discarding the observations at less than 5 ms. R code in f-motpol1.R

2.2 B-splines

We first visualize B-splines before using them. The left panel of Figure 2.3 shows seven B-splines, shifted vertically to separate them. The right panel provides a more standard presentation. For either panel, the middle curve shows one complete B-spline, which strongly resembles a normal density. The other curves are shifted copies of this middle curve, but truncated at the left or right boundary.

These are so-called cubic, or degree 3, B-splines. Each B-spline consists of four polynomial segments, each of degree 3, that begin and end at specific values of x called knots. In Figure 2.3, the knots are located at the integer numbers 0 to 4. At the inner knots (1 to 3) two polynomial segments of the same B-spline meet; their values and those of the first and second derivative are equal on both sides of each knot. Together these (degree $+1$) polynomial segments form one B-spline basis function (resembling a normal density).

The knots divide the domain of x into four sections of equal length. The number of B-splines is seven because they have degree 3. In both panels a vertical broken line visualizes the evaluation of the B-splines for one value of x.

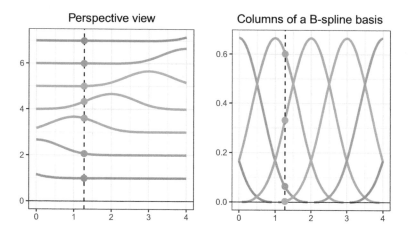

Figure 2.3 B-splines in perspective. In the left panel, the splines are offset vertically, in the right panel they are plotted on top of each other. R code in `f-persp.R`

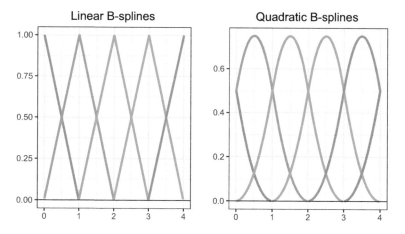

Figure 2.4 Linear (left) and quadratic (right) B-spline bases illustrated. R code in `f-B-lin-quad.R`

Only four of the evaluations have a nonzero value; which four is determined by the value of x. It is easy to check this by imagining a vertical line anywhere in the two panels. The number four is determined only by the degree of the B-splines and does not depend on their number. Said differently, even in a large basis with many B-splines, only four of them are nonzero for any x. Figure 2.4 shows linear and quadratic B-splines for the same choice of knots.

With x of length m and n B-splines, we form the basis matrix

$$B = [b_{ij}] = [B_j(x_i)] = \begin{bmatrix} B_1(x_1) & B_2(x_1) & \dots & B_n(x_1) \\ B_1(x_2) & B_2(x_2) & \dots & B_n(x_2) \\ \vdots & \vdots & \vdots & \vdots \\ B_1(x_m) & B_2(x_m) & \dots & B_n(x_m) \end{bmatrix},$$

where $i = 1 : m$ and $j = 1 : n$. Note that the elements of x do not have to be evenly spaced. They can have any value on the chosen domain, their order is immaterial, and repeated values are allowed.

Like with other basis functions, $\mu = B\alpha$ gives us values of a curve, at the positions determined by x. Given a vector y of data to be fitted, linear regression gives us, in principle, an estimate of the coefficients: $\hat{\alpha} = (B'WB)^{-1}B'Wy$. This is only true when $B'WB$ can be inverted, which is only the case when every B-spline has enough support, meaning that there are no columns in B with only zeros. For the moment we assume that this is the case. In Section 2.3, we will introduce penalties to solve the support problem.

Given the properties of the chosen B-splines (domain, number of segments, and degree of the splines), a basis matrix $B^\star$ can be computed for any desired new $x^\star$. Multiplication with the coefficients then gives a curve $\hat{f}(x^\star) = \hat{f} = B^\star\hat{\alpha}$. Generally the observed x does not form a nice grid, but one can choose a detailed $x^\star$ for plotting the fit.

The coefficients $\hat{\alpha}$ form the skeleton of a B-spline fit. A plot of them already gives a good impression of what a detailed curve f would look like, especially when the number of splines is large; we can get a glimpse of this by looking ahead to the different panels found in Figure 2.8. Although one generally speaks of a non-parametric model, in fact the influence of each B-spline coefficient on a curve fit can be seen very clearly. In a parametric model with a power functions basis, this is much more difficult.

To characterize a B-spline basis, we use the number of segments on the chosen domain. The number of B-splines is this number plus the degree of the B-splines. It is also the number of columns of B (or $B^\star$). The number of segments is independent of the degree of the B-splines and lends itself well to the human tendency to prefer numbers like 10, 20, or 50.

Returning to the motorcycle data, Figure 2.5 shows two B-spline fits, with slightly different choices of the domain. The left parts of the curves are quite different from each other, whereas the right parts are essentially identical. This illustrates the local behavior of B-splines, in contrast to polynomial fits (Figure 2.2).

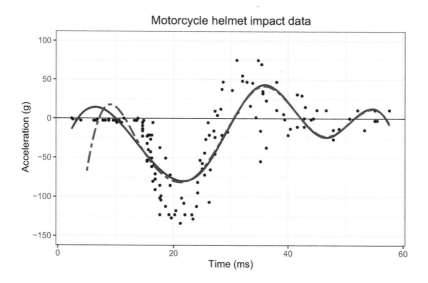

Figure 2.5 The motorcycle data, fit with cubic B-splines (five segments). Blue curve: based on all data; red broken curve: after discarding the observations at less than 5 ms. R code in f-mot-bsp.R

B-splines are zero over the largest part of the domain of x. As we have seen, this limited support makes them respond only locally to data, which is an advantage. On the other hand, it makes them vulnerable to sparse or missing data. Figure 2.6 presents two fits to the motorcycle data, one using 10 and the other using 20 segments. In the latter case, the rightmost B-splines are poorly supported, leading to $B'B$ being almost singular and the presence of so-called variance inflation. These consequences are illustrated by the downward swing near the end of the fitted curve.

Figure 2.7 shows B-spline fits to simulated data. The curve is smooth with a small basis and more wiggly with a larger one. One may get the impression that more splines in B automatically lead to a more detailed and wiggly curve $B\alpha$. While this is often true, it is not necessary. In fact, the smoothness of $\mu = B\alpha$ depends on α, not only on B. Consider Figure 2.8, which shows a variety of curves μ using the *same* B-spline basis, with different α. The values of the coefficients are plotted in the graphs to show that the smoother curves correspond to a less erratic α. As noted above, a plot of α alone already gives a strong impression of what the curve will be.

Figure 2.8 also displays the main idea of P-splines: use a rich B-spline basis with relatively many columns, say 20 or even 50, and control the smoothness of the coefficients α. To achieve such control, we need a measure for the

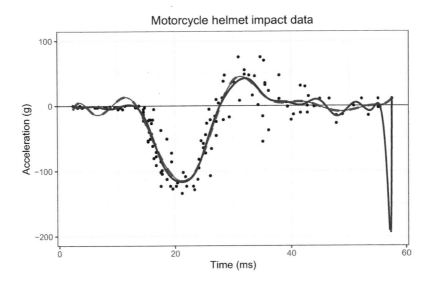

Figure 2.6 The motorcycle data fit with cubic B-splines using 10 (red broken curve) and 20 (blue solid curve) segments. R code in f-mot-bsize.R

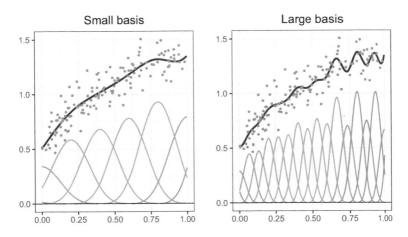

Figure 2.7 Two cubic B-spline fits to the same simulated data, with a small basis (left) and with a larger one (right). R code in f-bsize.R

roughness of α, so that we can penalize for it in a properly chosen objective function. Excellent candidates for measuring roughness are differences in adjacent elements of α, and we will consider a variety of differencing orders, e.g., first, second, or even higher.

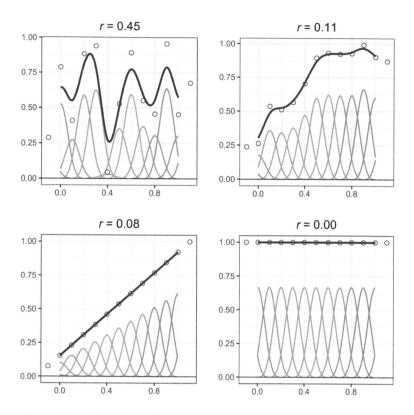

Figure 2.8 An illustration of how roughness of the mean μ can vary dramatically while using exactly the same basis B. The roughness of the curve only depends on the roughness of the coefficients α, measured by r. The red circles show the values of the individual coefficients associated with their corresponding B-splines. R code in f-brough2.R

2.3 Penalized Least Squares

In this section, we introduce penalties that are based on differences of neighboring elements of α. First-order differences are defined as $\Delta\alpha_j = \alpha_j - \alpha_{j-1}$. Here Δ is an operator, not a number. Second-order differences are obtained by applying the operator twice: $\Delta^2\alpha_j = \Delta(\alpha_j - \alpha_{j-1}) = \Delta\alpha_j - \Delta\alpha_{j-1}$, and higher orders follow by induction. With $\Delta^d\alpha$, we indicate dth ordered differences of all elements of α. Note that $\Delta^d\alpha_j$ does not exist for $j < 1 + d$. If α has n elements, $\Delta^d\alpha$ has $n - d$ elements.

Both for theoretical and numerical work, it is convenient to have matrix operations for differences, so that $\Delta\alpha$ can be written as $D_1\alpha$ and $\Delta^2\alpha$ as $D_2\alpha$, and so on for higher orders. The required matrices show patterns as in the low dimensional examples below:

$$D_1 = \begin{bmatrix} -1 & 1 & 0 & 0 \\ 0 & -1 & 1 & 0 \\ 0 & 0 & -1 & 1 \end{bmatrix}, \quad D_2 = \begin{bmatrix} 1 & -2 & 1 & 0 & 0 \\ 0 & 1 & -2 & 1 & 0 \\ 0 & 0 & 1 & -2 & 1 \end{bmatrix}. \quad (2.4)$$

In R, these matrices are obtained simply by D=diff(diag(n),diff=d), for $d < n$.

To measure the roughness of α, we use the sum of the squares of differences of order d:

$$R = R(\alpha) = \sum_{j=1+d}^{n} (\Delta^d \alpha_j)^2 = \alpha' D_d' D_d \alpha = ||D_d \alpha||^2. \quad (2.5)$$

A derived measure is

$$r = \sqrt{R/(n-d)}.$$

Figure 2.8 gives an impression of r for four different choices of the α vector, each with decreasing roughness. Note that in the limit all elements of α are equal and $r = 0$. In contexts where it is not explicitly needed, we will drop the subscript in D_d, and simply use the notation D. Typically we use a second-order penalty ($d = 2$) in this book.

Now that we have a measure of roughness associated with the B-spline coefficient vector, we can use it as a penalty to minimize the following objective function:

$$Q = (y - B\alpha)' W (y - B\alpha) + \lambda ||D\alpha||^2. \quad (2.6)$$

The second term is the penalty measuring the roughness of α. Its influence is determined by λ, a positive number, which is sometimes referred to as a tuning parameter. Standard B-spline smoothing results when $\lambda = 0$. Initially we will assume that λ is chosen by the user. In Chapter 3, we will present procedures for finding a reasonable data-driven or model-based choices for λ.

Equation (2.6) now technically presents the essence of P-splines: regression on a rich B-spline basis, combined with a discrete roughness penalty on the coefficients. As mentioned, we recommend using many splines to avoid any discussion about the size of the basis. The default choice can be 50, unless prior knowledge of flexibility indicates more. There is no way in which this simple recipe can go wrong; even 1,000 B-splines will work well with only 10 observations. In most of our examples, we will use 20 to 50 segments, unless indicated otherwise. Often 50 is (far) more than needed, but we suggest this number to emphasize that it is impossible to have too many B-splines.

Setting the derivative of Q, with respect to α, equal to zero produces the penalized least squares equations:

$$(B'WB + \lambda D'D)\alpha = B'Wy, \quad \text{or} \quad \hat{\alpha} = (B'WB + \lambda D'D)^{-1}B'Wy.$$

The solution depends on the value of λ, giving easy control over smoothness. Note that $B'WB$, $D'D$, and $B'Wy$ only have to be computed once. The entire smoothing problem is now driven by the value of λ. Remarkably, $B'WB+\lambda D'D$ is of full rank, even though this is certainly not the case for $D'D$, and potentially not for $B'WB$. This is the reason that it can do no harm to have many basis functions in B, allowing very flexible fits to our data, even for the case of $n \gg m$. Eilers et al. (2015) provide an example, smoothing 10 data points with 40 segments on the basis. The appendix of that paper also contains a proof.

Figure 2.9 displays the penalty in action for a simple scatter plot. As λ increases, the objective Q places more and more weight on the roughness

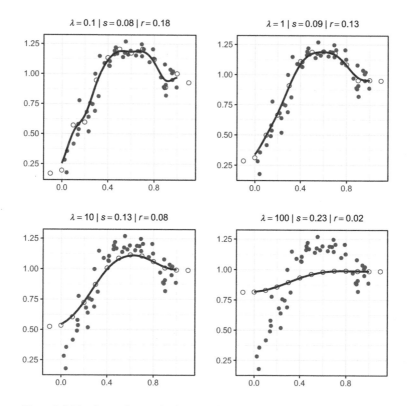

Figure 2.9 The first-order penalty in action for various values of λ. Also shown are the standard deviations of the residuals (s) and the roughness measure (r). Cubic B-splines, 20 segments. R code in f-d1pen.R

measure R, and the minimization of Q produces fitted curves that become increasingly more smooth. This feature is also observed through the estimated coefficients $\hat{\alpha}$: they fluctuate less as the penalty increases. This is expressed numerically by r. On the other hand s, the standard deviation of the residuals, increases.

The smooth fit tends toward a horizontal line as λ gets larger, and it is easy to see why this is the case. If the differences between neighboring coefficients are small, they will essentially have identical values.

The tendency toward a horizontal line can make the curve fit inflexible, generating a strong bias. Second-order differences are more attractive and generally give a smoother curve without increasing the sum of squares of the residuals; see Figure 2.10. They are nothing more than difference of differences, and the simple line of R code is provided just below (2.4) with $d = 2$.

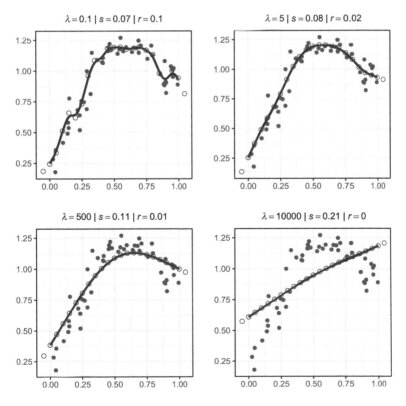

Figure 2.10 The second-order penalty in action for various values of λ. Also shown are the standard deviations of the residuals (s) and the roughness measure (r). Cubic B-splines, 20 segments. R code in f-d2pen.R

In holds that with differences of order d, the limit of heavy smoothing will be a polynomial of degrees $d - 1$. It is the best-fitting (least squares) polynomial of that degree. In Section 2.8, we discuss the limiting behavior of P-splines in more detail.

2.4 Interpolation and Extrapolation

As explained in Section 2.2, to get fitted values, we only need the B-spline basis matrix B and the estimated $\hat{\alpha}$. We can also interpolate to any desired resolution by evaluating the same B-splines, but now on a finer grid of x and multiplying it by $\hat{\alpha}$.

P-splines offer a second type of interpolation, one of the coefficients of B-splines that does not have support. As if by magic, they are filled in automatically. Eilers and Marx (2010) present a detailed analysis that we summarize here. The penalized least squares equations are the key. We have that

$$(B'WB + \lambda D'D)\alpha = B'Wy. \tag{2.7}$$

Assume that several neighboring elements of $B'Wy$ are zero because of zero weights in W. The corresponding rows and columns of $B'WB$ will then also be zero, and we will have that

$$\lambda \check{D}'\check{D}\check{\alpha} = 0, \tag{2.8}$$

where $\check{\alpha}$ and $\check{D}$ contain only the affected rows of α and columns of D. Equation 2.8 is a homogeneous linear difference equation of order $2d$. The solution is an exact polynomial in j, the index of the coefficients, of degree $2d - 1$. With a first-order penalty, interpolation is linear, and with a second-order penalty it is cubic. This holds for the coefficients. When "fleshing out" the curve with B-splines, some rounding of the shape will occur at the boundaries of interpolated regions.

Extrapolation is just as easy as interpolation. Pseudo-observations with zero weights are added at one or both ends of the data, extending the domain of x. The corresponding y-values can be any arbitrary number, but zero is an obvious choice. P-spline fitting automatically gives extrapolated B-spline coefficients from which an extrapolated curve fit can be calculated.

We do not get linear, but constant, extrapolation when $d = 1$. The explanation is found in the upper left and lower right corners of $D'D$. Consider extrapolation at the left boundary with $d = 1$. Then $\check{D}'\check{D}$ would be the upper left block of

$$
D'D = \begin{bmatrix}
1 & -1 & 0 & 0 & \cdots \\
-1 & 2 & -1 & 0 & \cdots \\
0 & -1 & 2 & -1 & \cdots \\
0 & 0 & -1 & 2 & \cdots \\
\vdots & \vdots & \vdots & \vdots & \ddots
\end{bmatrix}.
$$

The first row of $\check{D}'\check{D}\check{\alpha} = 0$ forces $\check{\alpha}_1 = \check{\alpha}_2$, leaving $\check{\alpha} \equiv c$ as the only possibility, where c is computed automatically to connect to the observed data smoothly.

With second-order differences, we have that

$$
D_2'D_2 = \begin{bmatrix}
1 & -2 & 1 & 0 & 0 & 0 & \cdots \\
-2 & 5 & -4 & 1 & 0 & 0 & \cdots \\
1 & -4 & 6 & -4 & 1 & 0 & \cdots \\
0 & 1 & -4 & 6 & -4 & 1 & \cdots \\
\vdots & \vdots & \vdots & \vdots & & \ddots
\end{bmatrix}. \tag{2.9}
$$

In the first two rows, the values of the elements are such that they "kill" quadratic and cubic terms, like the linear term was annihilated for $d = 1$.

We used zero weights for existing data as example for explaining inter- and extrapolation. The situation is a little different when there are simply no observations for large parts of the domain of x. As a result, some (or many) of the B-splines in the basis matrix have no support and the corresponding columns of B will contain only zeros. They do not contribute to $B'WB$ and $B'Wy$, and the corresponding rows of the latter and rows of columns of the former contain only zeros. We thus get the same results as for the analysis with zero weights.

Figure 2.11 demonstrates interpolation and extrapolation of data having a large gap in the central region of x. The basis matrix has three unsupported B-splines in the center and five at each end.

Automatic interpolation is extremely convenient. We do not have to worry about lack of support when choosing the number of B-splines in a basis. The function bbase in our package JOPS is happy to compute a basis with (many) unsupported B-splines. Many high-profile packages, like mgcv and gamlss, use algorithms that simply refuse to do such.

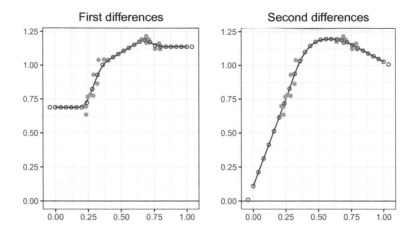

Figure 2.11 P-spline extrapolation and interpolation of a large gap in the x data, with penalty order $d = 1$ (left) and $d = 2$ (right). The gray dots show the data, and the blue circles show the values of the B-spline coefficients. The fitted curve is shown in red. R code in f-extrapol1.R

2.5 Derivatives

In some applications, we are not only interested in a fitted curve, but also in its derivative(s). A typical example is the growth speed of children. We use the fact that

$$\frac{d}{dt} \sum_j B_j(t; p)\alpha_j = \sum_j B_j(t; p - 1)\Delta\alpha_j / h, \qquad (2.10)$$

where p the degree of the B-splines and h the distance between the knots, which is equal to the length of the domain of x divided by the number of segments. When $\hat{\mu} = B\hat{\alpha}$, we get

$$\frac{d}{dt}\hat{\mu} = \tilde{B}(D\hat{\alpha})/h, \qquad (2.11)$$

where $\tilde{B}$ contains the B-spline basis of degree $p - 1$, and D forms first-order differences. Derivatives of order k can be computed in a similar way:

$$\frac{d^k}{dt^k} \sum_j B_j(t; p)\alpha_j = \sum_j B_j(t; p - k)(\Delta^k\alpha_j)/h^k. \qquad (2.12)$$

A condition is that $p > k$, otherwise the B-splines of degree $p - k$ will be zero everywhere.

Figure 2.12 shows an example for a sample of 1,000 boys from the data set boys7482 in the R package AGD. Note that the growth speed does not go to zero

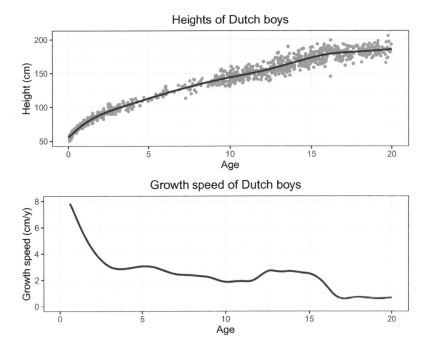

Figure 2.12 Height against age of 1,000 Dutch boys. Top panel: observations and fitted trend (50 cubic segments, $\lambda = 100$). Bottom panel: first derivative of the trend. R code in f-slope-height.R

at age 20, as one would expect for human height. In Section 8.7 we show how an extra penalty can force the slope to be zero from a specified age.

2.6 The Effective Dimension

For standard (unpenalized) regression models, we have the estimated mean $\hat{\mu} = B\hat{\alpha} = Hy$, where the least squares solution for α is $\hat{\alpha} = (B'WB)^{-1}B'Wy$. The "hat" matrix is defined as

$$H = B(B'WB)^{-1}B'W, \tag{2.13}$$

such that $\hat{\mu} = Hy$. For a general (full rank) regressor matrix B of dimension $m \times n$, we have the trace(H) = trace$((B'WB)^{-1}B'WB)$ = trace$(I) = n$ because the identity matrix is of dimension n. This result holds due to the invariance of the trace operator under cyclical permutation, i.e., trace(AB) = trace(BA) for general matrices A and B of proper dimension. Thus, for standard multiple regression, the trace(H) yields the exact dimension of the fit. This result is developed further and extended by Hastie and Tibshirani (1990) in a manner to compute the effective dimension of a smooth fit $\hat{\mu} = Hy$, where H is a general smoother matrix and the *effective dimension*, ED = trace(H).

A more principled proposal comes from Ye (1998). This work states that the effective model dimension is

$$\text{ED} = \sum_i \partial \hat{y}_i / \partial y_i. \qquad (2.14)$$

In the linear case, this gives again ED $= \sum_i h_{ii} = $ trace(H). At first, this definition of ED may not look impressive, but in fact it is powerful. The partial derivatives can be decomposed into separate and quantifiable contributions of individual components within larger models. Examples are the mixed models presented in Chapter 3 and the additive models found in Chapter 4.

This definition of the effective dimension also applies to P-splines, now with $H = B(B'WB + \lambda D'D)^{-1}B'W$. Using cyclic permutation, we find

$$\text{ED} = \text{trace}(H) = \text{trace}(G) = \text{trace}(B'WB(B'WB + \lambda D'D)^{-1}). \qquad (2.15)$$

Because G is an n by n matrix and generally much smaller than H, the latter definition is computationally more attractive.

There is also a monotone relationship between ED and λ. When λ approaches zero, ED approaches n (assuming support for all B-splines). The limit for increasing λ is ED $= d$. We see this relationship more completely in Figure 2.13. Note that y does not occur in the definition of ED; it is purely a

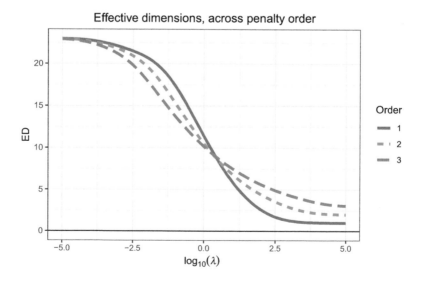

Figure 2.13 ED versus $\log_{10}(\lambda)$, by penalty order using 20 segments on the basis. R code in f-Peffdim.R

property of the design of the model (basis plus penalty for given λ). We will find in Section 2.8, that for large λ, the fitted curve approaches a polynomial of degree $d - 1$.

2.7 Standard Errors

The covariance matrix of $\hat{\alpha} = (B'WB + \lambda D'D)^{-1}B'Wy$, or that of the estimated coefficients, is

$$\hat{C} = \text{cov}(\hat{\alpha}) = \hat{\sigma}^2(B'WB + \lambda D'D)^{-1}, \qquad (2.16)$$

where $\hat{\sigma}^2 = ||y - B\hat{\alpha}||^2/(m - \text{ED})$. This is sometimes called the Bayesian covariance matrix. Its derivation is outlined in Appendix F, where it is also compared to an alternative, the sandwich estimate.

The diagonal of $B\hat{C}B'$ gives the variance of the fitted values, $\hat{\mu} = B\hat{\alpha}$. From its square root, we can construct error bands.

The underlying assumption in these equations is that we fill in the true λ, which is of course unknown. One hopes that "optimal smoothing" (see Chapter 3) will give a good estimate. Figure 2.14 displays an "optimal" P-spline fit (as determined by leave-one-out cross-validation) with twice standard error bands for the motorcycle data.

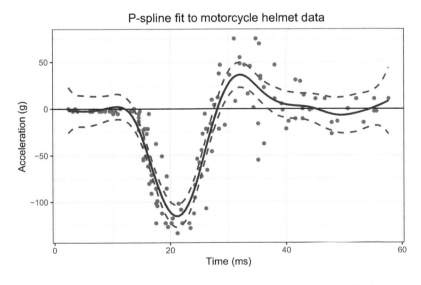

Figure 2.14 P-spline fit to the motorcycle helmet data, with twice standard error bands (20 cubic segments, second-order penalty). R code in f-se.R

2.8 Heavy Smoothing and Polynomial Limits

In the penalized least squares objective

$$Q = S + \lambda R = (y - B\alpha)' W (y - B\alpha) + \lambda ||D\alpha||^2,$$

the second term becomes dominant for large λ, which essentially forces $D\alpha \approx 0$.

If $\alpha_j = \sum_{k=0}^{d-1} \gamma_j j^k$, i.e., when the coefficients follow a polynomial of degree $d - 1$, then $||D\alpha||^2 = 0$ exactly. This is easy to prove when $\alpha_j = a + bj$. It follows

$$\Delta \alpha_{j+1} = \alpha_{j+1} - \alpha_j = a + b(j+1) - (a + bj) = b, \qquad (2.17)$$

for any j, and $\Delta^2 \alpha_{j+1} = \Delta b = 0$. Generalizations to higher-order differences are straightforward.

As λ increases, $\hat{\alpha}$ approaches a polynomial, and so will $B\hat{\alpha}$. The limiting polynomial is not arbitrary: it minimizes the sum of squares in the first term of the objective, hence the fit is the least squares polynomial. This bridge between P-splines and polynomials can be useful: sometimes strong smoothing is indicated by the data, and the P-splines can be replaced by a simple parametric model.

2.9 P-splines as a Parametric Model

A polynomial fit to data is commonly called a parametric model. A handful of coefficients fully determines the curve. Often it is suggested that a parametric model is desirable because one knows "what the parameters stand for." Yet, beyond a cubic polynomial this is dubious: it is almost impossible to relate the value of one coefficient of a higher power of x directly to the shape of the curve.

On the other hand, smoothing methods often are termed non-parametric or semi-parametric models, implying that there are no (or very few) parameters with a clear interpretation. This is certainly true for kernel smoothers and local likelihood methods. Truncated polynomials have clearly defined parameters, but they cannot be precisely interpreted (Eilers and Marx, 2010).

P-splines are different. As illustrated for cubic P-splines in Figure 2.15, the values of the coefficients are close to the value of the fitted curve directly above the peak of the corresponding B-spline. The interpretation of the parameters is easy: they closely predict the fitted curve at the center of the corresponding B-spline.

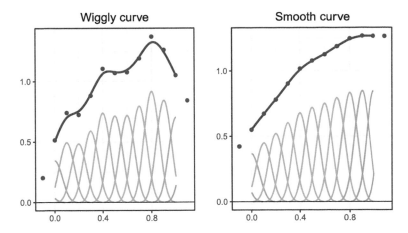

Figure 2.15 The values of the coefficients of the B-splines (red dots) lie close to the fitted curve (blue line). The smoother the curve, the closer the coefficients are to each other. R code in `f-bcoeff.R`

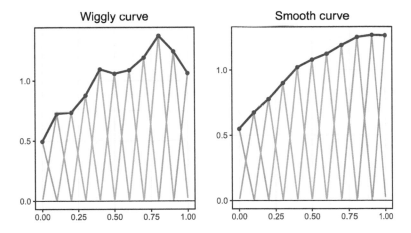

Figure 2.16 The values of the coefficients of linear B-splines (red dots) lie on the fitted curve (blue line). R code in `f-bcoeff-lin.R`

Linear P-splines have an almost perfect interpretation of the coefficients, as Figure 2.16 shows. The fitted curve linearly interpolates the coefficients. A piecewise linear curve with many knots can be acceptable in many applications, especially for visualization. A basis of linear B-splines can be computed in a few line of R code, as shown in Appendix C.1.

In view of the excellent interpretability of explicit coefficients, we should call P-splines a "proper parametric" model.

2.10 Whittaker: P-splines without B-splines

We obtain interesting and useful results when we replace B by an identity matrix, leading to $\hat{\mu} = (I + D'D)^{-1}y$. This is only meaningful if the locations of the observations are evenly spaced, and if we are interested in fitted values only on those locations. The number of coefficients will be equal to the number of observations (missing data can be handled with zero weights).

What results is the Whittaker smoother, originally designed for smoothing ("graduation") of life tables (Whittaker, 1923). The original algorithm used third-order differences. This smoother gradually became less used as the popularity of the smoothing spline was rising. P-splines can be considered as "Whittaker on steroids," with a skeleton defined by a discrete penalty, on which B-splines lay the muscles.

An advantage of the Whittaker smoother, when the application allows its use, is the extreme simplicity of the basis. There is neither the need to choose the number of knots nor the degree of the splines. All the pleasant properties of the penalty remain. Interpolation and extrapolation are automatic, and strong smoothing leads to polynomials, among other properties.

The equations for the Whittaker smoother are extremely sparse. Using sparse matrix algorithms (Eilers, 2003), extremely long data series can be smoothed in a fraction of a second. Unfortunately, calculation of the full hat matrix, $H = (I + \lambda D'D)^{-1}$, is not efficient because the inverse is large and not sparse. For computing its diagonal, Frasso and Eilers (2015) provides efficient R code (for $d = 2$), based on an algorithm by Hutchinson and de Hoog (1986). Its computation time and memory use only grow linearly with the length of the data series. It can also be used to compute standard errors, as the covariance matrix of $\hat{\mu}$ is $\hat{\sigma}^2 H$, so the square root of its diagonal gives the standard errors of the fitted $\hat{\mu}$.

The B-spline basis is reduced to a minimum and replaced by the identity matrix. The choice of number and degree of the splines do not play any role. This is what makes the Whittaker smoother a good vehicle for studying discrete penalties.

2.11 Equivalent Kernels

Hastie and Tibshirani (1990) show that linear smoothers can be better understood and more directly comparable if they are expressed as equivalent kernels. An equivalent kernel shows in detail how individual values in the input vector contribute to the smooth output. Consider the P-spline "hat" matrix

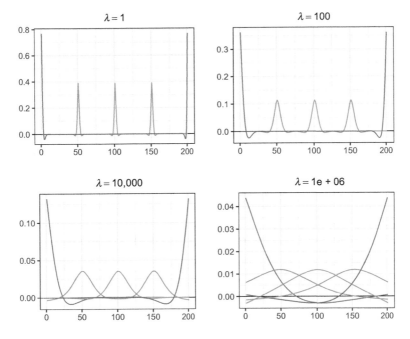

Figure 2.17 Illustration of equivalent kernels. The differently colored curves show the values in rows 1, 51, 101, 151, and 201 of the 201 by 201 hat matrix of the Whittaker smoother with penalty order 2. The titles of the panels show the value of λ. R code in f-eff-kernels.R

$H = B(B'B + \lambda D'D)^{-1}B'$ and how it transforms y into $\hat{y} = Hy$. Row i of H tells us how $\hat{y}_i = \sum_j h_{ij} y_j$ is formed as a weighted sum of all observations. The elements in row i form the equivalent kernel. Figure 2.17 shows, for different values of λ, the equivalent kernels in selected rows (1, 51, 101, 151, and 201) of a 201 by 201 hat matrix. It is based on the Whittaker smoother.

When λ is small, most of the elements in a row of H are close to zero, indicating that any element of $\hat{y}$ is only influenced by a few observations close to it. When λ is large, almost all observations contribute to each $\hat{y}_i$. It easy to see that $\sum_j h_{ij} = 1$ for all i, because if e is defined as an m vector of all ones, then $e = He$. Hence $\hat{y}_i$ is a proper weighted mean of y, with the weights in the ith row of H. Borrowing from systems theory, we can interpret $\hat{y} = Hy$ as the description of a linear system, with y as input, and H as describing how it is transformed to the output $\hat{y}$.

Note that at the boundaries the equivalent kernels get a strongly asymmetrical shape, but they do not cross the boundaries. This is simply impossible. The vanilla kernel smoother is different. All equivalent kernels have the same shape, implying that those near the boundaries spread out beyond them. See also the discussion of boundary effects in density estimation in Section 3.3.

From its definition follows that H is symmetric. Consider the special case that y consists of all zeros, except for one $y_j = 1$, which is often called an impulse signal. In such a case, Hy is equal to column j of H. Previously, we looked at rows of H that told us how all observations contribute to one element of $\hat{y}$; we now look at how one element of the input vector is distributed over the whole output vector.

In Section 8.5, we will present variations of the penalty and show their effects on equivalent kernels for some of them.

2.12 Smoothing of a Non-normal Response

In many applications, the response will not be normal. Common examples include Poisson distributed counts or binomial responses. P-splines can be directly transplanted into the generalized linear model (GLM) framework. For an introduction to GLM, we recommend Dobson and Barnett (2018) and Fahrmeir and Tutz (2001).

The GLM introduces three parts: the random component, the linear predictor, and the link function. The random component specifies the probability distribution of y. It can be any member of the exponential family, with mean $\mu = E(y)$, but we will restrict ourselves to the Poisson and binomial. The second component is the linear predictor, which we model with B-splines, $\eta = B\alpha$. The last component is the link function g: $\eta = g(\mu)$. Common (canonical) link functions include the logarithmic link (for Poisson) and the logit link (for binomial), which will be our choices throughout this book.

Maximum likelihood estimation is standard for the GLM. Because we want to introduce a penalty, we find it convenient to switch from maximizing the log-likelihood to minimizing the deviance, which is essentially (apart from a constant) minus two times the log-likelihood. We use Poisson smoothing to explain this idea.

2.12.1 Poisson Smoothing

Assuming independent observations, the Poisson likelihood is

$$L = \prod_{i=1}^{m} \frac{e^{-\mu_i} \mu_i^{y_i}}{y_i!}.$$

Neglecting the (constant) contribution from $y_i!$, the log-likelihood is

$$\ell(\mu; y) = \log(L) = \sum_{i=1}^{m}(y_i \log(\mu_i) - \mu_i). \qquad (2.18)$$

For convenience, we choose to work with the deviance, which is $\mathrm{dev}(\mu; y) = -2\ell(\mu; y) + 2\ell(y; y)$. Using deviance, a penalty can be attached in a similar way as it was to the sum of squares of residuals in (2.6). We now have an objective function in the form

$$Q = \mathrm{dev}(\mu; y) + \lambda ||D\alpha||^2$$
$$= 2\sum_{i=1}^{m}(y_i \log(y_i/\mu_i) - (y_i - \mu_i)) + \lambda ||D\alpha||^2, \qquad (2.19)$$

which for Poisson responses and the log link becomes a function of α through $\mu = \exp(\eta) = \exp(B\alpha)$. The goal is to minimize Q with respect to α, which is the solution to $\partial Q/\partial\alpha = 0$. Re-expressing with the chain rule, we find

$$0 = \frac{\partial Q}{\partial\alpha} = \frac{\partial Q}{\partial\mu}\frac{\partial\mu}{\partial\eta}\frac{\partial\eta}{\partial\alpha}.$$

Note that the third term simplifies to $B = \partial\eta/\partial\alpha$, and for Poisson (log link) the second term is $\mu = \partial\mu/\partial\eta$. The partial derivatives then yield the penalized likelihood equations

$$B'(y - \mu) = \lambda D'D\alpha, \qquad (2.20)$$

which remain nonlinear in α. The Newton–Raphson method applies a first-order Taylor approximation to the derivative on the left-hand side of (2.20) (about $\tilde{\alpha}$),

$$B'(y - \mu) \approx B'(y - \tilde{\mu}) - B'\tilde{W}B(\alpha - \tilde{\alpha}),$$

with $\tilde{\eta} = B\tilde{\alpha}$, $\tilde{\mu} = \exp(\tilde{\eta})$, and $\tilde{W} = \mathrm{diag}(\tilde{\mu})$, effectively providing a second-order approximation at a first-order price. The matrix $H = -B'WB$ is the so-called Hessian matrix, which is $H = -B'\partial\mu/\partial\alpha'$. Here the Newton–Raphson is equivalent to the Method of Scoring because $E(H) = H$. This finally gives the linear system of equations

$$(B'\tilde{W}_t B + \lambda D'D)\tilde{\alpha}_{t+1} = B'\tilde{W}_t(\tilde{\eta}_t + \tilde{W}_t^{-1}(y - \tilde{\mu}_t)). \qquad (2.21)$$

This system has to be solved iteratively. The subscript t indicates the iteration number. Starting values are only needed for the linear predictor η, which set

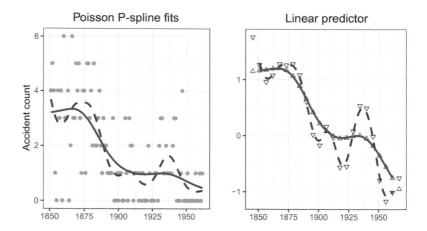

Figure 2.18 Yearly counts of British coal mining disasters, smoothed with a
Poisson model. P-spline fits with a cubic B-spline basis with 20 segments and
a second-order penalty, for both $\lambda = 1$ and $\lambda = 100$ (left). The corresponding
linear predictors and the B-spline coefficients are also shown (right). R code in
f-coal-smooth.R

up the GLM weights and working vector to initialize the iterations. We set
$\tilde{\eta}_0 = \log(y + 1)$, giving

$$\tilde{\alpha}_{t+1} = (B'\tilde{W}_t B + \lambda D'D)^{-1} B'\tilde{W}_t \tilde{z}_t, \qquad (2.22)$$

with $\tilde{z}_t = \tilde{\eta}_t + \tilde{W}_t^{-1}(y - \tilde{\mu}_t)$ as a working dependent vector. We find that (2.22)
reflects an iterative re-weighted (penalized) least squares solution. Usually
convergence is quick, needing only a handful of iterations. The working vector
is a foundational to effective dimension, standard error bands, among other
things, as outlined in Section 2.12.3 ahead.

The stage is now set to fit a smooth curve through a series of counts. We
use data on the annual number of major accidents in British coal mines, from
1851 to 1962. They are based on the data set coal in R. The observations,
the fitted values, and the linear predictors are plotted in Figure 2.18, for both
light and heavy penalization. The coefficients of the B-splines are plotted
too, emphasizing again how they form the skeleton of the smooth linear
predictor.

The generalized linear P-spline smoother is ideal for histograms, which are
also a series of counts. See Section 3.3 for details, including the choice of
domain, the influence of the bin width, and the optimal choice of λ.

P-splines have a property that we call the conservation of moments, which
is of great value for density estimation. Let c be the vector of counts in the bins

of a histogram of length m, and let $\hat{\mu}$ be the smooth fit. Given the penalty of order d, it holds for all $\lambda \geq 0$:

- For $d = 1$, $\sum_{i=1}^{m} y_i = \sum_{i=1}^{m} \hat{\mu}_i$ (proper density);
- For $d = 2$, the above holds and also $\sum_{i=1}^{m} x_i c_i = \sum_{i=1}^{m} x_i \hat{\mu}_i$ (same mean);
- For $d = 3$, the above hold and also $\sum_{i=1}^{m} x_i^2 c_i = \sum_{i=1}^{m} x_i^2 \hat{\mu}_i$ (same variance).

The conservation property can be extended to higher moments using higher-order penalties. Notice that $d = 3$ is especially useful because both the variance and mean of the smoothed histogram are the same as those of the raw histogram, even with strong smoothing. Most other algorithms would increase the variance. Moreover, the polynomial limits for large λ have a clear interpretation: when $d = 2$, the linear predictor becomes linear in x, and we get an exponential distribution. For $d = 3$, the smooth approaches the normal distribution.

Even with narrow bins, the counts in histograms generally do not form a long data series. The length may be around 100 or so. This is small enough to use the identity matrix as the P-spline basis, as described for the Whittaker smoother in Section 2.10.

In some hazard modeling applications, the goal of smoothing of counts is not to get a smooth estimate of μ itself, but rather of a smooth hazard (or intensity), say h. Then $E(y_i) = \mu_i = h_i u_i$, where u is the exposure, usually a population size. The smoothing of the hazard can be achieved by taking $h = \exp(B\alpha)$ and $U = \text{diag}(u)$, which leads to $\mu = U \exp(B\alpha)$. The classical approach is to use $\mu = \exp(B\alpha + \log u)$, where $\log(u)$ is called the offset. This clearly runs into problems when some elements of u are zero. It can occur that both y and u are zero in some places. A typical example is extrapolation. Multiplication by U avoids logarithms of zeros.

2.12.2 Binomial Smoothing

For binomial responses, y denotes the number of *successes* among t independent trials ($0 \leq y \leq t$). We estimate a smooth curve for the binomial parameter π, which represents the probability of observing a success for any given trial. It follows that $\mu = t\pi$. The same statements hold true for Bernoulli responses, but now with the restrictions $y = 0$ or 1 and $t = 1$, and $P(y = 1) = \pi = \mu$. In the GLM framework, the response distribution is now set to the binomial, and we choose the (canonical) link function to be the logit. The model is

$$g(\mu) = \log\left(\frac{\pi}{1-\pi}\right) = \eta = B\alpha, \qquad (2.23)$$

where π is the binomial "success" probability. Equivalently,

$$\pi = \frac{1}{1 + \exp(-B\alpha)},$$

and for m independent binomials, each with t_i trials $(i = 1 : m)$

$$Q = 2 \sum_{i=1}^{m} \left(y_i \log\left[\frac{y_i}{\mu_i}\right] + (t_i - y_i) \log\left[\frac{t_i - y_i}{t_i - \mu_i}\right] \right) + \lambda||D\alpha||^2. \quad (2.24)$$

Neglecting the parts of Q that do not depend on μ, the following simplification results

$$Q = -2 \sum_{i=1}^{m} [y_i \log \mu_i + (t_i - y_i) \log(t_i - \mu_i)] + \lambda||D\alpha||^2, \quad (2.25)$$

which further simplifies in the (ungrouped) Bernoulli setting. Using the same linearization technique that was presented for Poisson smoothing, we arrive at equations similar to (2.21), but now with $W = \text{diag}(\mu(1 - \pi))$. A convenient choice for starting values is $\tilde{\pi}_0 = (y_i + 1)/(t_i + 2)$ or $\tilde{\eta}_0 = \log(\tilde{\pi}_0/(1 - \tilde{\pi}_0))$.

We revisit the kyphosis case study presented in Hastie and Tibshirani (1990) (data set kyphosis in R). The binary response is presence (1) or absence (0) of postoperative spinal deformity in children. There are 81 observations (17 present, 64 absent). We model the probability of occurrence as a function of age. The data and the fitted curves for the probabilities are plotted in Figure 2.19 (left panel) for two levels of smoothing ($\lambda = 1$ and $\lambda = 100$). The corresponding linear predictors are also displayed in the right panel.

2.12.3 GLM Effective Dimension and Standard Errors

Upon convergence, it is useful to view (2.21) as weighted linear smoothing of the working dependent variable $\hat{z} = \hat{\eta} + \hat{W}^{-1}(y - \hat{\mu})$, with weights $\hat{W}$. We can then interpret

$$H = B(B'\hat{W}B + \lambda D'D)^{-1}B'\hat{W} \quad (2.26)$$

as the "effective" hat matrix and

$$ED = \text{trace}(H) = \text{trace}((B'\hat{W}B + \lambda D'D)^{-1}B'\hat{W}B)$$

as the effective dimension. For the covariance matrix of $\hat{\alpha}$, we find the Bayesian form to yield

$$\text{cov}(\hat{\alpha}) = \phi(B'\hat{W}B + \lambda D'D)^{-1}, \quad (2.27)$$

where ϕ denotes a scale parameter. With normal responses (and the identity link function), a scale parameter, $\phi = \sigma^2$ was presented. For the binomial and

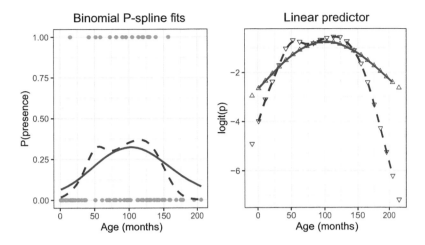

Figure 2.19 Kyphosis binomial response fit with basis using 20 segments (left). The dashed (solid) line indicates light (heavy) penalization using $\lambda = 1$ and 100, respectively. The corresponding linear predictor, and the P-spline coefficients are also shown (right). R code in f-kypho-smooth.R

Poisson forms – that are generally associated with the exponential family – we find $\phi = 1$ (see table 2.1 of Fahrmeir and Tutz [2001]). A common problem with Poisson modeling is the presence of overdispersion or $\phi > 1$. In such cases, we can estimate the scale parameter with $\hat{\phi} = \text{Dev}(\hat{\mu}; y)/(m - \text{ED})$. Other estimators of ϕ replace deviance with the Pearson chi-square statistic.

The covariance of $\hat{\eta}$ follows immediately as $\Gamma = B\text{cov}(\hat{\alpha})B'$, and approximate standard errors for the linear predictor can be constructed using the square root of the diagonal elements of Γ. Thus, twice lower and upper bounds for η follow from $\hat{\eta} \pm 2se(\hat{\eta})$. Representing these limits as (L, U), the corresponding limits for $\hat{\mu}$ follow as $(h(L), h(U))$, where $h(\cdot)$ denotes the inverse link function.

In addition to the inherent GLM weights, prior weights can also be useful in generalized linear smoothing. Assuming that such prior weights are now provided in the vector v and $V = \text{diag}(v)$, then $V\tilde{W}$ should replace $\tilde{W}$ everywhere in the fitting algorithm, and $V\hat{W}$ should replace $\hat{W}$ in the effective hat matrix and derived results.

On the scale of the linear predictor, the features of automatic interpolation and extrapolation, as well as polynomial limits for large λ, follow for the GLM as they did for normal responses on the linear predictor. For example, when smoothing binomial data with the logit link function and a second-order penalty, the limiting result with heavy smoothing is the same as linear logistic regression.

2.13 Notes and Details

This chapter lays the foundation for the rest of the book. P-splines combine a rich and evenly spaced B-spline basis with a simple difference penalty on the coefficients. Smoothing becomes an extension of (generalized) linear regression, with a single tuning parameter, avoiding tinkering with the size and number of B-splines. Interpolation and extrapolation are essentially automatic.

The difference penalty of P-splines is a simplification of the work of O'Sullivan (1986). He derived a matrix, very similar to our discrete difference matrix D, based on the integrated square of the second derivative of the fitted curve. Whereas pure differences are trivial to construct, O'Sullivan's approach is complicated for higher-order derivatives. Recently published algorithms simplify the computations (Wand and Ormerod, 2008; Wood, 2017). As long as knots are evenly spaced, we do not see any advantages in these works. Wand and Ormerod (2008) claim better performance of what they termed O-splines, but Eilers et al. (2015) show that a wrong B-spline basis had been used for their comparisons.

We emphasize that the discrete difference penalty is not meant at all to be an approximation to a continuous penalty. It is simple, and it is powerful, and it is all we need. It also puts no demands on the degree of the B-spline. To base a penalty on, say, fourth derivatives of the fitted curve, the B-splines should have at least degree 4, or else the derivative disappears. P-splines do not have this limitation. In the next chapter we will see for histogram smoothing that splines of zero order combine perfectly with a third-order difference penalty.

The penalty can be interpreted as the condition that the B-spline parameters α closely obey a linear difference equation. The coefficients of the equation form rows of the Pascal triangle with alternating signs. Many specialized variations are possible; some of them are discussed in Chapter 8.

A few years after we published our paper on P-splines, Ruppert and Carroll (2000) proposed to use a mixed model with truncated power functions (TPF) for smoothing, an approach that is extended by Ruppert et al. (2003). Quantiles of x are used for the knots. This approach underestimates the power of a (difference) penalty. Indeed, if there is no penalty, quantiles as knots guarantee support for all basis functions, which is a good thing. A penalty is a more elegant solution. In Eilers and Marx (2010), we show that evenly spaced knots are to be preferred for TPF.

In many publications we noticed the temptation to optimize the number of splines. Based on the TPF model with quantile-based knots, Ruppert (2002) and Ruppert et al. (2003) present formulas that boil down to one spline per four unique x, with a certain maximum. This advice has been cited many times for guidance on penalized B-splines. We propose to simply forget optimizing the number of splines and just take a large number of them.

Asymptotic results on P-splines have been obtained by Hall and Opsomer (2005), Kauermann et al. (2009), Li and Ruppert (2008), and Claeskens et al. (2009). They all consider the limited situation in which more data become available on the same domain. A more realistic setting is smoothing of (seasonal) time series, that grow in length as more observations are collected. It is clear that the number of P-splines must then grow too.

The R function lsfit() finds the solution of $B'WB\hat{\alpha} = B'Wy$ for given B, y and $W = \text{diag}(w)$. It can also be used for penalized regression through data augmentation, i.e., $\hat{\alpha} = (B'_+ W_+ B_+)^{-1} B'_+ W_+ y_+$, where

$$B_+ = \begin{bmatrix} B \\ \sqrt{\lambda}D \end{bmatrix} \quad y_+ = \begin{bmatrix} y \\ 0 \end{bmatrix} \quad \text{and} \quad w_+ = \begin{bmatrix} w \\ 1 \end{bmatrix}.$$

In this way, standard and widely available fitting algorithms that only accept B, y, and w can be tricked into solving penalized regression, including P-splines. If there are multiple penalties or additive structures, they too can be handled by additional augmentations. In this book, we have used lsfit() with data augmentation in some of our programs.

3

Optimal Smoothing in Action

We have introduced the principle of P-splines and explained a number of their properties. Thus far, we made a subjective choice when setting λ, the tuning parameter. That approach is fine for exploring data, but what we really need is an automatic procedure to let the data decide on the weight of the penalty. We term this optimal smoothing, and it is what we will explore in this chapter.

A fruitful idea is to look beyond how the model fits a data set, while evaluating the model on new, but similar, data. Seldom are we lucky enough to get additional data, but we can mimic the situation with cross-validation (CV). Akaike's information criterion (AIC) is also based on hypothetical new data, but does not try to generate them, as in CV. Rather, it corrects the deviance by adding a term, two times the effective model dimension. A numerical search procedure finds the minimum of CV or AIC by systematically varying λ.

Mixed models take another approach by assuming that spline coefficients are generated by a random process. The splines form a curve, to which noise is added. Two variances are estimated from the data: one for the noise and the other for the coefficients. Their ratio is equal to λ. Standard mixed model software can be used, but we show how to simplify the algorithm and make it faster.

Bayesian P-splines have the same structure as the mixed model, but the variances (and the coefficients) are estimated with a simple Gibbs sampler. The Laplace approximation proves to be an attractive alternative, especially for generalized linear smoothing. We explore two different algorithms, in the context of density estimation.

Optimal smoothing can go astray if the data show serial correlation or outlying observations. We present examples to warn our readers. The V-curve is a promising remedy.

We discuss some details that can be overlooked by inexperienced users: the proper choice of the domain for density estimation and transformation of the independent variable in scatterplot smoothing.

3.1 Cross-Validation

There exist many variants of cross-validation, but we consider only one: leave-one-out, which we will sometimes refer to as LOOCV. The idea is to leave out each observation in turn, fit a model to obtain a prediction for it, and measure how close that is to the observed value. If $\hat{\mu}_{-i}$ is the prediction of y_i, based on all other observations, the standard error of prediction is

$$CV = \sqrt{\sum_{i=1}^{m}(y_i - \hat{\mu}_{-i})^2/m}. \tag{3.1}$$

As it stands, the definition of CV is expensive because the model has to be estimated m times. The organization of the computations can be streamlined by using 0/1 weights, with a zero for the left-out observation, but much work is still needed.

For any linear model with $\hat{\mu} = Hy$, it holds that

$$y_i - \hat{\mu}_{-i} = (y_i - \hat{\mu}_i)/(1 - h_{ii}). \tag{3.2}$$

This is a well-known fact, but it is one that is not obvious. Hyndman (2014) adapted a proof from Seber and Lee (2003), for the case of linear regression without a penalty. In Appendix C.2, we extend his result to penalized linear regression.

As we learned in Chapter 2, the "hat" matrix for P-splines is $H = B(B'WB + \lambda D'D)^{-1}B'W$. As it is an m by m matrix, it is inefficient to first compute it in full and then extract the main diagonal. Instead, we form the element-by-element product of B' and $(B'B + \lambda D'D)^{-1}B'$ and take the sums of the columns of this matrix.

The recipe now is to choose a grid of values of λ, compute CV for each λ, and locate the minimum. A large range should be explored. A linear grid for λ itself is not a good idea; we always use a linear grid for $\log_{10}(\lambda)$. Figure 3.1 shows P-spline fits for a few choices of λ, with numerical values of CV; it also shows a profile of LOOCV, with a minimum close to $\lambda \approx 10$. There is no need to determine λ with high precision, as the fitted curve hardly changes when λ changes by 10% or less.

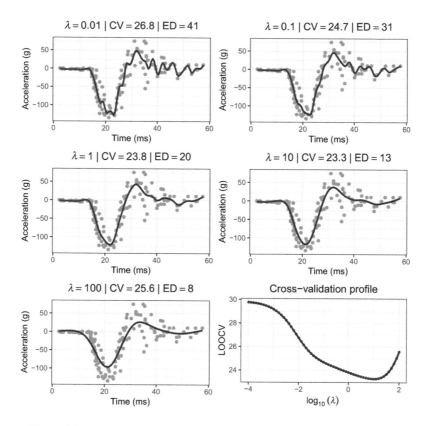

Figure 3.1 P-spline smooth fits to motorcycle acceleration data for various λ (20 segments, $d = 2$). CV is minimized for $\lambda \approx 10$ (bottom, right). R code in f-cv-plot.R

3.2 Akaike's Information Criterion

In principle, cross-validation can be used for generalized linear smoothing too, using linearization in the prediction and the deviance to measure the distance of $\hat{\mu}_{-i}$ to y_i. This is far from common. More popular is the minimization of Akaike's information criterion (AIC), which is defined as

$$AIC = \text{dev}(\mu; y) + 2 \, ED, \qquad (3.3)$$

where ED is the effective (model) dimension. AIC is a measure of how well a model will fit new data; it is a compromise measure between fidelity to the data and complexity of the model (Akaike, 1974).

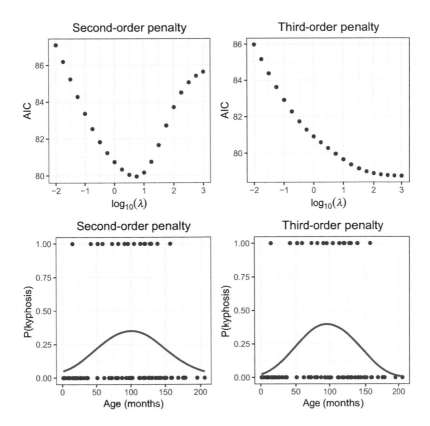

Figure 3.2 Kyphosis: optimal P-spline fit based on AIC using regressor age for binomial response kyphosis and logit link for $d = 2, 3$. R code in f-kyphopt.R

For Poisson and binomial distributions, we presented the respective deviance formulas in (2.19) and (2.24). For the effective dimension, we have

$$\text{ED} = \text{trace}((B'\hat{W}B + \lambda D'D)^{-1}B'\hat{W}B), \tag{3.4}$$

using the converged GLM weights.

As with cross-validation, we vary $\log_{10}(\lambda)$ on a linear grid, covering a wide range, and search for the minimum of AIC. Figure 3.2 displays the AIC profile and the optimal fit for the kyphosis data, using both a second- and third-order penalty. We find that with $d = 3$, λ can be made very large, indicating that a parametric generalized linear model with a quadratic polynomial in age would fit the data well.

3.3 Density Estimation

A histogram is a series of counts, and P-splines with a Poisson model can be directly applied to smooth it. Viewed as a GLM, the optimal weight of the penalty can also be obtained using AIC. Although histograms are discrete, the B-spline coefficients allow the evaluation of a continuous density at any required resolution. Somewhat surprisingly, very narrow bins in the histogram give excellent results. To support this last claim, Figure 3.3 shows two histograms of the eruption times of the Old Faithful geyser in Yellowstone National Park, Wyoming (data set `faithful` in R), using narrow (width 0.05), as well as very narrow (width 0.02) bins. AIC profiles are shown in the left panels and the corresponding optimal P-spline smooths in the right panels, with virtually the same results.

The domain of the B-splines should be chosen with care. An example is the suicide data set (Silverman, 1986), giving the lengths of treatment spells of suicidal patients, shown in Figure 3.4. Because treatment time cannot be negative, the left boundary should be zero. The upper panels display the results fitting the density where the B-spline basis is only supported on the interval

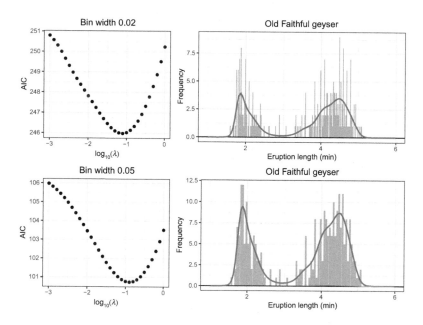

Figure 3.3 P-spline density estimation for Old Faithful eruption length using bin widths 0.02 (top row) and 0.05 (bottom row). B-splines with 20 segments and second-order penalty. The left column shows the AIC profiles, the right column the histograms and fits. R code in `f-geyseropt.R`

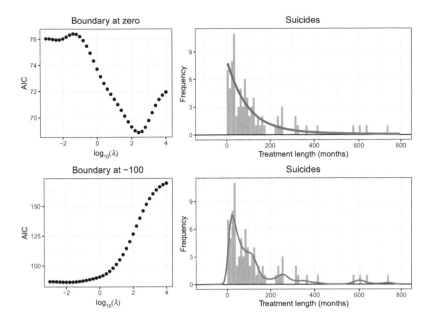

Figure 3.4 Optimal P-spline density based on AIC for suicide data using different lower domain limits (20 cubic segments, $d = 2$). R code in f-suicide-opt.R

(0, 800). We find that AIC indicates $\lambda \approx 200$. The result closely resembles an exponential density, as expected with a large λ and $d = 2$. The proper left boundary implicitly states that the density is zero for negative values. The bottom panels use an artificial left limit (-100), implying that the density is nonzero in between -100 and 0, although no negative data have been observed. This leads to a much smaller optimal λ and lighter smoothing.

Even in the case when there are no natural boundaries to the data, we should take care. Unless the bins are explicitly specified, a histogram function like hist() in R will choose (approximately) minimum and maximum of the data as boundaries. This implies that no observations are possible beyond these boundaries, which usually is not true. We advise to specify the boundaries explicitly and to pad the histogram with enough zeros on both sides.

3.4 Mixed Models

Mixed models originally were introduced to handle correlated observations. The prototypical application is to reading performance in schools. Because all pupils in a particular class have the same teacher, their performance may be similar. A proper model then is $y = \mu + Zc + \epsilon$, where Z is an indicator matrix, connecting pupils to their class, μ is an overall mean, and c contains the class parameters. Thus $z_{ij} = 1$ if pupil i belongs to class j, otherwise it is zero, and column j indicates which pupils are in class j.

If we treat c (and μ) as parameters in a classical regression model, we can estimate a value for every class. This is not what a mixed model does. It rather assumes that the elements of c are realizations of a random variable, drawn from a normal distribution (with unknown variance). In contrast, μ is assumed to be fixed.

Often the only goal of a mixed model is to properly take into account the correlation between observations, especially when confidence intervals of (linear functions) of fixed effects are studied.

The model can be generalized. An explanatory variable $u = [u_i]$ also may have been observed. Instead of an overall mean μ, an overall regression line $\beta_1 + u_i\beta_2$ can be assumed. With X as a matrix with $x_{i1} = 1$ and $x_{i2} = u_i$, the model now becomes $y = X\beta + Zc + \epsilon$, and the elements of c represent shifts with respect to the overall regression line. Many variations of X and Z are possible, and multiple X and/or Z are allowed.

P-splines can be written as a mixed model. With a proper choice of X and Z, we can write $B\alpha + \epsilon = X\beta + Zc + \epsilon$, replacing the penalty term $||D\alpha||^2$ by $||c||^2$. This penalty can be handled out of the box by software for mixed model estimation. That is not the case for a penalty based on differences. Several variations are possible for the choice of Z, and the details are described in Appendix E. The elements of ϵ and c are independent normal variables, with variances σ^2 and τ^2, respectively. It turns out that $\lambda = \sigma^2/\tau^2$, and thus it follows that we have to estimate two variances to determine the amount of smoothing.

The R package nlme provides the function lme( ) to fit a linear mixed model. The necessary code is

```
grp = 0 * x + 1  # Artificial group, to trick lme
lml <- lme(y ~ x, random = list(grp = pdIdent(~ Z - 1)))
cfix = fixef(lml)          # Coefficients for X
cran = unlist(ranef(lml))  # Coefficients for Z
```

A little trick is needed here. The function lme( ) expects a grouping variable, but we do not have any groups; this explains the vector grp in the first line. After fitting the model, matrices X^* and Z^* can be computed on a fine grid for x. A detailed curve then is obtained as $\mu^* = X^*\hat{\beta} + Z^*\hat{c}$. Figure 3.5 shows results for the motorcycle data, using $Z = BD'(DD')^{-1}$ (see Appendix E.1).

In lme( ), we have the option to use maximum likelihood (ML) or residual maximum likelihood (REML). The differences between results are minimal for

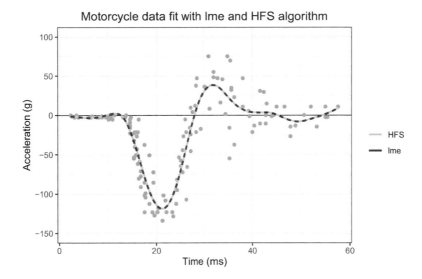

Figure 3.5 Automatic smoothing of the motorcycle data with a mixed model using the lme function (solid blue line) and with the HFS algorithm (broken red line), both with $\lambda \approx 0.01$. R code in f-mot-lme-mix.R

P-splines, especially when using many B-splines. This is not surprising: REML essentially corrects degrees of freedom of the model for the number of fixed effects, which is small (2) in our application.

Appendix E.2 shows how an algorithm of Harville (1977) can be simplified in such a way that there is no need to use specialized mixed model software. Appendix E also shows how the fixed part of the model can be eliminated. There is then no need for both model terms $X\beta$ and Zc, as we can work directly with only $B\alpha$. The associated details are also in the appendix, and here we only present the bottom line.

The steps in the iterative algorithm follow below. A reasonable starting value is $\lambda = 1$.

- Estimate the coefficients from $(B'B + \lambda D'D)\alpha = B'y$.
- Let $G = (B'B + \lambda D'D)^{-1}B'B$.
- Let $\mathrm{ED} = \mathrm{trace}(G)$, the effective model dimension.
- Let $\tau^2 = ||D\alpha||^2/(\mathrm{ED} - d)$.
- Let $\sigma^2 = ||y - B\alpha||^2/(m - \mathrm{ED})$.
- Update $\lambda = \sigma^2/\tau^2$.

When we apply this scheme to the motorcycle impact data, we get five-digit precision for λ in seven iterations. Figure 3.5 shows the fitted curve so obtained.

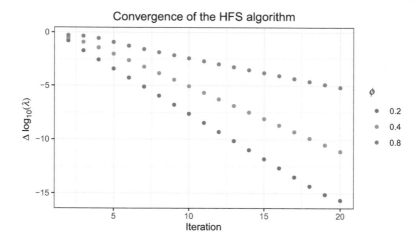

Figure 3.6 Speed of convergence of the HFS (Harville–Fellner–Schall) algorithm
for different values of the standard deviation of the noise (ϕ) in the simulation. R
code in f-HFS-convergence.R

The presented algorithm is an extension of the work of Harville (1977) and
a special case of the ones proposed by Fellner (1986) and Schall (1991); we
indicate it by the acronym HFS. Because we can work with the B-spline basis
matrix itself, sparseness is conserved, and even very large data sets can be
handled with ease, using a package like spam for sparse matrix operations.

With a small simulation, we give an impression of how the speed of
convergence of the HFS algorithm depends on the amount of noise. The data
were generated as $y = \sin(10x) + \phi\epsilon$, for $\phi = 0.2, 0.4$, or 0.8. Figure 3.6 shows
that convergence is faster for cleaner data.

An improvement is to treat the problem as a case of root finding. At
convergence $\lambda = \sigma^2/\tau^2$, hence $\log(\lambda) - \log(\sigma^2) + \log(\tau^2) = 0$. We can
define $f(\lambda) = \log(\lambda) - \log(\sigma(\lambda)^2) + \log(\tau(\lambda)^2)$, where $\sigma(\lambda)^2$ and $\tau(\lambda)^2$ are
computed after smoothing with λ. The *regula falsi* (RF) algorithm (Gentle,
2009) starts from trial values $\kappa_1 = \log(\lambda_1)$ and $\kappa_2 = \log(\lambda_2)$ at both sides of
the root, such that $f_1 = f(\lambda_1)$ and $f_2 = f(\lambda_2)$ have different signs. Cutting the
horizontal axis with the line connecting (κ_1, f_1) and $\kappa_2, f_2)$ gives an estimate of
the root, say $\tilde{\kappa}$, and $\tilde{\lambda} = \exp(\tilde{\kappa})$. If $f(\tilde{\lambda})$ has the same sign as $f(\lambda_1)$, it replaces
λ_1, otherwise it replaces λ_2. A new iteration then follows, and so on.

Figure 3.7 shows that the RF algorithm converges much faster than HFS. The
starting values were deliberately chosen to be a bit extreme ($\log_{10}(\lambda_1) = -2$
and $\log_{10}(\lambda_1) = 3$), showing that there is no need to be very precise. In principle
more advanced root-finding algorithms could be used, but there is no real need

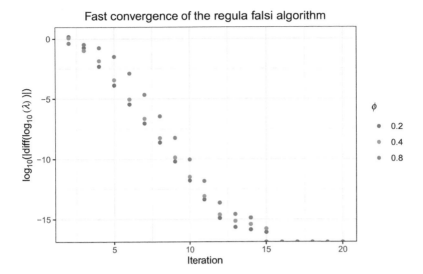

Figure 3.7 Improved speed of convergence of the HFS (Harville–Fellner–Schall) algorithm when combined with the *regula falsi* algorithm for root finding. Three different values of the standard deviation (ϕ) of the noise in the simulation are presented. R code in `f-regula-falsi.R`

for them in the present simulation. Figure 3.7 shows that 10 RF iterations are more than enough.

3.5 Bayesian P-splines

Lang et al. (2003) present a Bayesian variant of P-splines that is very similar to the simplified mixed model. In the latter, we update the variances in each iteration by recomputing their expected values from sums of squares and effective dimensions. The spline coefficients are updated too, by solving the penalized least squares equations. In the Bayesian approach, new values are simulated repeatedly from proper conditional distributions.

Assuming that starting values for τ and σ are available, we repeat the steps below many times. The number of observations is m, the number of B-splines is n, and d is the order of the differences.

- Solve for $\tilde{\alpha}$ in $(B'B/\sigma^2 + D'D/\tau^2)\tilde{\alpha} = B'y/\sigma^2$.
- Simulate a new α from a normal distribution with expectation $\tilde{\alpha}$ and covariance $(B'B/\sigma^2 + D'D/\tau^2)^{-1}$.

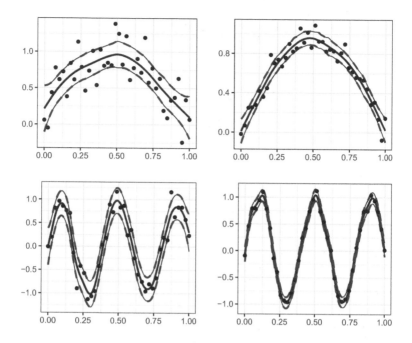

Figure 3.8 Smoothing of simulated data with Bayesian P-splines (20 cubic segments, second-order penalty) for different combinations of smoothness and noise level. The number of Markov steps was 1,000. Blue curves: expect values; red curves: plus and minus two standard deviations. R code in f-bayes-show.R

- Compute $\tilde{\tau}^2 = ||D\alpha||^2/n$ and $\tilde{\sigma}^2 = ||y - B\tilde{\alpha}||^2/m$.
- Simulate a new $\tau^2 = \tilde{\tau}^2/u$, with u drawn from a χ^2 distribution with $n - d$ degrees of freedom.
- Simulate a new $\sigma^2 = \tilde{\sigma}^2/u$, with u drawn from a χ^2 distribution with m degrees of freedom.

This is a simplification of the algorithm of Lang and Brezger. They assume inverse-Gamma priors for σ^2 and τ^2. We will come back to this in what follows.

Figure 3.8 shows this algorithm in action on simulated data, for different choices of the frequency of a sine wave and the size of the random errors. The algorithm is fast, achieving several thousand Monte Carlo Markov chain (MCMc) steps per second, on a standard notebook computer, using a few tricks for fast computation of sums of squares beforehand. Because all coefficients are updated at the same time, the mixing of the Markov chain is excellent, so that relatively short runs are sufficient.

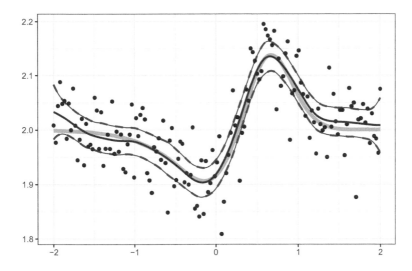

Figure 3.9 Smoothing of simulated data with Bayesian P-splines (20 cubic segments, second-order penalty). The true curve is represented by the thick gray line. It consists of sums and differences of logistic functions. The thinner blue line shows the fit and the red broken lines the two standard deviation lines above and below it. The number of Markov steps was 1,000. R code in f-jullion.R

Lang and Brezger use an inverse-Gamma prior for the variances, with shape parameter $a = 1$ and scale parameter b, a (very) small number. Jullion and Lambert (2007) show that this choice favors strong smoothing, and they propose alternatives. It appears that our simplified algorithm does not have such problems. Figure 3.9 shows a simulation with a P-spline fit, inspired by equation (2) in Jullion and Lambert (2007).

In the examples above, the observation errors are normal, allowing the use of the Gibbs sampler, which is efficient and needs no tuning. This is not the case with other conditional distributions, like Poisson or binomial. A Metropolis–Hastings step must then be included, complicating the computations. We will not explore this in detail, but instead switch to recently developed algorithms. One is a general approach called INLA (integrated nested Laplace approximation) (Rue et al., 2009), and another is a fast Laplace approximation developed for P-splines by Gressani and Lambert (2018). They call it LPS for Laplacian P-splines.

Wang et al. (2018) present a section on P-splines with INLA. One of their examples is density estimation, which we adapt for the Old Faithful data, giving the results shown in Figure 3.10. INLA provides summary statistics, e.g., mean, standard deviation, and quantiles of the estimated spline coefficients. They can

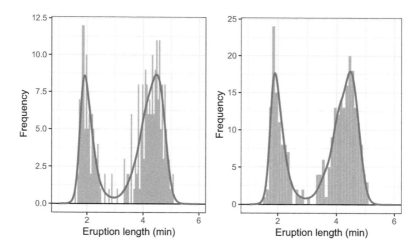

Figure 3.10 Smoothing of a histogram of Old Faithful eruption times, using INLA, with 20 segments in the basis and an "RW2" prior, which implies a second-order penalty. Left: bin width 0.05; right: bin width 0.1. R code in `f-INLA-geyser2.R`

be used to compute the linear predictor, with error bands, on a fine grid. An error band for a density is not very meaningful because it ignores the fact that a density has to integrate to one, so we do not present it.

INLA fits a latent Gaussian field to the observations, meaning that there is a separate parameter for each bin in the histogram. Basis functions, such as B-splines, initially played no role in INLA. In later years, they were included as second-class citizens: the basis matrix is used to introduce constraints, to force the parameters for the observations to be linear combinations of the basis functions. This is not extremely elegant. Also we cannot use a penalty matrix of our choice: INLA offers built-in roughness priors, using first- and second-order random walks.

The idea of Gressani and Lambert (2018) is simple and effective: compute, for a number of λs: (1) the mode of the log-likelihood; (2) a quadratic approximation to the posterior density, and (3) use that as a weight. The P-spline parameters at each trial value of λ are saved and finally combined using a weighted average. An illustration follows.

In the specific case of density estimation, for each trial λ, $\hat{\alpha}$ is computed, which is simply the penalized likelihood estimate. The Laplace approximation is a multivariate normal density centered at $\hat{\alpha}$, with covariance matrix $(B'\hat{M}B + \lambda D'D)^{-1}$, where $\hat{M} = \text{diag}(\hat{\mu})$. Note that this is the Bayesian covariance estimate of $\hat{\alpha}$ (see Section 2.7). Using the Laplace approximation and a (gamma) prior density for λ, the (non-normalized) posterior probability density of λ_k, say π_k, is calculated. We then compute $\hat{\lambda} = \exp\left(\sum_k \pi_k \log(\lambda_k)/\sum_k \pi_k\right)$, a weighted average. Similarly, a weighted average of the $\hat{\alpha}$ obtained for each trial λ gives a final estimate, say $\hat{\hat{\alpha}}$. Gressani and Lambert (2018) give a recipe for estimating the posterior covariance.

Figure 3.10 provides the INLA results for Old Faithful density estimation. We find that INLA is very close in comparison to the LPS fit, with differences of less than 1.5% of the maximum of the fitted density. Although LPS is about seven times faster than INLA (0.3 versus 2.1 seconds), this is not a crucial advantage because both algorithms are fast. More important with LPS, we can plug in any penalty matrix we like, as the next example will show.

We illustrate LPS with a nonstandard penalty on an interesting data set about paper stamps. Basford et al. (1977) describe an analysis of the thickness of Hidalgo stamps from Mexico. See Figure 3.11 for a histogram display of stamp thickness. The authors fit a mixture of seven or eight normal densities with equal standard deviations, assuming that different batches of paper have

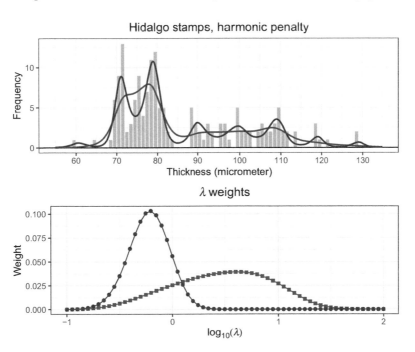

Figure 3.11 Top: smoothing of a histogram of the thickness of 162 Hidalgo stamps, using Laplacian P-splines. Bottom: the posterior weights for λ. Red curve: 30 segments, second-order penalty. Blue line: harmonic penalty with period of 10 micrometer. R code in f-LAPS-stamps-harmonic.R

been used to produce the stamps. We do not believe this to be true. The modes all appear near multiples of 10 micrometer. Thickness is measured with a so-called micrometer, in which a screw is turned until it is blocked by the object under study. Paper is a soft material, so the "end point" is vague. In such a situation digit preference (DP) occurs, the human tendency to round inexact measurements to "nice numbers," like multiples of 10 or 5. Our explanation is that DP is at work here. Camarda et al. (2008) present a sophisticated model for DP. We keep it simple here, assuming the logarithm of the density follows a repeating pattern with a period of 10 micrometers.

A harmonic penalty (see Section 8.2 for details) with period 10 μm is used in Figure 3.11. A linear grid for $\log_{10}(\lambda)$ is explored, running from -2 to 2, in steps of 0.1. The B-spline basis matrix has 30 segments. Computation takes about 0.15 seconds. To show the influence of the prior, we use a random sample consisting of one-third of the complete data. Apparently, the standard second-order penalty does not pick up the periodicity, while the harmonic penalty does. When we use all data, as shown in Figure 3.12, the evidence is so strong that

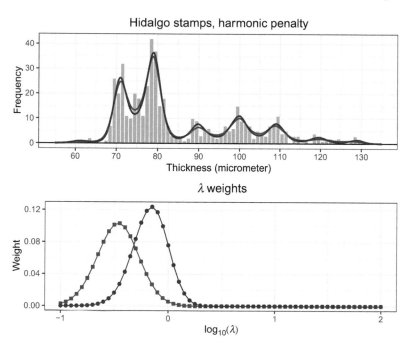

Figure 3.12 Top: smoothing of a histogram of the thickness of 486 Hidalgo stamps, using Laplacian P-splines. Bottom: the posterior weights for λ. Red line: 30 segments, second-order penalty. Blue line: harmonic penalty with period of 10 micrometer. R code in f-LAPS-stamps-harmonic-all.R

the two penalties give very similar results. If we compare the lower panels of Figures 3.11 and 3.12, we see that the distributions of the weights get sharper with more data. In Figure 3.11 we see that the distribution of the weights is much sharper when the harmonic penalty is used.

3.6 Dangers of Automatic Smoothing

We must be careful when using an automatic procedure for choosing λ. We start with an example that illustrates digit preference in the original Old Faithful data.

There exist two data sets containing the Old Faithful eruption times: one is faithful in standard R, and the other geyser in the package MASS. The latter is based on Azzalini and Bowman (1990), which contains a list of the raw data. During the original data collection, nightly observations were crudely recorded as either "long" or "short." In the geyser data set, these were converted to exactly 4.0 and 2.0 minutes, respectively. The help file in R provides further details.

Figure 3.13 shows the influence on the histogram, which now displays two large spikes. AIC responds by choosing a rather small value of λ because it interprets the peaks as real data. The number of raw observations here is 299, while there are 272 observations in the faithful data set. It is not completely clear how the two data sets are related, as we found that there are far more than 27 letter codes in the table presented by Azzalini and Bowman (1990). Because our goal is only to give a warning to automatic smoothing, we do not investigate the issue further.

For these data, we know where the problem comes from: the two bins at 2.0 and 4.0. We introduce weights that are 1 everywhere, except for the two problematic bins, where they are zero. Then we minimize the weighted penalized deviance and search for the λ that minimizes AIC. We find that $\log_{10}(\lambda) = -0.8$ is optimal. The resulting density estimate is more realistic, as is shown in Figure 3.14.

In the Old Faithful example, it is clear that the Poisson assumption does not hold, and it is also clear which of the isolated data points are the culprits. Figure 3.15 shows an example where violations occur in many places. The data are death counts of males living in Greece during the year 1960 (Perperoglou and Eilers, 2010). We vary the numbers of B-splines in the basis to be either 10 or 40, using a second-order penalty. In both cases, the minimum of AIC is not pronounced. If we would trust the result for the small basis, which is shown in the upper right panel, we might get the impression that we have a decent fit to the

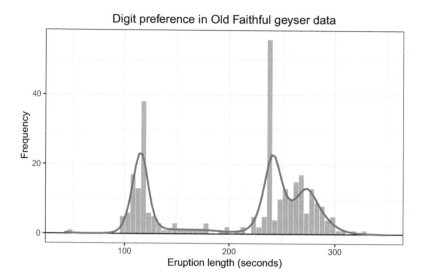

Figure 3.13 Digit preference in Old Faithful eruption times. Uncertain nightly observations have been rounded to exactly 2 and 4 minutes. Optimal $\log_{10}(\lambda) = -1.5$ determined by AIC. Cubic B-spline basis with 20 segments and third-order penalty. R code in `f-geyser-with-DP.R`

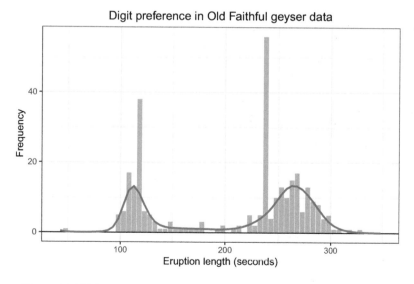

Figure 3.14 Using weights to remedy digit preference in Old Faithful eruption times. Uncertain nightly observations have been rounded to exactly 2 and 4 minutes. These bins have been given zero weights. Optimal $\log_{10}(\lambda) = -0.8$ determined by AIC. Cubic B-spline basis with 20 segments and third-order penalty. R code in `f-geyser-weights.R`

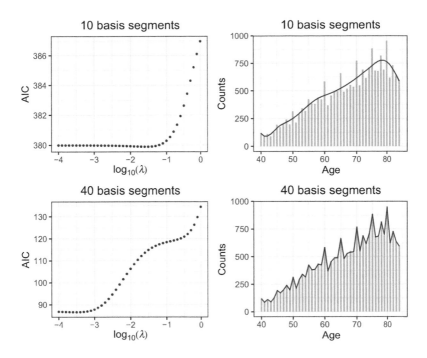

Figure 3.15 Counts of male deaths in Greece, in 1960, versus age. In the top row a cubic basis with 10 segments was used. The upper left panel shows the profile of AIC and the upper right panel the data and the minimum AIC fit. Bottom row: ditto, using 40 segments in the basis. R code in f-Greece-AIC.R

data. But the large basis gives a very rough result, warning us that the Poisson assumption is wrong and that we need an improved smoothing algorithm that can handle the apparent overdispersion.

The effective dimension and the deviance give interesting insights. With 10 segments, the cubic B-spline basis matrix has 13 columns. The effective dimension of the fitted model is 12.9, almost equal to the nominal dimension. With 40 segments, the nominal dimension is 43, and 42.6 is reported for the effective dimension, again quite close. For the small basis the deviance is very large, 354.1, while for the large basis it is 1.51, extremely small.

Although it is not shown here, the HFS algorithm gives essentially the same results. In this case, HFS estimates the variance of the differences of the coefficients, but assumes that the variance of the residuals, σ^2, is 1. However, we can relax this assumption and estimate σ^2 from the data using $\hat{\sigma}^2 = \sum r_i^2/(m - \text{ED})$, where $r_i = (y_i - \hat{\mu}_i)/\sqrt{\hat{\mu}_i}$. This is a variant of quasi-likelihood (McCullagh and Nelder, 1989). Figure 3.16 shows results for 10 and 40 segments; they are almost indistinguishable.

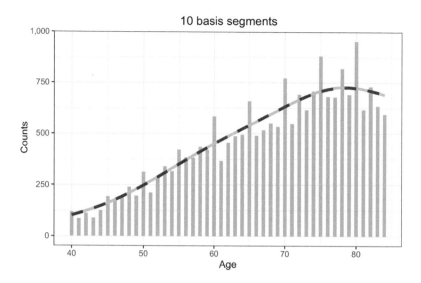

Figure 3.16 Counts of male deaths in Greece, in 1960, versus age. P-spline fit with quasi-likelihood for 10 (broken blue curve) and 40 (pink curve) segments in the basis. The two curves are almost identical. R code in f-Greece-QL.R

An alternative approach to overdispersion, using the same data, is presented in Section 8.4. There random effects are added to the linear predictor, one for each observation, and estimated using penalized likelihood.

3.7 L- and V-curves

We next present a more recent development, the V-curve (Frasso and Eilers, 2015). It is easy to compute and handles serial correlation well. The roots of the V-curve lie in ridge regression, which minimizes the penalized sum of squares $||y - X\alpha||^2 + \lambda||\alpha||^2$, where X is an arbitrary matrix of regressors with possibly more columns than rows. The penalty $\lambda||\alpha||^2$ constrains the size of α, shrinking it toward zero. As with smoothing, the "best" value of λ is to be determined from the data. Hansen (1992) proposes the L-curve, a plot of $\log(||y - X\alpha||^2)$ against $\log(||\alpha||^2)$ for a grid of values of $\log(\lambda)$. If the spacing of the grid is fine, the plotted dots present a "curve." In Hansen's examples, the curve has the shape of an L with a rather sharp corner. Hansen advises to choose the value of λ that corresponds to the corner and found good results.

Frasso and Eilers (2015) explore the L-curve for P-splines, plotting $\log(||y - B\alpha||^2)$ against $\log(||D\alpha||^2)$. We illustrate this approach with the

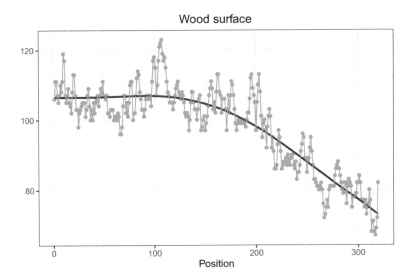

Figure 3.17 Detailed measurements along a line on the surface of a sanded piece
of wood. The gray dots and thin line show the data. The thick blue line shows the
trend, with tuning of λ based on the V-curve. R code in f-wood-surf.R

data shown in Figure 3.17, which are detailed measurements of the surface
of a sanded piece of wood (Pandit and Wu, 1993). The noise in the data is
strongly correlated, and consequently cross-validation (LOOCV) indicates
very light smoothing. At first sight, this comes as a surprise because we clearly
see a smooth trend plus noise. However, the guiding principle of LOOCV
is to optimize predictions of single left-out observations, based on smooth
interpolation. If there is serial correlation, it is better to stay close to neighbors
than to use a smooth trend for prediction.

The L-curve is illustrated in the left panel of Figure 3.18 for the wood data,
using the Whittaker smoother. There is no sign of a sharp corner, only a small
wiggle, as if an L shape has been bent to become almost flat. This makes it
difficult to locate a suitable λ. However, the dots are closer together in the
neighborhood of the "corner," which suggests to plot the distance between
the dots against $\log_{10}(\lambda)$ (actually the average of the logarithms of the two λ
belonging to adjacent dots). This is called the V-curve, and it is shown in the right
panel. A clear minimum can now be located, indicating $\log_{10}(\lambda) \approx 2.8$ as a good
choice. The crossing broken lines in the left panel cross at the corresponding
position on the L-curve. Computations for the V-curve are fast because no
hat matrix is needed. It is sufficient to compute $\hat{\alpha}$, $||y - B\hat{\alpha}||^2$ and $||D\hat{\alpha}||^2$.
Especially when B is large and sparse, this can be a strong advantage.

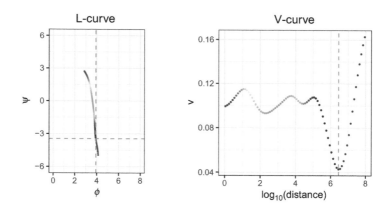

Figure 3.18 L-curve and V-curve for the wood surface data. R code in f-L-and-V-wood.R

Frasso and Eilers (2015) present several applications of the V-curve. They find that it clearly outperformed mixed model fits that explicitly estimated an autoregressive error structure. Computation is very fast, and it even works well in cases where an autoregressive error structure cannot be estimated.

3.8 Transformation of the Independent Variable

Many statisticians are familiar with transformation of a dependent variable. Generally the goal is to achieve errors that are more or less normally distributed and thus suitable for (penalized) least squares fitting. In contrast, transformation of the independent variable has been relatively neglected in the literature. An example will show that such a transformation can be useful. Figure 3.19 shows a scatterplot of the body mass index (BMI) of Dutch boys by age. The data are available in the R package AGD (16 observations have been omitted; the ones with BMI less than 10 or larger than 30). The trend has been computed with a B-spline basis having 50 segments, and λ has been determined with the HFS algorithm; its value is 13.7. After 13 iterations (starting from $\lambda = 10$), the relative change in λ is less than 10^{-5}. The effective dimension is 26.0.

The very steep increase of BMI at very young ages forces the fitted curve to be very flexible. This results in unwanted wiggly behavior at the older ages. In Figure 3.20, the square root of age is used as the independent variable.

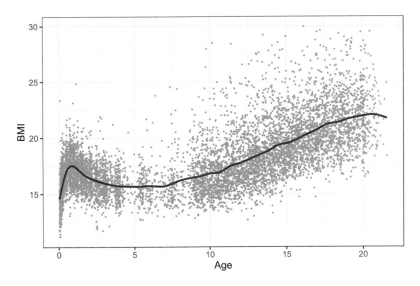

Figure 3.19 Body mass index of Dutch boys against their age. Trend determined with the HFS algorithm. B-spline basis with 50 segments and second-order penalty. R code in f-BMI-lin.R

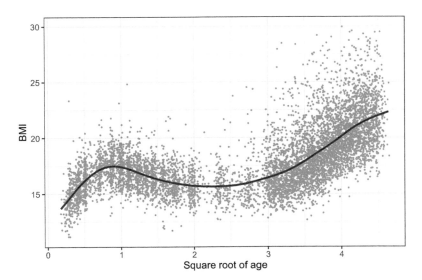

Figure 3.20 Body mass index of Dutch boys versus the square root of their age. Trend determined with the HFS algorithm. B-spline basis with 50 segments and second-order penalty. R code in f-BMI-sqrt.R

Young ages are expanded, removing the previously observed steep increase in this region. Five iterations of the HFS algorithm are enough to converge to $\lambda = 275.5$, and a very smooth curve is obtained. The effective dimension is now 13.4.

If desired, the fitted curve can be transformed back to age. In our experience many growth data show a steep increase at young ages. The data set that we used here also contains height and weight measurements, which exhibit similar patterns. It would truly be a step forward if the square root of age would be adopted on a broad scale for display and analysis of growth data. To make for easy reading of the scale, a separate axis with markers at pleasant positions on a linear scale can be added. An example with growth charts for children with the Ellis–van Creveld syndrome can be found in Verbeek et al. (2011).

3.9 Notes and Details

We have avoided the discussion of explicit models for correlated errors. Currie and Durbán (2002) and Kauermann et al. (2011) analyze P-splines with autoregressive errors, in a mixed model setting. They also provide R software. Frasso and Eilers (2015) show that the success rate of an autoregressive model depends on the type of noise. They also gave an example (the price of orange juice), where AR models fail, while the V-curve worked well.

We evaluated CV or AIC on a relatively detailed grid of values of $\log_{10}(\lambda)$ and searched for the minimum. If there is only one λ this works fine, and the profile can provide an impression whether or not the minimum is sharply defined. In the chapters ahead (e.g., Chapter 4), we will encounter models with multiple λs. It is then more convenient to use numerical optimization.

4

Multidimensional Smoothing

We now turn to multidimensional models, with multiple explanatory variables and one response. We mainly study the two-dimensional case, although our models allow more dimensions.

We first present the linear additive model, which is essentially a sum of unidimensional models, without interactions. We collect B-spline basis matrices and penalties in one large structure, fitting all terms simultaneously. For a non-normal response leads we introduce the generalized additive model (P-GAM). A simple modification leads to the varying coefficient model (VCM), allowing coefficients in a linear regression model to vary smoothly with an additional variable.

To handle general interactions, we introduce tensor products of B-splines and simultaneous penalties on the rows and columns of coefficients. An alternative is a additive decomposition of effects, having individual penalties, called PS-ANOVA. Both algorithms are very fast, doing spatial smoothing of data sets with thousands of observations in a few seconds. Large rectangular grids can be smoothed even faster, using the so-called array algorithm.

Interpolation and extrapolation occur automatically, as in the case of one dimension. There we have that the fitted curve is not influenced by the amount of extrapolation, In two dimensions this is no longer the case because the penalties interact.

With multidimensional models come multiple smoothing parameters. Two-dimensional PS-ANOVA has five of them. The streamlined algorithm for mixed model estimation quickly finds a solution. Partial effective dimensions play an important role in the estimation of variances, but also in the interpretation of the importance of model components.

4.1 Generalized Additive Models

An additive model fits a response variable y by a sum of smooth functions of the regressors, x_j for $j = 1 : p$ (Hastie and Tibshirani, 1990). To keep the notation simple, in this chapter x_j indicates a whole vector of length m.

For a normal response, the additive model is

$$\mu = E(y) = \sum_{j=1}^{p} f_j(x_j) = \eta, \qquad (4.1)$$

where the $f_j(\cdot)$ are smooth functions. For non-normal responses the linear predictor $g(\mu) = \eta$ is modeled as a sum of smooth functions, where $g(\cdot)$ is the monotone link function, and y is assumed to have a distribution in the exponential family. This broader framework gives the generalized additive model (GAM).

Consider a simple model with two components:

$$\mu = f_1(x_1) + f_2(x_2) = B_1\alpha_1 + B_2\alpha_2. \qquad (4.2)$$

The model is ill-defined because any constant shift δ in $f_1(x_1)$ can be compensated by a shift $-\delta$ in $f_2(x_2)$. We will come back to this issue below.

To build the linear predictor, we column join B_1 and B_2 and stack α_1 and α_2 to get

$$\eta = [B_1 \mid B_2] \begin{bmatrix} \alpha_1 \\ \alpha_2 \end{bmatrix} = B\alpha.$$

A difference penalty is placed on each vector α_j, with separate tuning parameters λ_1 and λ_2. To avoid cluttered notation, we do not indicate order and size of each differencing matrix; in general they may be different. The penalized least squares objective is

$$S = ||y - B\alpha||^2 + \lambda_1||D_1\alpha_1||^2 + \lambda_2||D_2\alpha_2||^2. \qquad (4.3)$$

The explicit solution follows from the normal equations

$$(B'B + P)\alpha = B'y, \quad \hat{\alpha} = (B'B + P)^{-1}B'y, \qquad (4.4)$$

which are the same equations as for unidimensional P-splines, but now using a block-diagonal matrix

$$P = \begin{bmatrix} \lambda_1 D_1' D_1 & 0 \\ 0 & \lambda_2 D_2' D_2 \end{bmatrix}.$$

To handle weights, in a diagonal matrix W, the first term in (4.3) should be changed to $(y' - B\alpha)'W(y - B\alpha)$.

In the generalized linear case, we compute α that minimizes the penalized deviance function

$$\text{dev}(\alpha;\ B,\ y) + \lambda_1||D_1\alpha_1||^2 + \lambda_2||D_2\alpha_2||^2,$$

which then leads to the iterative scheme similar to (2.22)

$$\tilde{\alpha}_{t+1} = (B'\tilde{W}_t B + P)^{-1} B'\tilde{W}_t \tilde{z}_t, \tag{4.5}$$

where $\tilde{W}_t$ is a diagonal matrix with the working GLM weights, and $\tilde{z}_t = \tilde{\eta}_t + \tilde{W}_t^{-1}(y - \tilde{\mu}_t)$ is the working dependent variable, at iteration t. We call this model a P-GAM.

As mentioned, the above systems are singular, as for any offset δ, $\alpha_1 + \delta$ and $\alpha_2 - \delta$ will give the same solution. Therefore we add a small ridge penalty, replacing P by $P^+ = P + \kappa I$, with I an identity matrix and κ a small number, like 10^{-6}. This puts a penalty on the size of α, forcing the solution to be the one with minimum norm.

We illustrate the additive model with the `ethanol` data set in R. The dependent variable is the concentration of nitrous oxides (NOx) in the exhaust gas of a combustion engine. The explanatory variables are the compression ratio of the engine (C) and the equivalence ratio (air to ethanol) (E) of the fuel. Figure 4.1 presents several summary panels, showing the design points of C and E, the estimates of $f_1(C)$, $f_2(E)$, and a plot of the observations versus the fitted values. The model fits quite well to the data; the standard deviation of the residuals is 0.22. We used 10 segments for each basis and a second-order penalty. The penalty parameters are $\lambda_C = 1$ and $\lambda_E = 0.1$, with $\kappa = 10^{-6}$ (these values were subjectively chosen).

Figure 4.2 shows a contour plot of the fitted surface. It is dominated by the effect of the equivalence ratio. It has a simple structure, as it is the sum of two functions, one along E and the other along C. In Sections 4.5 and 4.12, we analyze the same data, using tensor product P-splines, which allow a more complicated structure of the surface.

The additive model allows a useful breakdown of the effective dimension and the hat matrix, giving a partial effective dimension for each model component. From (4.4), we find that the hat matrix is $H = B(B'B + P^+)^{-1}B'$. Let $Q = (B'B + P^+)^{-1}$. Because $B = [B_1|B_2]$, we find that $H = B_1 Q B_1' + B_2 Q B_2' = H_1 + H_2$, expressing the hat matrix as a sum. As ED $= \text{trace}(H) = \text{trace}(H_1) + \text{trace}(H_2)$, we arrive at a sum for the effective dimension. We also can prove that ED$_1 = \text{trace}(K_{11})$ and ED$_2 = \text{trace}(K_{22})$, where $K = (B'B + P^+)^{-1}B'B$ is a partitioned matrix with blocks K_{11} and K_{22} on its diagonal. Here the size of K_{11} is equal to that of $D_1'D_1$, and K_{22} has the size of $D_2'D_2$. In the case of a GAM, the decomposition works as well, on the scale of the linear predictor.

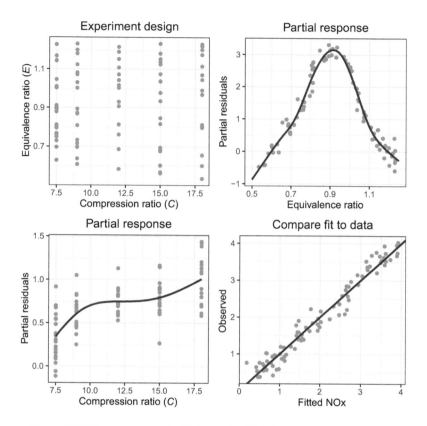

Figure 4.1 Fitting a generalized additive model (GAM) to the ethanol data. Design points for compression ratio (C) and equivalence ratio (E) (top, left); the additive smooth components (top, right) and (bottom, left); observed versus fitted values (bottom, right). R code in f-ethanol-gam.R

Several properties of P-splines carry over to the GAM. When λ_j gets large, the corresponding additive component will approach a polynomial of degree $d_j - 1$, with d_j denoting the order of the differences in the penalty for component j. The partial effective dimension will approach d_j.

The (Bayesian) covariance matrix of the estimated coefficient vector is

$$\mathrm{Cov}(\hat{\alpha}) = \sigma^2 (B'B + P^+)^{-1}. \tag{4.6}$$

To estimate σ^2, we need to correct for the effective model dimension and for the implicit polynomial components that are in the null space of the penalty

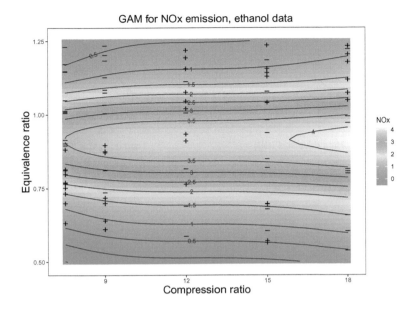

Figure 4.2 Additive model for the ethanol data. Image and contours of the fitted surface. R code in f-ethanol-gam-surf.R

matrices. This is further discussed in Appendix E. Hence, for the P-GAM model,

$$\hat{\sigma}^2 = ||y - \hat{\mu}||^2/(m - \text{ED}). \qquad (4.7)$$

With non-normal extensions, computation of the standard error bands for the linear predictor follows the same pattern, utilizing GLM weights as in (2.27), while replacing the estimate of σ^2 with a dispersion parameter ϕ. The inverse link operation is required on the limits, to get bands for the expected values.

4.2 Varying Coefficient Models

The main idea of the varying coefficient model (VCM) is to allow regression coefficients to vary smoothly with another variable, generating coefficient curves (Hastie and Tibshirani, 1993). Assume that we have explanatory variables as for a GAM, but there is an extra variable t, which might be time or any other continuous or ordinal variate. We do not consider nonlinear functions of the xs, as in a GAM, but rather focus on the classic linear regression model setting. The coefficients of this model are allowed to change smoothly with t.

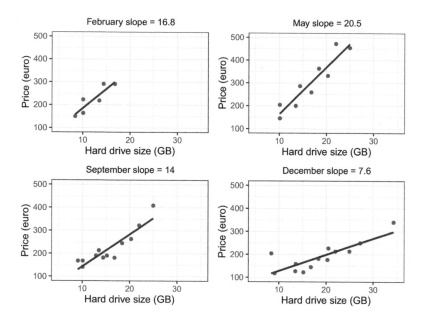

Figure 4.3 IBM hard drives: price versus size, in four different months, with linear regression lines. R code in f-vcm4up.R

To illustrate the VCM, we use historical data on the prices of IBM hard disk drives, as advertised in a monthly Dutch computer journal from February 1999 through January 2000. In each month, for a handful of drives, we have the capacity in gigabytes (GB) and the price (in Dutch guilders, converted here to euros). The price/capacity ratio (euro/GB) changes over time, reflecting technological and economic advances. For a number of months, drives with different capacities are available, so it is possible to do a linear regression for each of these months separately. Figure 4.3 gives an impression. A plot of the monthly slopes of the regression lines gives an impression of the trend, which is provided in Figure 4.4 (the dots).

There are no data for August 1999, and the pattern of the dots is noisy. We could use P-splines to compute a smooth trend directly on these monthly snapshots of slopes, while (e.g.) using the inverse variances of these slope estimates as weights. This approach would not admit data for months where only one disk drive was advertised. The VCM is a more elegant and useful solution. It automatically interpolates the missing month and extrapolates the trend into future months.

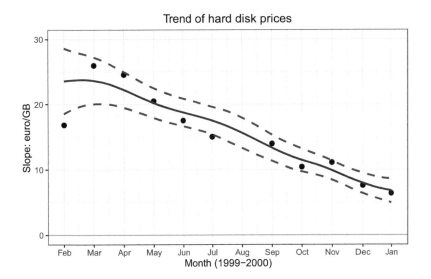

Figure 4.4 IBM: estimated varying slope, combining all monthly data. The individual data points represent the estimated slopes using the data month by month. R code in f-vcmsmooth.R

The VCM combines all data into one model, allowing intercept and the slope to vary smoothly with t:

$$\mu(t) = \beta_1(t) + x(t)\beta_2(t). \tag{4.8}$$

Introducing the B-spline basis B, computed from t, we can write

$$\mu = B\alpha_1 + XB\alpha_2 = B\alpha_1 + U\alpha_2 = R\alpha,$$

where $R = [B \mid U]$ and $\alpha' = [\alpha_1' \mid \alpha_2]'$. We see that the structure is identical to that of the additive model, and we can use the same penalized least squares algorithm for estimation, i.e., minimizing

$$S^\star = ||y - R\alpha||^2 + \lambda_1||D_1\alpha_1||^2 + \lambda_2||D_2\alpha_2||^2, \tag{4.9}$$

with the explicit solution

$$\hat{\alpha} = (R'R + P)^{-1}R'y, \tag{4.10}$$

where the penalty matrix is the familiar $P = \text{block diag}(\lambda_1 D_1' D_1, \lambda_2 D_2' D_2)$.

Generally the VCM is not ill-conditioned, so an extra ridge penalty, as for the GAM, is not needed. Due to the scaling of the rows of B by X in $U = XB$, it is no longer the case that $\alpha_1 + \delta$ and $\alpha_2 - \delta$ give the same μ.

Figure 4.4 shows the estimated trend of the price per gigabyte. After a slight increase in early 1999, the disks did quickly get cheaper: within a single year, the consumer received more than double the size for the same price. We used 10 segments for each basis and a second-order penalty. Optimal tuning was set at $\lambda = 100$ for both the varying intercept and slope, with the effective dimensions of 2.2 and 7.7, respectively. The ridge parameter was set at $\kappa = 10^{-6}$.

Details of the GAM (effective dimensions, standard errors, etc.) directly carry over to the VCM setting; as they are straightforward extensions, we do not expand on them here.

The VCM fits naturally into the GLM framework, with a link function $g(\cdot)$: $g(\mu) = R\alpha = \eta$. We illustrate it with a model for monthly counts of polio cases in the United States (as reported to the U.S. Centers for Disease Control) during the years 1970 through 1984 (data set polio in the R package gamlss.data). The counts are assumed to follow Poisson distributions. To handle the strong seasonal pattern, the logarithms of their expectations are modeled with a VCM having five components: a trend plus smoothly modulated sine and cosine functions, each with periods of 12 and 6 months. The model follows as

$$\log(\mu(t)) = f_0(t) + \sum_{k=1}^{2}(f_{1k}(t)\cos(k\omega t) + f_{2k}(t)\sin(k\omega t)), \qquad (4.11)$$

where $\omega = 2\pi/12$ for $t = 1 : 216$. In matrix notation, we have

$$\log(\mu) = B\alpha_0 + \sum_{k=1}^{2}(C_k B\alpha_{ck} + S_k B\alpha_{sk}) = R\alpha, \qquad (4.12)$$

where $R = (B \mid C_1 B \mid C_2 B \mid S_1 B \mid S_2 B)$ and α is the corresponding augmented coefficient vector. Here $C_k = \mathrm{diag}(\cos(k\omega t))$ and $S_k = \mathrm{diag}(\sin(k\omega t))$, $k = 1 : 2$.

There is one common B-spline basis matrix B for modeling each of the smooth functions, but coefficients vectors are different. We choose 20 segments for the basis and a second-order penalty for each term. Each sine and cosine term has a separate λ. To optimize their values, we use the Harville–Fellner–Schall algorithm (see Section 3.4), updating iteratively λ_j by $\widetilde{\mathrm{ED}}_j/||D\tilde{\alpha}_j||^2$. Convergence is quick: after 10 iterations, starting from $\lambda_j = 1$ for all j, the maximum relative change in the λs is less than 10^{-5}.

Figure 4.5 displays some results. Both seasonal components are strong. There is generally a downward trend, with an upward bump at the end of the seventies. The effective dimensions of all five components fall in a narrow

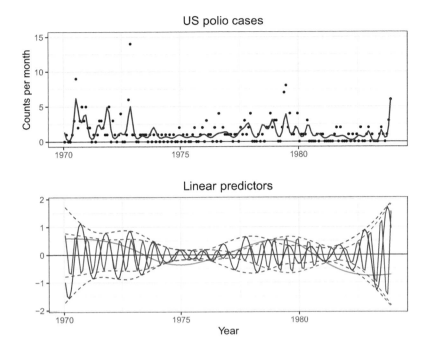

Figure 4.5 Polio data. Top: observed monthly counts and fitted values of the varying coefficient model. Bottom: the components of the linear predictor, a smooth trend (green) and modulated (co)sines with periods of 6 (red) and 12 (blue) months (bottom). The broken lines show the varying amplitudes. R code in f-polio-vcm.R

band, from 5.2 to 7.1. The varying amplitude of component k is computed as $\sqrt{f_{1k}(t)^2 + f_{2k}(t)^2}$.

The use of a modulated (co)sine function for modeling of seasonal counts has been proposed by Eilers et al. (2008). The bilinear modulation model is a generalization, in which the (co)sines are replaced by a nonparametric periodic function (Marx et al., 2010).

4.3 Tensor Product Models

To make P-splines work with interactions in two dimensions, we need to generalize the basis *and* the penalties. Tensor products will be used for the former goal (Dierckx, 1993). Instead of a vector of spline coefficients, there will now be a matrix. There will be two penalties, one down all columns of this matrix and another along all rows. The penalties can have different values of λ, allowing anisotropic smoothing.

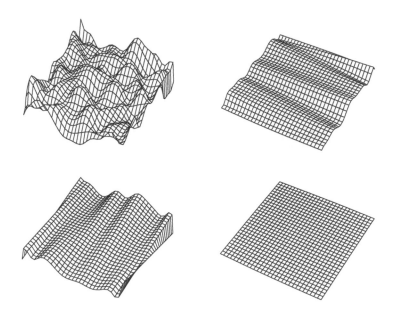

Figure 4.6 Examples of tensor product surfaces, with various degrees of interaction. See the text for explanation. R code in f-tensor4up.R

The concept of tensor product P-splines is not complicated, but the implementation demands are. The elegance of directly applicable matrix operations, as in one-dimensional regression, is gone. Still we need to introduce them to solve linear systems of equations. With Kronecker products and vectorization of matrices, this can be achieved. For large problems this leads to very long computation times and memory overflow. Fortunately, for data on a rectangular grid, rearrangement of the computations, with the so-called array algorithm, saves orders of magnitude in memory use and computation time. The technical details are in Appendix D, but we present an outline in this chapter.

Figure 4.6 gives an impression of the variety of surfaces that are possible with tensor product P-splines. All panels were generated with the tensor product of two B-spline bases, each having 10 segments. In the upper left panel, the coefficients are random. In the lower left panel, a light second-order penalty has been applied in both directions. In the upper right panel, a strong second-order penalty is applied in the y direction and a light one in the x direction. In the lower right panel a very strong second-order penalty works in both directions, resulting in a bilinear surface.

4.4 Tensor Product Bases

The principles of tensor products of B-splines are relatively easy, but they can lead to complicated expressions with many indices. Before doing so, we use a conceptual presentation, similar to how we introduced B-splines in Chapter 2.

We start with data Y on a grid with m rows and $\breve{m}$ columns. A matrix W, of the same size, contains weights. These may represent uncertainties in the data, but W can also be a matrix with ones and zeros, where zeros indicate missing data. As we will see, automatic interpolation works for tensor product P-splines, like in the one-dimensional case. Let x and $\breve{x}$ indicate the coordinates of rows and columns of Y, respectively. Based on x, the m by n B-splines basis matrix B can be computed, and based on $\breve{x}$, we have the $\breve{m}$ by $\breve{n}$ basis matrix $\breve{B}$.

The tensor products are $b_{ik}\breve{b}_{jl}$, with $i = 1 : m$, $j = 1 : \breve{m}$, $k = 1 : n$ and $l = 1 : \breve{n}$. The expected value of y_{ij} is formed by

$$\mu_{ij} = \sum_k \sum_l b_{ik}\breve{b}_{jl}\alpha_{kl} = \sum_k \sum_l c_{ijkl}\alpha_{kl}, \tag{4.13}$$

and the coefficients form an n by $\breve{n}$ matrix $A = [\alpha_{kl}]$. A much more compact way to write (4.13) is

$$M = [\mu_{ij}] = BA\breve{B}'. \tag{4.14}$$

If we wish to evaluate the fit in more detail, in one or both dimensions for a given A, it is sufficient to evaluate B-spline basis matrices on a more detailed grid, using the design parameters that were used for B and $\breve{B}$.

In one dimension the B-spline coefficients form the skeleton of a fit. The same is true for tensor products. The four-dimensional array C in (4.13) holds the tensor product of B and $\breve{B}$. For fixed k and l, $[c_{ijkl}]$ defines a matrix that is filled with the outer product of column k of B and column l of $\breve{B}$. The left panel of Figure 4.7 shows one such outer product as a surface. An impression of the entire two-dimensional basis is given in the right panel of that figure, looking at all combinations of k and l. Note that, to improve the display (avoiding too much overlap), only every second basis function has been plotted.

In three dimensions or more, this tensor product scheme holds as well. The notation gets awkward, but the principle is straightforward. In this book we will not go into applications beyond two dimensions. For further information, see Section 4.11 at the end of this chapter.

The equation (4.13) is elegant, but how can we use it to fit a surface to data? In our notation, we use the squared Frobenius norm, $||U||_F^2$, which indicates the sum of the squares of all the elements of a matrix, and $\odot$ indicates

One tensor product   **A tensor product basis**

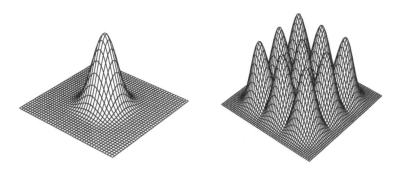

Figure 4.7 Left: one tensor product basis function, the building block. Right: sparse representation of a complete tensor product B-spline basis. R code in f-tensor-show.R

element-wise product of two matrices: $[u_{ij}] \odot [v_{ij}] = [u_{ij}v_{ij}]$. To estimate A, we define the objective function

$$S = ||W^{\frac{1}{2}} \odot (Y - M)||_F^2 = ||W^{\frac{1}{2}} \odot (Y - BA\breve{B}')||_F^2. \qquad (4.15)$$

Here we denote $W^{\frac{1}{2}} = [\sqrt{w_{ij}}]$. We vectorize A, W, and Y, while additionally turning the tensor products of B-splines into an $m\breve{m}$ by $n\breve{n}$ matrix. This is achieved by computing $\alpha = \text{vec}(A)$, $w = \text{vec}(W)$, $y = \text{vec}(Y)$, and $\mathcal{B} = \breve{B} \otimes B$, where $\otimes$ indicates the Kronecker product, and the *vec* operator stacks the columns of a matrix on top of each other into one vector.

We then have

$$S = (y - \mathcal{B}\alpha)'\mathcal{W}(y - \mathcal{B}\alpha), \qquad (4.16)$$

where $\mathcal{W} = \text{diag}(w)$. The explicit solution is

$$\hat{\alpha} = (\mathcal{B}'\mathcal{W}\mathcal{B})^{-1}\mathcal{B}'\mathcal{W}y. \qquad (4.17)$$

Naturally the vector $\hat{\alpha}$ can be reshaped into the n by $\breve{n}$ coefficient matrix $\hat{A}$. No penalties are involved yet; we will add them in the next section.

Thus far, the Y data have been presented on a grid. This may not be the case in general, as data may be scattered. We then have quadruples (x, $\breve{x}$, y, w), with the vectors x and $\breve{x}$ being arbitrary coordinate positions, associated with the vector of responses y and vector of weights w. One-dimensional B-spline basis matrices B and $\check{B}$ are computed, based on x and $\check{x}$. The expected values are given by

$$\mu_i = \sum_k \sum_l b_{ik} \check{b}_{il} \alpha_{kl} = \sum_k \sum_l c_{ikl} \alpha_{kl}. \tag{4.18}$$

We now obtain a three-dimensional array C, connecting values at scattered data points to a matrix of coefficients. The objective function can be written as in (4.16), but the definition of $\mathcal{B}$ has to be changed, as it no longer is a Kronecker product. The number of rows of $\mathcal{B}$ is equal to the number of observations, and each row of $\mathcal{B}$ is the Kronecker product of the corresponding rows of $\check{B}$ and B. Symbolically: $\mathcal{B}(i, :) = \check{B}(i, :) \otimes B(i, :)$. A convenient notation is $\mathcal{B} = \check{B} \square B = (\check{B} \otimes 1'_n) \odot (1'_{\check{n}} \otimes B)$, called the "box" product of $\check{B}$ and B of dimension $m^\star$ by $n\check{n}$, where $m^\star$ is the number of observations (Eilers et al., 2006). The name comes from the LaTeX code box for the rectangle symbol. Note that $m^\star = m\check{m}$ for data on a grid.

4.5 Two-Dimensional Penalties

We now come to the penalties. In two dimensions they are almost indispensable. Equation (4.17) will only work if we are fortunate, i.e., when all basis functions are well supported by the data locations. This can be the case when data on a grid are complete, but many practical data sets have "holes," missing corners, or irregular domains. With scattered data points in a plane, it is almost certain that some or many tensor products have no support.

In one dimension, the P-spline penalty is $\lambda ||D\alpha||^2$, while α is a vector. Eilers and Marx (2003) extend the idea to two dimensions. Here we have $\check{n}$ such vectors in the columns of A. With DA, we form a matrix of differences of the columns. To construct a penalty, we square and add them up. This can be written as $||DA||_F^2$. We can apply a similar procedure to the rows of A by computing $||\check{D}A'||_F^2 = ||A\check{D}'||_F^2$ and summing the penalties:

$$\text{Pen} = \lambda ||DA||_F^2 + \check{\lambda} ||A\check{D}'||_F^2, \tag{4.19}$$

which can be combined directly with the objective function in (4.15). Note that there are two λs, which can have different values, allowing anisotropic smoothing according to row and column orientations.

To apply the penalty to $\alpha = \text{vec}(A)$, a construction with Kronecker products is required:

$$\text{Pen} = \lambda ||(\check{I} \otimes D)\alpha||^2 + \check{\lambda} ||(\check{D} \otimes I)\alpha||^2 = \lambda \alpha' P \alpha + \check{\lambda} \alpha' \check{P} \alpha, \tag{4.20}$$

with $P = (\check{I} \otimes D)'(\check{I} \otimes D)$ and $\check{P} = (\check{D} \otimes I)'(\check{D} \otimes I)$, where I, $\check{I}$ are identity matrices of proper dimensions. As the coefficients remain on a grid, the penalty does not depend on whether the data are scattered or on a grid because in either case there is the (full) coefficient matrix A.

The bottom line is that (4.17) changes to

$$\hat{\alpha} = (\mathcal{B}'\mathcal{W}\mathcal{B} + \lambda P + \check{\lambda}\check{P})^{-1}\mathcal{B}'\mathcal{W}y. \tag{4.21}$$

The structure of this equation is the same as that for one-dimensional P-splines: a sum of weighted inner products of a basis with itself and a penalty matrix (here $\lambda P + \check{\lambda}\check{P}$) on the left, with a weighted inner product of the basis matrix and the observations on the right.

Figure 4.8 shows a fit to the ethanol data, using a second-order penalty with $\lambda_C = 1$ for the compression ratio and $\lambda_E = 0.1$ for the equivalence ratio, with 10 segments in each basis. The standard deviation of the residuals is 0.17, which is a 23% reduction from the P-GAM fit. Comparisons of fits in Figure 4.8 relative to Figure 4.2 also shows that the tensor product surface is more complicated and nonadditive.

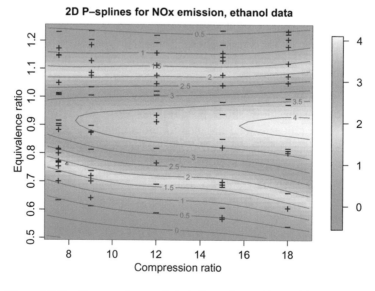

Figure 4.8 The blue $+$ and $-$ symbols indicate the positions of the data points and the signs of the residuals. Each basis has 10 segments and a second-order penalty, with $\lambda = 1$ (for the C axis) and $\check{\lambda} = 0.1$ (for the E axis). R code in f-ethanol-psp2.R

4.6 Interpolation and Extrapolation

In Section 2.4, we showed how to do interpolation and extrapolation with P-splines. Thanks to the penalty, coefficients of B-splines without support are automatically estimated. In the univariate setting, interpolation at new positions between the data points, say x^*, requires a new basis matrix B^* to be computed using the same design parameters (domain of x, number of segments, and degree of the B-splines). Multiplying B^* by the coefficient vector gives the desired result. Extrapolation is similar, but one has to choose the domain of the B-spline basis large enough, so that it covers the extrapolation region.

The same principles work for tensor product P-splines. Thanks to the penalties, all elements of the coefficient matrix are estimated automatically, and detailed basis matrices allow computation of the fitted surface on an arbitrary grid.

In most cases, it is wise to limit the domain on which a fitted surface is computed and displayed, as unrealistic extrapolation can occur. Figure 4.9

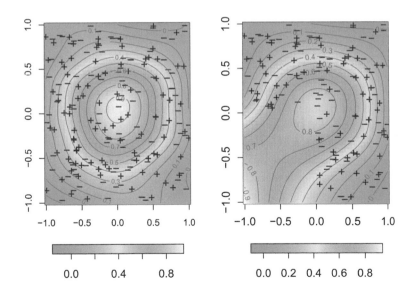

Figure 4.9 Fitting of scattered data with tensor product P-splines: complete data (left) and a data subset after removal of data in the lower left corner (right). The surface is extrapolated automatically, but it looks unrealistic. R code in f-psp-corner.R

illustrates the issue for simulated data in which one of the corners is missing. Although a fitted surface is obtained without any problems, its extrapolation in the lower left corner looks doubtful. It may be better to curb the boundaries of the display, visually like using a cookie cutter. Naturally the choice of the proper region depends on the pattern of the data. Figure 4.16 (ahead in Section 4.12) illustrates an additional example for real data, involving a precipitation anomaly in the United States.

In one dimension, the fitted curve does not change when the domain is extended to allow extrapolation. This is not the case in two (or more) dimensions, because the penalties interact. As far as we know this problem has not been treated in the literature. See also Section 8.9 about extrapolation of mortality tables.

4.7 Smoothing on Large Grids

In principle vectorization and a Kronecker product basis allow us to fit two-dimensional P-splines to data on any grid. However, in practice we find that this approach chokes on large data sets. The bottleneck comes from the computation of the inner product $B'WB$. Suppose Y is a matrix with 1,000 rows and 1,000 columns, which is not unusually large for images, and let each basis have 30 B-splines. Then B has 1 million rows and close to a thousand columns, or almost 1 billion elements. With 8-byte floating point numbers just storing this matrix demands 8 GB of memory, and the computation of $B'WB$ is computationally taxing. In Appendix D, we describe the array algorithm (Currie et al., 2006; Eilers et al., 2006) that solves both problems, reducing the demands on memory space and computation time by several orders of magnitude for gridded data.

To provide a numerical example, Figure 4.10 shows a smooth surface computed from a data matrix with simulated noisy data, having 500 rows and 500 columns, while using tensor products with 20 segments in both directions. On an average (notebook) computer, this result is obtained in far less than a second.

A surprising property of two-dimensional smoothing is that quite sparse data can turn out to be informative. Figure 4.11 shows 200 data points that were randomly selected from a 200 by 200 source image, like the one in the left panel of Figure 4.10 (without the noise). A quite good estimate of the true image is obtained.

Data   **Smoothed**

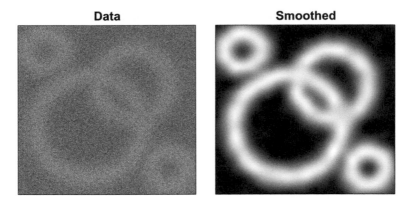

Figure 4.10 Smoothing of a noisy image with 500 rows and 500 columns, with 20 times 20 segments in the tensor product basis, second-order penalties, and both λs set to 1. R code in f-ring.R

Data   **Smoothed**

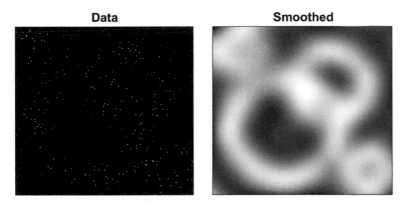

Figure 4.11 Smoothing on a 200 by 200 grid with only 200 non-missing data points. Tensor product basis with 20 times 20 segments, second-order penalties, and both λs set to 1. R code in f-scatring.R

4.8 Generalized Two-Dimensional Smoothing

In two dimensions, the structure of the penalized normal equations is identical to those for one-dimensional P-splines. This means that the extension to generalized linear smoothing (Section 2.12) is straightforward. For this generalization, it is crucial that the array algorithm allows arbitrary weights. We use two-dimensional histogram smoothing as an example.

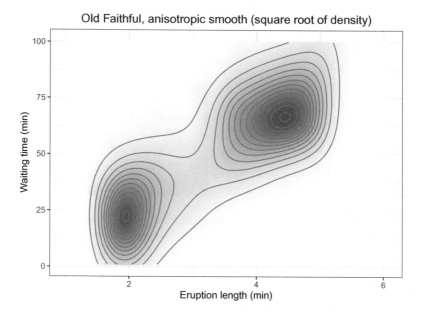

Figure 4.12 Density estimation with anisotropic smoothing, second-order differences, and 10 times 10 segments on in the basis. R code in f-geyser-aniso.R

If data pairs (u, v) are available, they can be counted in a matrix with, say, 100 rows and 100 columns, giving the count matrix Y. Assume that y_{ij} follows a Poisson distribution with expected value μ_{ij}, and let $M = [\mu_{ij}] = \exp(BA\check{B}') = \exp(N)$ (using the log link function), with $N = [\eta_{ij}]$ denoting the linear predictor. Given a current estimate $\tilde{N}$ of the solution, we improve it through penalized regression of the working variables $Z = [z_{ij}]$, with weights $\tilde{M}$, on a tensor product basis, where $z_{ij} = (y_{ij} - \tilde{\mu}_{ij})/\tilde{\mu}_{ij} + \tilde{\eta}_{ij}$ and $\tilde{\mu}_{ij} = \exp(\tilde{\eta}_{ij})$.

Figure 4.12 shows the estimated joint density of waiting time and eruption duration of the Old Faithful geyser. A grid with 100 by 100 bins was used for the histogram, and 10 by 10 segments were used in the tensor product B-spline basis. Smoothing takes a fraction of a second for one pair of values of λ and $\check{\lambda}$.

The log link ensures that $\hat{M}$ is positive everywhere. The marginal one-dimensional densities follow from $\hat{M}$ (after normalization to make it sum to 1); they can be used to compute smooth conditional densities.

4.9 Optimal Two-Dimensional Smoothing

To determine the amount of smoothing for density estimation, we can use AIC, as in one dimension. In the isotropic case, with equal λs for both axes, it is practical to explore a grid of, say, 20 values for $\log_{10}(\lambda)$, as we did for one-dimensional histogram smoothing (see Section 3.3). The profile of AIC for the Old Faithful data (not shown) has a relatively sharp minimum.

For anisotropic smoothing, when $\lambda \neq \breve{\lambda}$, a two-dimensional grid search is feasible, at least in principle, but it means much computation, working through several hundreds of pairs of tuning parameters. It is more attractive to use a function for numerical optimization; `ucminf`, in the R package with the same name, works well. Figure 4.12 shows the result. With $\lambda = 0.0043$ and $\breve{\lambda} = 0.31$. the minimum of AIC is 1237.6. Figure 4.13 shows the result of isotropic smoothing. For $\lambda = \breve{\lambda} = 0.037$, the minimum of AIC is 1241.3. Less than 20 function evaluations were needed in either case. The differences between the estimated densities are small.

For one-dimensional P-spline smoothing, the diagonal of the (effective) hat matrix is straightforward to obtain. In two dimensions, this is far more

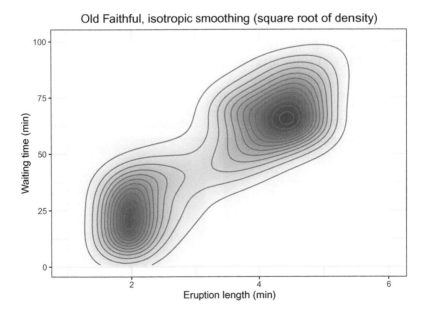

Figure 4.13 Density estimation with isotropic smoothing, second-order differences, and 10 times 10 segments on in the basis. R code in `f-geyser-iso.R`

challenging. It is very inefficient and almost impossible (because of the large memory demand) to compute the complete $\mathcal{H} = \mathcal{B}(\mathcal{B}'\mathcal{W}\mathcal{B} + \text{Pen})^{-1}\mathcal{B}'\mathcal{W}$ and then extract its diagonal. Appendix D shows how to use the array algorithm to compute a matrix H of the same size as Y, such that $h_{ij} = \partial\hat{y}_{ij}/\partial y_{ij}$. This way we get the required diagonal of $\mathcal{H}$, nicely packed in a matrix.

If only the effective dimension is needed, we can use the fact that

$$\text{trace}(\mathcal{H}) = \text{trace}(G) \quad \text{with} \quad G = (\mathcal{B}'\mathcal{W}\mathcal{B} + \text{Pen})^{-1}\mathcal{B}'\mathcal{W}\mathcal{B}. \qquad (4.22)$$

The number of rows (and columns) of G is $n\check{n}$. It can be computed efficiently from matrices in the linear system of equations for estimating the P-splines coefficients.

With linear isotropic smoothing, when the same λ is used for both penalties, fitting a mixed model is not different from the one-dimensional case. We solve the same type of penalized normal equations. For a mixed model, the sums of squares of differences of coefficients and the effective dimension are easily computed and in turn give us λ.

The same is true for Bayesian smoothing. We saw in Section 3.5 how to apply Markov chain Monte Carlo using only the inner products $B'WB$, $D'D$ and $B'Wy$. For tensor products, they are replaced by $\mathcal{B}'\mathcal{W}\mathcal{B}$, Pen and $\mathcal{B}'\mathcal{W}y$. Figure 4.14 shows Bayesian tensor product smoothing in action.

| 20 and 20 segments, $\lambda = 1.1$ | 50 and 20 segments, $\lambda = 2.1$ |

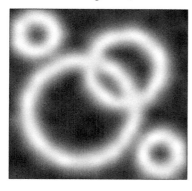

Figure 4.14 Bayesian isotropic smoothing of a noisy image (see Figure 4.10 for the data). Left: using bases with 20 segments. Right: one basis with 50, the other with 20 segments. The different sizes of the bases lead to artefacts because the surface has much more freedom in the horizontal direction. R code in f-quasi-iso.R

4.10 Issues with Isotropic Smoothing

We called two-dimensional smoothing with one penalty parameter as isotropic, which is in contrast to anisotropic smoothing, which has a penalty parameter for each dimension. This terminology is not strictly correct: the numbers of B-spline segments in the one-dimensional B-spline basis matrices play a role too.

Figure 4.14 shows smoothing of the simulated rings data that appeared in the left panel of Figure 4.10. In the left panel of Figure 4.14, 20 segments were used in both directions, and no artefacts are visible. In the right panel of the same figure, the segments were set to 50 and 20, and now vertical streaks occur. Reversing the number of segments to be 20 and 50, respectively, the streaks were found to be horizontal (not shown). When smoothing spatial data, we recommend to choose the numbers of segments in such a way that the segments have the same length for both dimensions.

4.11 Higher Dimensions

In principle, extension of tensor product P-splines to three or more dimensions is relatively uncomplicated, although the many required indices makes the notation unattractive. Lee and Durbán (2009) use three-dimensional P-splines for spatiotemporal smoothing of concentrations of air pollution in Europe. Currie et al. (2006) smooth mortality tables with three dimensions (year, month, age), which also shows the array algorithm in action for three dimensions, while presenting general formulas. In more than two dimensions, the computational gains are truly impressive.

In one dimension it is easy to be cavalier about the size of the B-spline basis. This is not the case in two or more dimensions. Already in 2 dimensions a tensor product basis of 30 by 30 segments approaches one 1,000 coefficients, where in 3 dimensions 10 segments yield this number. On the other hand, we must be realistic: enormous amounts of detailed data are needed to estimate interactions in 3 or more dimensions. These will not be available most of the time.

4.12 Nested Bases and PS-ANOVA

Appendix E shows how P-splines can be written as a mixed model: $B\alpha = X\beta + Zc = [X \mid Z]\theta$, with $\theta' = [\beta' \mid c']'$. We consider the case where X and Z

are derived from the difference penalty: $Z = B(DD')^{-1}D$. With second-order differences, X has two columns, one a constant and the other a linear sequence, which we indicate by x.

In two dimensions, the tensor product of $[X \mid Z]$ and $[\check{X} \mid \check{Z}]$ forms a proper basis, and we can write $M = [\mu_{ij}] = [X \mid Z]\Theta[\check{X} \mid \check{Z}]'$ for the fitted surface. It can be decomposed in four components:

$$M = X\Theta_{11}\check{X}' + X\Theta_{12}\check{Z}' + Z\Theta_{21}\check{X}' + Z\Theta_{22}\check{Z}'. \qquad (4.23)$$

The first term in (4.23) represents a bilinear surface described by the four coefficients in Θ_{11}. The second term contains the outer products of 1 and x with two smooth functions in the other dimension. Similarly, the third term represents outer products of 1 and $\check{x}$ with two smooth functions of x. The final term is a sum of many tensor product of individual basis functions. It describes a complicated smooth interaction surface.

The idea of nested bases is to reduce the number of terms in $Z\Theta_{22}\check{Z}'$, i.e., using less B-splines when computing the matrices that occur in this product, for example, using one-third or one-half of the original number of segments. This approach has been proposed by Lee et al. (2013), who termed it PS-ANOVA because it gives a decomposition similar to classical ANOVA. If $\underline{B}$ and $\check{\underline{B}}$ are bases with less knots, $\underline{B}\,\underline{\alpha} = X\beta + \underline{Z}\,\underline{c}$ and $\check{\underline{B}}\,\check{\underline{\alpha}} = \check{X}\check{\beta} + \check{\underline{Z}}\,\check{\underline{c}}$, the last term of (4.23) becomes $\underline{Z}\,\Theta_{22}\,\check{\underline{Z}}'$.

A direct advantage of this strategy is that the number of coefficients is reduced to about one-ninth to one-fourth of what would otherwise be needed, giving a massive reduction of the computation time. Another advantage is that the model is additive in many cross-products, and we can put roughness penalties on each component separately. This makes it straightforward to use the HFS algorithm.

A fitted PS-ANOVA model gives an interesting and useful view of the estimated surface. Each smooth term has an effective dimension, and a comparison to the nominal dimension (the number of coefficients) shows the relative importance of each term.

Figure 4.15 shows results for PS-ANOVA, as applied to the ethanol data set. The titles of the panels identify the components. In the lower right panel the labels C, E, and CE indicate the (fixed) linear effects of compression and equivalence ratios and their interaction. The random components f(C) and f(E) are one-dimensional smooth functions of C and E, while f(CE) is a two-dimensional smooth function; E:f(C) and C:f(E) are the two varying coefficient components. Note that f(·) stands for different functions; it is just a symbolic notation. We see from the partial effective dimensions that the main

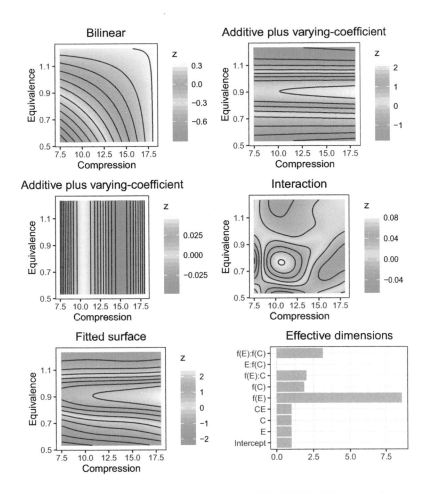

Figure 4.15 Smoothing of the ethanol data with PS-ANOVA. The panels show individual components of the model and their effective dimensions. See the text for explanation of the panels. R code in f-SpATS-ethanol.R

contribution to the fitted surface comes from the variation with the equivalence ratio, especially the additive component f(E).

It is easy to extend the model with extra terms, penalized or not. Rodriguez-Alvarez et al. (2018) describe an application in the analysis of agricultural field trials, where the row and column numbers of the plots in the field and the genotypes of the plants are included. This model is remarkably stable and reliable, as Velazco et al. (2017) report; it also is much easier to interpret than models based on variograms and kriging, which traditionally have a strong position in this field.

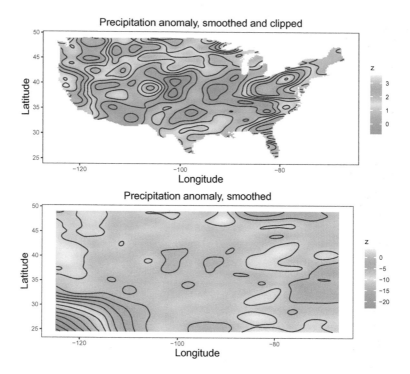

Figure 4.16 Smoothing of the precipitation anomaly in the United States (April 1948). with PS-ANOVA, using 30 segments for both longitude and latitude. See the text for explanation of the panels. R code in f-SpATS-precip-clip.R

PS-ANOVA can handle many observations efficiently. Figure 4.16 shows smoothing of data on the precipitation anomaly in April 1948, in the United States (data set USprecip in the package spam). It contains almost 12,000 observations spread over the United States. The number of segments used is 30, for both longitude and latitude. It takes less than 10 seconds to estimate the model on a computer with an Intel I3-3220 processor.

The lower panel of the figure shows the complete rectangular surface, of which the lower-left corner bends down strongly. This corner region lies far away from the mainland data, and the bend is simply a consequence of automatic extrapolation. The scale of fit (associated with the lower panel) is also dramatically changed, making it very difficult to judge the fitted surface. The upper panel is more useful: it shows only the pixels that lie within the boundaries of the United States.

4.13 Notes and Details

Analogous to one-dimensional P-splines, the system in (4.21) gives the covariance matrix of the estimated coefficients as $(\mathcal{B}'\mathcal{W}\mathcal{B} + \lambda P + \breve{\lambda}\breve{P})^{-1}$, from which standard error of the coefficients and a fitted curve or surface can be derived directly.

Hastie and Tibshirani (1990) introduce the generalized additive model (GAM). They propose backfitting for estimation, which is used in the package gam. Marx and Eilers (1998) propose the P-GAM as an attractive alternative, which was introduced in Section 4.1. The disadvantages of backfitting have been documented by Schimek (2009): slow convergence, no tools for automatic smoothing, unstable estimates, and lack of standard errors. Wood (2017) offers a superior alternative in his package mgcv, which can also handle VCMs. It provides a suite of choices for basis functions and penalties, while allowing models to be specified in the formula syntax of R. Wood's work is a massive product: the reference manual has over 300 pages. The software is actively being maintained and expanded. Unfortunately, it is currently rather rigid when it comes to choosing your own knots for the B-splines.

The additive and varying coefficient models show how easy it is to build a model with several smooth components. Obviously, other linear regressors or factors can be added. Their coefficients will not be penalized, and the corresponding blocks on the diagonal of the penalty matrix will contain only zeros. Functional regressors (signals or spectra, see Chapter 7) can be included as well. Tensor product models also fit into this scheme. This too is the case for classical mixed models with a multilevel structure because they can be written as penalized regression. Eilers and Marx (2002) propose the acronym GLASS (generalized linear additive smooth structures), while Fahrmeir et al. (2004) call their variant STAR (structure additive regression). The package R2BayesX can fit many varieties of these models; Umlauf et al. (2015) provide an extensive description with applications. Marx (2010) presents large-scale P-spline VCMs.

5
Smoothing of Scale and Shape

In previous chapters, our goal was to estimate a curve for the expected value of our data. There were variations in the objective function, sums of squares or the log-likelihood. The scale, i.e., the variance or standard deviation of the data distribution, was not explicitly modeled. For the Poisson and binomial distributions, the scale is a known function of the mean. For the normal distribution, we assumed constant variance and obtained a formula to estimate it from the data.

In this chapter, we want to obtain a more detailed picture of the distribution of our observations, y, conditional on the explanatory variable, x. To obtain smooth quantile curves, we combine ideas from quantile regression with roughness penalties. We encounter various technical challenges because the objective function of quantile regression is an asymmetrically weighted sum of absolute values of residuals. If we also change to absolute values in the roughness penalty, we can use linear programming. An alternative is to keep the sum of squares in the penalty and use iterative weighted least squares.

A limited case of quantile smoothing only estimates a curve for the median, which is very robust against outliers.

Expectiles are defined by an asymmetrically weighted sum of squares in the objective function. They are easy to compute. Compared to quantiles, a set of smooth expectile curves generally gives a more realistic impression of the conditional distribution. We show how to compute a conditional density of y, given x, from a set of expectiles.

Rather than modeling quantiles or expectiles, we can assume a parametric form for the conditional distribution and let its parameters vary smoothly. The GAMLSS model, with the `gamlss` package, was designed for this purpose. It covers a very large terrain, but we show only a few applications relevant to P-splines.

5.1 Quantile Smoothing

It is well known that if we minimize $S = \sum_{i=1}^{m}(y_i - g)^2$, the solution is $g = \sum y_i/m$, the arithmetic mean. Computation is trivial. This is not the case if the objective is changed to $S = \sum_{i=1}^{m}|y_i - g|$, where the solution is given by the median. To find the solution, the data are sorted, and the middle value (or the mean of the two middle values, if m is even) is taken. This solution only works if there are no covariates. With covariates, linear programming is needed, leading to a special case of quantile regression (Koenker, 2005), for which the function rq() in the R package quantreg is available. This work makes median smoothing with unpenalized B-splines straightforward: minimize $S = ||y - B\alpha||^1$, where B is the basis matrix, and $|| \cdot ||^1$ denotes the sum of absolute values. In fact, B and y can be directly plugged into rq().

Penalized median smoothing requires more care and extra work. For one, the sum of squares of differences (that we have used in many places) is not easy or natural to combine with the sum of absolute residuals. However, a sum of absolute values of differences in the penalty does lead to a clean solution. We call the former a quadratic or L_2 penalty and the latter an L_1 penalty.

Consider the objective function

$$Q = ||y - B\alpha||^1 + \lambda||D\alpha||^1. \tag{5.1}$$

The function rq takes a response vector and a design matrix as inputs. There is no explicit way to include a penalty, but it can be handled by data augmentation. Let $(B^+)' = [B' \mid \lambda D']'$ denote the design matrix, and let $y^+ = [y' \mid \mathbf{0}']'$ be the response vector: the rows of B are extended by λD, and y is extended by vector with $(n - d)$ zeros. The minimization of $Q = ||y^+ - B^+\alpha||^1$ then gives the desired solution. Figure 5.1 shows an example of median smoothing for the motorcycle data. To emphasize its robustness, two extreme outliers have been introduced, at 5 and 50 ms. They change the fit of standard P-splines quite strongly, but the median smoother is unaffected.

Unfortunately, median smoothing with a large B-spline basis and an L_1 penalty has an unpleasant property: the fitted curve tends toward a piecewise-linear shape, rounded by the splines. In Figure 5.1, with only 10 B-spline segments, the artefact is not visible, whereas in Figure 5.2 with 50 segments, it is pronounced. The sum of absolute values in the penalty with second-order differences is the culprit: when λ is large, α is forced toward a piecewise-linear series. A simple solution is to use third-order differences in the penalty, as illustrated in Figure 5.2. The curve now has a piecewise quadratic shape, which is more pleasing to the eye.

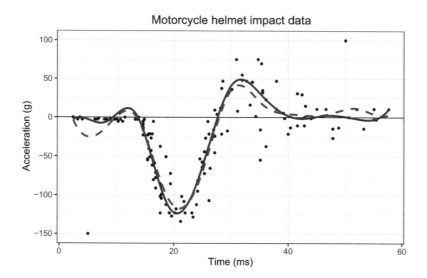

Figure 5.1 Median smoothing of the motorcycle data with two artificial extreme outliers. Cubic P-splines, with 10 segments on the domain from 0 to 60 ms, and $\lambda = 0.01$ (solid blue line). The broken red line shows the fit of standard P-splines with the same parameter settings. R code in `f-mot-median.R`

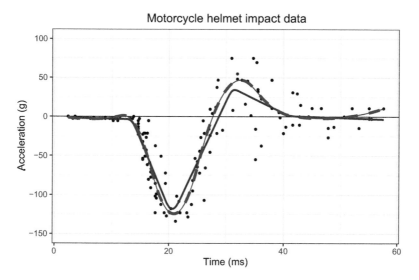

Figure 5.2 Median smoothing of the motorcycle data using cubic P-splines, with 50 segments on the domain from 0 to 60 ms, second-order differences, and $\lambda = 10$ (blue full line). The piecewise-linear shape is a consequence of the sum of absolute values in the penalty. With third-order differences, the curve becomes piecewise quadratic (red broken line). R code in `f-mot-median-d3.R`

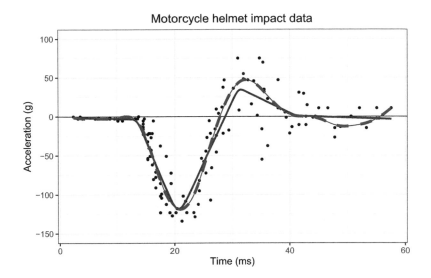

Figure 5.3 Median smoothing of the motorcycle data using cubic P-splines, with 50 segments on the domain from 0 to 60 ms. The piecewise-linear curve (solid blue line) is obtained with absolute values in the penalty ($\lambda = 10$). The smoother curve (broken red line) is obtained with squares in the penalty ($\lambda = 1$). R code in `f-mot-median-iter.R`

If we drop linear programming and switch to an iterative algorithm, we can combine the sum of absolute values of the residuals with a sum of squares in the penalty. The key observation is to note that (for any scalar u) $|u| = u^2/|u| = wu^2$, with $w = 1/|u|$. Using this identity, we can write a sum of absolute values as a weighted sum of squares. Extending u to be a vector, it follows that $|u| = Wu^2$ with $W = \mathrm{diag}(w)$ and $w_i = 1/|w_i|$ (Schlossmacher, 1973). There is a chicken-and-egg problem here because we need u to compute w and W. A solution that works well in practice is to perform standard P-spline fitting, which provides an initial estimate $\tilde{\alpha}$, compute residuals $\tilde{u} = y - B\tilde{\alpha}$, and weights $\tilde{w}_i = 1/|\tilde{u}_i|$. The objective function can now be written as $(y - B\alpha)'\tilde{W}(y - B\alpha) + \lambda||D\alpha||^2$, a standard case of P-spline smoothing. Generally, in median (and quantile) regression, some of the residuals will be exactly zero, causing the iterative algorithm to become unstable. Our solution is to use $w_i = 1/\sqrt{u_i^2 + \beta^2}$, with β a small number, say 10^{-4} times the range of y. Figure 5.3 shows the results of median smoothing with the two types of penalties.

To switch from medians to more general quantiles requires only a small step. To obtain the τth quantile curve, we give weight τ to positive residuals and $1 - \tau$ to the negative ones, with $0 < \tau < 1$. The objective function is

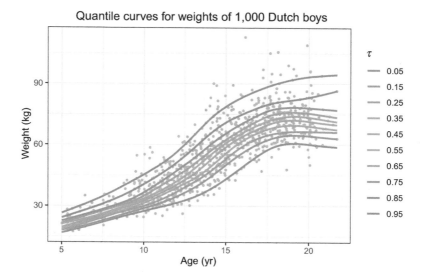

Figure 5.4 Quantile smoothing of body weights of 1,000 Dutch boys, with 20 cubic B-spline segments, using the iterative algorithm ($\beta = 0.001$ and $\lambda = 1$). R code in f-quant-curves-1000.R

$$Q = (y - B\alpha_\tau)'\tilde{W}_\tau(y - B\alpha_\tau) + \lambda||D\alpha_\tau||^2, \qquad (5.2)$$

with $w_{i(\tau)} = \tau v_i$ if $y_i > \hat{y}_i$, and $w_{i(\tau)} = (1 - \tau)v_i$ otherwise, where $v_i = 1/\sqrt{(y_i - \hat{y}_i)^2 + \beta^2}$.

When using the rq() function for quantile smoothing, a problem arises: it applies the τ value to all terms in the objective function, including the pseudo-observations, which incorrectly makes the penalty asymmetric too. In our package JOPS, we provide the function rqflex(), which allows an input vector with a separate value of τ for each (pseudo-)observation. Our function is a translation of the Matlab functions available at www.econ.uiuc .edu/~roger/research/rq/rq.m.

Figure 5.4 shows an example, where nine quantile curves have been computed with the quadratic difference penalty. The data are weights of Dutch boys at different ages, available in the R package AGD. A random sample of 1,000 boys has been used. With many observations, the quantile curves look good, and they cross only in a few places. This is not true when we sample only 100 boys, as shown in Figure 5.5, where the result is hardly useful. This is a general pattern: quantile curves for small data sets usually look disappointing.

To keep quantile curves from crossing, Schnabel and Eilers (2013b) propose the quantile sheet. Instead of fitting smooth quantile curves one by one, the

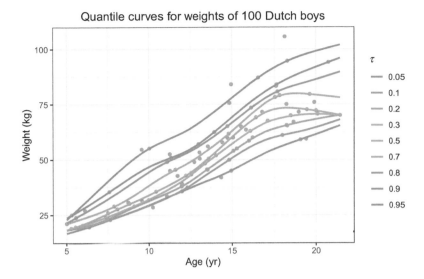

Figure 5.5 Quantile smoothing of body weights of 100 Dutch boys, with 20 cubic
B-spline segments, using the iterative algorithm ($\beta = 0.001$ and $\lambda = 1$). R code in
f-quant-curves-100.R

smooth surface $q(x, \tau)$ is estimated. It is called "sheet" and not "surface" to
avoid confusion with spatial quantiles, say $q(x, y; \tau)$, which are defined on a
spatial domain for a given value of τ. For the quantile sheet, τ is assumed
to vary from 0 to 1. For a chosen value, say τ^*, $q(x, \tau^*)$ is the corresponding
quantile curve; it is a cross section of the sheet. Similarly, $q(x^*, \tau)$ is the quantile
function at x^*, the inverse of the cumulative distribution.

We model the quantile sheet with a sum of tensor products of B-splines, as
described in Chapter 4:

$$q(x, \tau) = \sum_k \sum_l B_k(x) \breve{B}_l(\tau) \alpha_{kl}. \tag{5.3}$$

To fit the sheet to data pairs (x_i, y_i), we specify a grid of values of τ_j and
minimize the penalized objective function

$$S = \sum_i \sum_j w_{ij} |y_i - q(x_i, \tau_j)| + \text{Pen}, \tag{5.4}$$

with the asymmetric weights $w_{ij} = \tau_j$ if $y_i > q(x_i, \tau_j)$, and $w_{ij} = 1 - \tau_j$
otherwise. The penalty is based on differences of rows and columns of the
coefficient matrix A:

$$\text{Pen} = \lambda ||DA||_F^2 + \breve{\lambda} ||A\breve{D}'||_F^2, \tag{5.5}$$

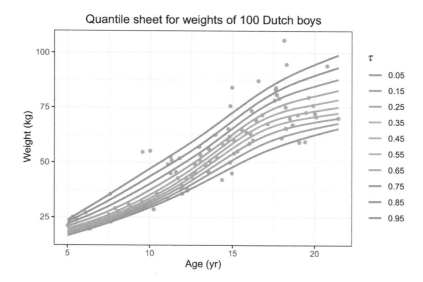

Figure 5.6 Quantile sheet for body weights of 100 Dutch boys, cubic tensor product P-splines segments, with 10 by 10 segments ($\beta = 0.001$ and $\lambda = 1$ for *Age* and for various τ). R code in f-quant-sheet-100.R

where $|| \cdot ||_F^2$ indicates the square of the Frobenius norm, i.e., the sum of the squares of all the elements of a matrix, and D and $\check{D}$ are (order 2) differencing matrices of proper dimensions.

The weighted sum of absolute values in the first term of the objective function in (5.4) can be handled by the iterative weighted least squares algorithm. The estimation of the quantile sheet then becomes a special case of fitting tensor product P-splines to data on a grid (see Section 4.7). As can be seen from the objective function in (5.4), each y_i is replicated once for each value of τ_j, so we have a grid of pseudo-observations and a grid of weights. For larger data sets the computations are much faster than those for estimating individual quantile curves.

The roughness penalty, along τ, pushes the sheet toward a smooth increase at every x. If strong enough, it makes the surface increase everywhere in the direction of τ, eliminating crossing quantile curves completely. Figure 5.6 shows a cross section of a quantile sheet for the weights of 100 boys. The grid for τ runs from 0.05 to 0.95, with 0.1 steps. When we compare with Figure 5.5, the improvement is clear.

5.2 Expectile Smoothing

In the previous section we showed how quantiles can be defined as the solution of the minimization of an objective function with asymmetric weights. Given a probability τ, it is $\sum w_i |y_i - g|$, with $w_i = \tau$ if $x_i > g$, and $w_i = 1 - \tau$ otherwise. Writing g as a function of (B-spline) regressors opened the road to quantile smoothing.

We can replace the sum of absolute values by a sum of squares, while keeping the asymmetric weights. Then τ is no longer a probability; we call it the *asymmetry* with values $0 < \tau < 1$. The minimizer of $\sum w_i (y_i - g)^2$, with asymmetric weights w, defines the expectile corresponding to τ (Newey and Powell, 1987). Expectiles do not have the easy intuitive interpretation that quantiles enjoy, but they are more useful.

One advantage of expectiles is their ease of computation by iterative weighted least squares. Starting from $w_i \equiv 0.5$, one computes $\tilde{g}$ as the weighted mean of y. From the signs of $(y - \tilde{g})$, the new weights follow for the next iteration. The objective function is convex, so convergence is guaranteed, and in practice this occurs after a handful of iterations. If g is a linear function of regressors, iterative weighted regression leads to the expectile regression.

Introduction of P-splines produces expectile smoothing (Schnabel and Eilers, 2009). The objective function in this setting becomes

$$Q = (y - B\alpha_\tau)' W_\tau (y - B\alpha_\tau) + \lambda ||D\alpha_\tau||^2, \qquad (5.6)$$

with $W_\tau = \mathrm{diag}(w_\tau)$ and $w_{i(\tau)} = \tau$ if $r_i > 0$, and $w_{i(\tau)} = 1 - \tau$ otherwise, where $r = y - B\alpha_\tau$. We do this for a series of values of τ. For each of them we get a separate coefficient vector $\hat{\alpha}_\tau$ that allows us to compute an expectile curve on a fine grid of x. Figure 5.7 shows expectile curves for the weights of the sample of 100 boys.

Note that (5.6) has the same form as (5.2): only the weights are different. For expectiles in (5.6), the weights are simply τ or $1 - \tau$, whereas for quantiles in (5.2), they were τv_i or $(1 - \tau)v_i$, where $v_i = 1/\sqrt{(y_i - \hat{y}_i)^2 + \beta^2}$ is iteratively updated.

Expectile curves look better than quantile curves, as the curves now show less crossings, especially for small data sets. This is an attractive property for data exploration, where the goal is to get a good impression of trend and spread. Quantiles are familiar, as they are connected to cumulative distributions and data sorting. Expectiles do not have such an intuitive interpretation. Their usefulness

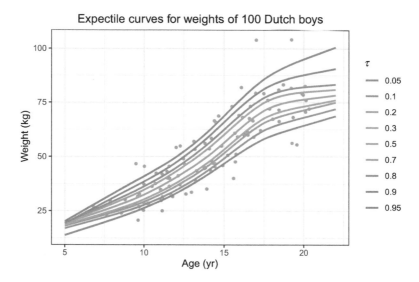

Figure 5.7 Expectile smoothing of weights of Dutch boys, with 20 cubic B-spline segments and $\lambda = 1$. R code in f-exp-curves-100.R

is increasingly being recognized, as we see a growing popularity in the literature.

To tune λ, approximate leave-one-out cross-validation can be used (Schnabel and Eilers, 2009). Given the weights in W_τ for the expectile curve $g(x; \tau)$, we have $\hat{g} = B\hat{\alpha}_\tau = B(B'W_\tau B + \lambda D'D)^{-1}B'W_\tau y$. Hence the hat matrix is $H = B(B'W_\tau B + \lambda D'D)^{-1}B'W_\tau$ and $h_{ii} = \partial\hat{e}_i/\partial y_i$. The prediction error, when leaving out observation i and recomputing the expectile curve, then is $(y_i - g_i)/(1 - h_{ii})$, as presented in Section 3.1. This assumes that the weights do not change when observation i is discarded, which is not strictly true. Some residuals may change sign because the fitted expectile curve will shift a little locally. However with a reasonably large number of observations, this effect should be minor. The result can be disappointing with small data sets, as Figure 5.8 shows. The indicated amount of smoothing is quite variable, and the curves cross in many places.

Expectiles have more to offer than visualization, as the computational recipe has a theoretical counterpart. For a given density $f(y)$, the expectile g_τ (corresponding to asymmetry τ) minimizes

$$S = (1 - \tau) \int_{-\infty}^{g} (y - g)^2 f(y)dy + \tau \int_{g}^{\infty} (y - g)^2 f(y)dy. \qquad (5.7)$$

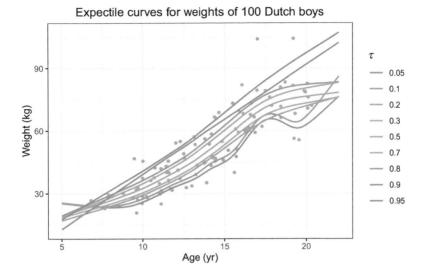

Figure 5.8 Expectile smoothing of weights of Dutch boys, with 20 cubic B-spline segments. For each curve λ was tuned with asymmetric cross-validation. R code in †-exp-curves-100-cv.R

The estimating equation sets (5.7) to zero. Let $F(y) = \int_{-\infty}^{y} f(u)du$ be the cumulative distribution and $G(y) = \int_{-\infty}^{y} uf(u)du$ the incomplete first moment of $f(\cdot)$. It then follows, with $G(\infty) = \mu$, that

$$\int_{-\infty}^{g} (y-g)f(y)dy = G(g) - gF(g)$$

$$\int_{g}^{\infty} (y-g)f(y)dy = G(\infty) - G(g) + g[1 - F(g)],$$

leading to an explicit equation for τ, given the expectile g:

$$\tau = \frac{G(g) - gF(g)}{2[G(g) - gF(g)] + g - \mu}. \tag{5.8}$$

Generally numerical inversion of (5.8) will be needed to compute an expectile for a given τ.

Like quantiles, expectiles can be used to compare distributions in an expectile–expectile plot (Schnabel and Eilers, 2009). In contrast to quantiles, they are well defined for discrete distributions.

Given a set of empirical expectiles, a smooth nonparametric density can be estimated (Schnabel and Eilers, 2013a). As for density estimation from a histogram (Section 3.3), we model its logarithm with P-splines. For

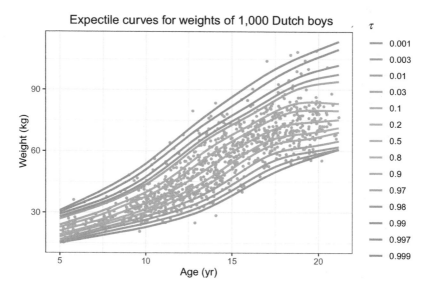

Figure 5.9 Expectile smoothing of weights of Dutch boys, with 20 cubic B-spline segments and $\lambda = 10$. R code in f-exp-curves-1000.R

illustration, we take the density of the weights of boys at age 15 from the results in Figure 5.9. For this age, we have values for nine conditional expectiles, as shown in Figure 5.10. Let $f_i = \exp(\eta_i)$ be a discrete approximation to the density $f(x_i)$, for $i = 1 : m$, with a suitably chosen grid for x. Let $\eta = B\alpha$ and $f_i = \exp(\eta_i)$. The expectiles are g_k for $k = 1 : p$, with corresponding asymmetries τ_k. We then have to fulfill p conditions $\sum_i \psi_{ik} f_i = 0$ with

$$\psi_{ik} = \tau_k \quad \text{if} \quad x_i > g_k, \quad \text{and} \quad 1 - \tau_k \quad \text{otherwise.}$$

A condition is that f should be a proper discrete density: $\sum_i f_i = 1$. Let v be a vector with p zeros and one 1, and define the matrix $\Psi = (\psi_{ik})$. Denote Ψ^+ to be Ψ, but extended with a row of ones. We then have the conditions $\Psi^+ f = v$.

Figure 5.10 shows the result, using a grid with steps of 1 kg for the density and $\lambda = 10$ (subjectively chosen). In the upper panel, the estimated pairs (g_j, τ_j) are plotted as dots. The curve shows the asymmetry as a function of the expectile, when using the estimated density in (5.8).

The objective function strives for closeness, but not to equality, of observed and modeled expectiles. This feature makes it robust against sampling variation. When expectile curves cross, estimated conditional expectiles will not form a strictly monotone sequence. The algorithm will happily accept non-monotone expectiles, so there will not be any technical problem. The quality of the density

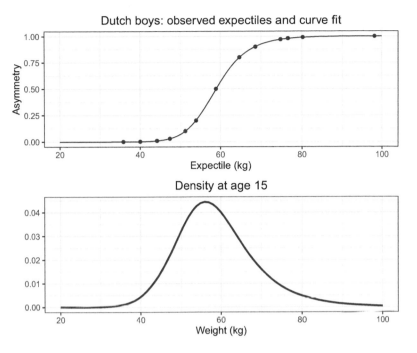

Figure 5.10 Boys' weights. Expectiles at age 15 were obtained from the individual expectile curves, shown in Figure 5.9. They are plotted in the upper panel. The right panel shows the density estimate obtained from the expectiles. R code in f-exp-curves-1000-dens

estimate will probably suffer, but we do not know how much; this is uncharted terrain, awaiting systematic research.

In Section 5.3, we fit a model with a parametric conditional distribution to the weights of the boys, using the package GAMLSS, and compare results.

If $g^\star(\tau)$ is an expectile of a given density, or of an observed sample $y^\star$, then it follows that the linear transformation $y = t + sy^\star$ changes $g^\star(\tau)$ to $g(\tau) = t + sg^\star(\tau)$. If we let the transformation parameters depend on x, we get an interesting and useful model for a data cloud. Schnabel and Eilers (2013a) propose the location-scale or "bundle" model for expectile curves. It is expressed as $g(x; \tau) = t(x) + s(x)c(\tau)$: there is a trend $t(x)$ for all expectile curves and a scale curve $s(x)$. The latter is multiplied by a function of τ, $c(\tau)$, which is independent of x. The distance between two expectile curves is $g(x; \tau_1) - g(x; \tau_2) = s(x)[c(\tau_1) - c(\tau_2)]$, meaning that the relative distances between expectile curves are the same everywhere. Thus the distribution of the observation errors has a constant shape, but a scale that depends on x, and it is shifted by $t(x)$. The bundle model is attractive because it summarizes a cloud of data points with three curves, of which $c(\tau)$ probably is the most informative, as it characterizes the shape of the distribution of the data.

Schnabel and Eilers (2013a) also discuss estimation of the bundle model. A simple algorithm would first estimate the mean curve, subtract it from the data, and fit $s(x)c(\tau)$ to the residuals. This can work well for a symmetric conditional distribution, but we get into trouble when it is strongly asymmetric. As the paper shows, it is necessary to update trend and scale function jointly.

The grid of values for τ was chosen in such a way that the corresponding expectiles of a standard normal distribution lie on a uniform grid, say from -4 to 4 in steps of 0.5.

Figure 5.11 shows the LIDAR data, which are available in the package SemiPar, presenting both the estimated bundle and the scale curve $s(x)$. The independent variable is the distance that laser light traveled before it was reflected back, while the dependent variable is the logarithm of the ratio

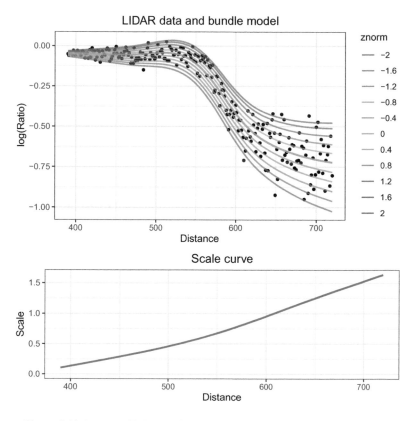

Figure 5.11 An expectile bundle for LIDAR data. Top panel: the bundle, where the mean curve $t(x)$ is shown in gray. Bottom panel: the scale curve $s(x)$. R code in f-lidar-bundle.R

of the intensity of received light to that of a reference laser source. The estimated expectiles are a smooth bundle of non-crossing curves. The bundle was estimated with 20 cubic B-spline segments and $\lambda = 10$ for both $t(x)$ and $s(x)$.

The underlying density can be estimated from $\hat{c}(\tau)$ by the same algorithm that was used for the weights of Dutch boys, shown in Figure 5.10.

The expectile sheet is the analogue of the quantile sheet, based on asymmetric least squares (Waltrup et al., 2015).

A valid question is why we should try to estimate expectile curves or sheets when we have good algorithms for two-dimensional density estimation, as shown in Section 3.3. One answer is that, with extra penalties, expectile curves can be forced to be monotone or follow other shape constraints. Also it is not clear how to combine density estimation with a bundle model.

5.3 Models for Shape and Scale Parameters

Quantile and expectile curves are useful data exploration tools. They give a visual impression of how the conditional distribution of the data varies with a covariate. Sometimes it is desirable to model the conditional distribution using an explicit parametric form, with smoothly changing parameters. This is the essence of what GAMLSS (generalized additive models for location, scale and shape) offers (Rigby and Stasinopoulos, 2005). The corresponding R package furnishes many continuous and discrete distributions, as well as a robust fitting algorithm. The GAMLSS book (Stasinopoulos et al., 2017) has almost 550 pages and covers much material. In a companion volume, the many available distributions are described in detail (Rigby et al., 2019).

The description of the model is simple. If the conditional distribution is assumed to be normal, smooth curves for the mean and the logarithm of the standard deviation are estimated. P-splines are one possibility, but other smoothers are available in the package. By modeling its logarithm, the estimate of the standard deviation will always be positive.

If the skewness of the data distribution cannot be neglected, prior transformation is an option. A classical choice is the Box–Cox transformation, with, e.g., $z = (y^{\nu} - 1)/\nu$ (for $\nu \neq 0$), after which the conditional distribution of z is modeled. In gamlss, the family BCCG (Box–Cox–Cole–Green) uses this transformation and assumes a normal conditional distribution as just described. The transformation parameter ν can be chosen to be a constant, or it can follow a smooth curve too.

To estimate the parameters of a model, gamlss sets up a system of penalized likelihood equations and solves them with an iterative algorithm.

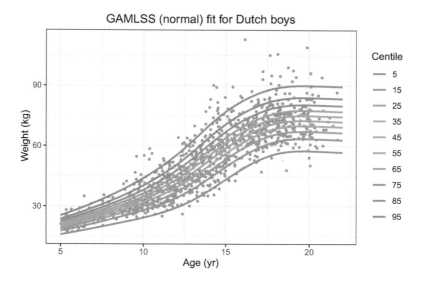

Figure 5.12 P-spline-based centile curves of the weights of a sample of 1,000 Dutch boys, using gamlss, assuming a normal conditional distribution with varying mean and standard deviation. R code in f-boys-normal.R

It also optimizes the amount of smoothing using AIC. Details can be found in Stasinopoulos et al. (2017) or Stasinopoulos and Rigby (2007).

To illustrate the use of gamlss, we return to the weights of boys that we previously analyzed. Initially we assume that a normal distribution, with a smoothly changing mean and standard deviation (as a function of age), is a reasonable model. The following call will do the trick: g <- gamlss(y ~ pb(x), sigma.formula = ~ pb(x)). Here pb() specifies the use of P-splines; other types of splines, or parametric functions, can be specified with the familiar model syntax of R. The default choice for the conditional distribution is the normal. It is straightforward to obtain estimates of curves on an arbitrary grid, using the predict function.

Figure 5.12 shows results, as centile curves. Note that gamlss automatically tuned the smoothing parameters, using AIC. We see that the distances between the centile curves are symmetric above and below the mean curve, as is the case for a normal distribution. The data do not seem to agree: they show positive skewness. A possible remedy is to apply the Box–Cox transformation. To this end, we change the model formula to g <- gamlss(y ~ pb(x), sigma.formula= ~ pb(x), nu.formula= ~pb(x), family = BCCG), specifying the distribution explicitly and allowing the transformation parameter ν to vary smoothly with x. Visually judging from Figure 5.13, this model fits the data better. The gamlss package

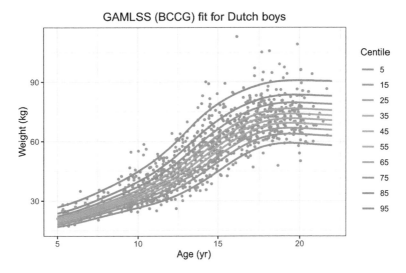

Figure 5.13 P-spline-based centile curves of the weights of a sample of 1,000 Dutch boys, using gamlss with the Box–Cox Cole–Green model. The model assumes a normal distribution after a power transformation of y. R code in f-boys-BCCG.R

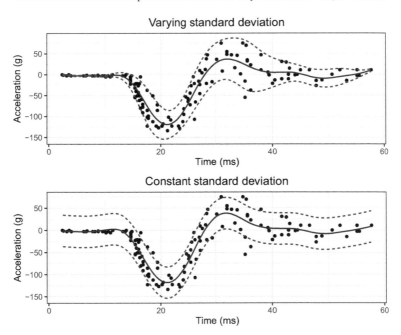

Figure 5.14 Estimation of smooth percentile curves (5, 50, and 95%) for the conditional data distribution of the motorcycle data using gamlss. Top: smoothly varying standard deviation. Bottom: constant standard deviation. R code in f-mot-gamlss.R

offers tools for objective comparison of models. AIC is a summary measure of model quality, which cannot directly diagnose in which places the fit of a model is good or not. A special display, called the worm plot, was designed to solve this problem (van Buuren, 2007), and it has been integrated into the gamlss package.

In Figure 5.14, we revisit the motorcycle data. It is clear that the spread of the data points around the mean curve is not constant. Initially the spread is very small, but it notably increases after about 15 ms. Using the specification g <- gamlss(y ~ pb(x), sigma.formula = ~ pb(x)) again, we can fit a proper model. The result, expressed as percentile curves, is shown in the top panel of Figure 5.14. Indeed the band for the data points is very narrow at the left, but we see that it also shrinks near the right boundary. If we leave out the formula for sigma.formula, gamlss tacitly assumed that the standard deviation is constant, with the result shown in the lower panel.

The model for the standard deviation has a strong influence on standard errors for the estimated mean curve, as is shown in Figure 5.15. With a varying

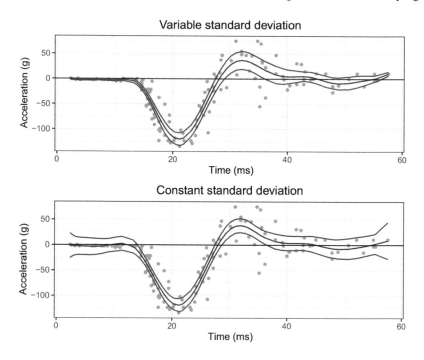

Figure 5.15 Motorcycle impact data. Estimated mean curves and 95% confidence bands, for two assumptions for the standard deviation of the (normal) error distribution. Top panel: varying standard deviation. Bottom panel: fixed standard deviation. R code in f-mot-gamlss2.R

standard deviation we get a more realistic result, showing a narrow confidence banded at the left.

5.4 Baseline Estimation

Many physical and chemical instruments produce a signal that consists of a series of peaks on top of a slowly varying background, often called the baseline. The positions and the heights of the peaks characterize the concentrations of chemical components, or physical properties of the material under study, and the baseline is a nuisance. Figure 5.16 shows an example, which is the diffractogram of indium oxide that is available in the R package diffractometry. To estimate the baseline, a very smooth expectile curve with τ set to a rather small number, like 0.04, works well in practice. This is shown in the top panel of Figure 5.16. After subtraction, the peaks are obtained. The asymmetric weights have a low value in the regions below peaks and thus make it easy to extract the peaks after baseline correction and also to analyze their properties.

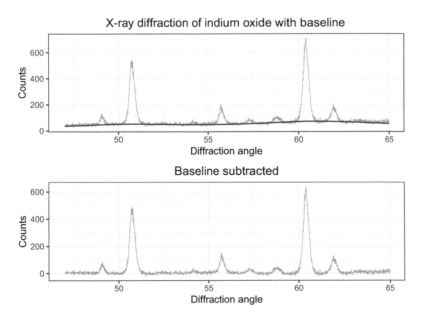

Figure 5.16 X-ray diffractometry scan of indium oxide. Estimation of a baseline by expectile smoothing with 40 cubic B-spline segments, $\lambda = 1,000$, and asymmetry $\tau = 0.04$. Top: data and baseline; bottom: after subtraction of the baseline. R code in f-baseline.R

The choice of λ is not very critical, but that of τ is. Where we have only baseline and no peaks, we wish the trend to steer through "the middle of the noise." In practice, visual inspection works quite well, and it was used for Figure 5.16. A more automatic approach is desirable, and de Rooi and Eilers (2012) propose a more complicated model that takes the distribution of the noise into account. It has been extended to two-dimensional data, estimating a "base surface" using tensor product P-splines (de Rooi et al., 2013).

The signal of a diffractometer actually consist of counts of photons, so it would be more appropriate to use conditional Poisson distributions with expected values that are a sum of both the baseline and the peaks. Such would lead to the more complicated penalized composite link model (PCLM) that is found in Chapter 6. Camarda et al. (2016) use the PCLM to estimate sums of smooth curves for counts in mortality tables.

5.5 Notes and Details

Quantile regression first began with the seminal paper by Koenker and Bassett (1978). It has seen a growing popularity ever since. Modern (interior point) algorithms for linear programming make computation fast and reliable (Portnoy and Koenker, 1997). B-splines are bases for regression, so they combine well with quantile regression. For a seamless combination, it is necessary to use the L_1 norm in the penalty, which can lead to a fit with large polynomial segments, as we saw in Figure 5.2.

Newey and Powell (1987) introduce asymmetry in least squares regression, but their paper saw very little response for the first 20 years after publication. However, in the last decade, expectiles have encountered growing recognition. They have very attractive properties, especially for smoothing. Computation is easy, and results look attractive. In contrast to quantiles, expectiles are well defined for (low) count data and discrete distributions.

For opinionated views on quantiles and expectiles in smoothing, we recommend the paper by Kneib (2013), and its colorful discussion.

6

Complex Counts and Composite Links

Chapter 2 showed how to smooth count data with P-splines. When constructing a histogram from raw continuous data, we are essentially free to use as many bins as we like. This is not the case if the data are given as rounded numbers or have already been collected in bins.

In this chapter, we look at data where we cannot directly observe raw counts, but instead have grouped, rounded, or mixed data. We introduce this subject using data on lead concentrations in the blood of New York children. The official reporting protocol specifies wide intervals of different sizes, but we are interested in density estimates on a fine grid. The composite link model (CLM), when extended with a roughness penalty (PCLM), is the ideal tool for this purpose. The primary CLM reference is Thompson and Baker (1981).

The PCLM specifies a composition matrix connecting latent expectations to the expected values of observed counts. Creative construction of this matrix allows systematic modeling of complex patterns of counts.

Problems with histograms can surface with data that look perfectly fine at first sight. We illustrate this with measurements of a blood parameter (RDW) that has a skewed distribution, suggesting a logarithmic transformation. The resulting histogram shows a strong systematic pattern, which is a consequence of rounding. The PCLM solves this with a composition matrix for the mapping from linear to logarithmic intervals. The PCLM can also handle density estimation with individual observations that each have a different censoring interval. Our example uses uncertain infection times of HIV patients.

Distributions for counts can be modeled as mixtures, in which the expected values of Poisson distributions are generated from a latent density. The negative binomial distribution is an example, with a (parametric) gamma latent density. Using the PCLM, we can compute a nonparametric estimate of the mixing density. We illustrate this application with counts of environmental complaints.

6.1 Histograms with Wide Bins

Figure 6.1 shows an example of coarsely aggregated data, summarizing observed concentrations of lead in the blood of New York children. The numbers are available in Hasselblad et al. (1980); the wide intervals are prescribed by a legal protocol. The coarse histograms are available for seven age groups for each of the years 1970 to 1976. The protocol changed the boundaries of the intervals in 1975. If we are interested in how means, standard deviations, or certain percentiles vary with time or age, such raw data are not very useful. Using the CLM, we will see how to compute a smooth estimate of the underlying distribution.

Given an observed vector y of length m, we assume that element y_i is drawn from a Poisson distribution with expectation μ_i. If our goal was to estimate a smooth μ, we would be in the realm of histogram smoothing, as discussed in Section 3.3. This makes sense if m is relatively large, but this is not the case of the New York blood data. We also assume that there is a latent (smooth) vector γ, such that $\mu = C\gamma$, where C is a given matrix (with details to follow). The length of γ is q, a relatively large number, say 20 to 100. Given y and C, we aim to estimate γ, even though it cannot be observed directly.

The structure of C is determined by the problem at hand. For illustration, consider a case with y having $m = 3$ elements and γ having $q = 15$ elements. We then have

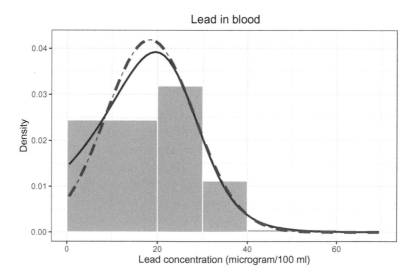

Figure 6.1 Raw density of lead concentrations in the blood of New York children and the estimated smooth density, based on optimal AIC. Solid line: second-order penalty; broken line: third-order penalty. R code in f-lead2.R

$$C = \begin{bmatrix} 1 & 1 & 1 & 1 & 1 & 0 & 0 & 0 & 0 & 0 & 0 & 0 & 0 & 0 & 0 \\ 0 & 0 & 0 & 0 & 0 & 1 & 1 & 1 & 1 & 1 & 0 & 0 & 0 & 0 & 0 \\ 0 & 0 & 0 & 0 & 0 & 0 & 0 & 0 & 0 & 0 & 1 & 1 & 1 & 1 & 1 \end{bmatrix}. \quad (6.1)$$

Here all three intervals contain five narrow bins, but clearly we can describe more general (unequal) widths with appropriate patterns of ones and zeros. We can also choose q to be larger or smaller, as we like.

We refer to these type of observations as complex counts, and we will present several examples. The combination of the composite link model (CLM) and P-splines gives us the penalized composite link model (PCLM).

To make γ positive, we model its logarithm with B-splines: $\log(\gamma) = B\alpha$. To make it smooth, we use a penalty. The B-splines are evaluated on the grid defined by the centers of the bins for γ. The model then becomes $\mu = C \exp(B\alpha)$. The P-spline model for a histogram without grouping is just a special case, with $C = I$, the identity matrix.

The objective function is the penalized Poisson deviance:

$$S = \mathrm{dev}(\alpha; B, y) + \lambda ||D\alpha||^2 = -2 \sum_{i=1}^{m} y_i \log(y_i/\mu_i) + \lambda ||D\alpha||^2. \quad (6.2)$$

Thompson and Baker (1981) provide an estimation algorithm for the unpenalized CLM, which we adapt to our case. When $\lambda = 0$, the likelihood equations are

$$\sum_{i=1}^{m} \frac{\partial S}{\partial \alpha_k} = \sum_{i=1}^{m} \frac{(y_i - \mu_i)}{\mu_i} \frac{\partial \mu_i}{\partial \alpha_k} = 0, \quad (6.3)$$

for all $k = 1 : n$. Because

$$\frac{\partial \mu_i}{\partial \alpha_k} = \sum_{j=1}^{q} c_{ij} \frac{\partial \gamma_j}{\partial \alpha_k} = \sum_{j=1}^{q} c_{ij} \gamma_j b_{jk},$$

we arrive at

$$\sum_{i=1}^{m} (y_i - \mu_i) g_{ik} = 0 \quad \text{with} \quad g_{ik} = \sum_{j=1}^{q} c_{ij} \gamma_j b_{jk} / \mu_i. \quad (6.4)$$

In matrix notation, we have $G = M^{-1} C \Gamma B$, where $M = \mathrm{diag}(\mu)$ and $\Gamma = \mathrm{diag}(\gamma)$. The unpenalized likelihood equations are finally $G'(y - \mu) = 0$. Adding the penalty gives

$$G'(y - \mu) = \lambda D' D\alpha. \quad (6.5)$$

For histogram smoothing that was presented in Chapter 2, we obtained the penalized likelihood equations

$$B'(y - \mu) = \lambda D' D\alpha. \quad (6.6)$$

We see that the only change in the PCLM is the replacement of the basis matrix B by the working matrix $G = M^{-1}C\Gamma B$, which, along with the working dependent variable and weights, is updated in each iteration. The iterative algorithm for computing an improved estimate of α from the current approximation $\tilde{\alpha}$ follows immediately:

$$(\tilde{G}'\tilde{W}\tilde{G} + \lambda D'D)\alpha = \tilde{G}'\tilde{W}(\tilde{G}\tilde{\alpha} + \tilde{W}^{-1}(y - \tilde{\mu})), \qquad (6.7)$$

with diagonal weight matrix $\tilde{W} = \tilde{M}$. The notation $\tilde{G}$ reflects and highlights that we indeed have a working regressor matrix in an otherwise standard GLM system of equations. To initialize the iterations, we set $\alpha_k \equiv \log\left(\sum_i y_i/n\right)$, making γ a uniform distribution that gives $\sum_i \hat{\mu}_i = \sum_i y_i$.

Quantities like covariance matrices and the effective dimension are straightforward to derive by replacing the matrix B with the converged $\hat{G}$ in the corresponding equations found in Section 2.12.3 for GLMs; see (2.27). For the covariance of $\hat{\alpha}$, we get

$$\mathrm{Cov}(\hat{\alpha}) = (\hat{G}'\hat{W}\hat{G} + \lambda D'D)^{-1}. \qquad (6.8)$$

The effective hat matrix is

$$H = \hat{G}(\hat{G}'\hat{W}\hat{G} + \lambda D'D)^{-1}\hat{G}'\hat{W}, \qquad (6.9)$$

while the effective dimension is

$$\mathrm{ED} = \mathrm{trace}(H) = \mathrm{trace}((\hat{G}'\hat{W}\hat{G} + \lambda D'D)^{-1}\hat{G}'\hat{W}\hat{G}). \qquad (6.10)$$

The covariance matrix and ED are only approximations because of the uncertainties in $\hat{W}$ and $\hat{G}$.

Returning to Figure 6.1, observed lead concentrations in the blood of New York children are provided in coarse intervals. Note that the leftmost bin is two times wider than the other ones. With unequal intervals, it is more meaningful to show densities instead of counts. The width of the bins for the latent distribution γ is 1 µg/100 mL. As just outlined, we model the observed counts with the total number of observations in this example being $m = 154$.

For the PCLM, ten B-spline segments were used, and $\log_{10}(\lambda)$ was varied on a grid in 0.1 steps; see Figure 6.2. Using a second-order penalty, the minimum of AIC ≈ 9.62 occurs for $\lambda = 3.2$, whereas with the third-order penalty, the minimum of AIC ≈ 9.59 occurs for $\lambda = 50.1$. As Figure 6.1 also displays, the estimated densities are essentially the same in their right tails, but do differ near the origin, as the third-order penalty allows a more flexible shape. With a

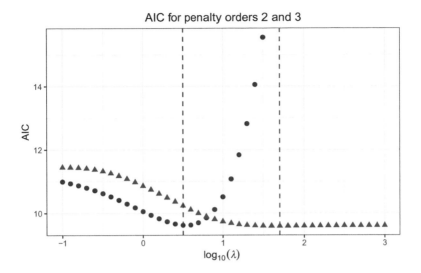

Figure 6.2 AIC profiles for the lead in blood data for second- (filled circles) and third-order (triangle) penalties. The vertical lines indicate the positions of the minima. R code in f-lead-AIC.R

third-order penalty, the profile of AIC is essentially flat for $\lambda > 100$, indicating a truncated normal distribution for γ; see Section 2.12.1.

Histograms with wide bins occur across many disciplines. For example, epidemiological studies commonly provide death counts for various diseases that are grouped into intervals of 5 or 10 years wide, with only one group for all ages above 85. In situations when one wishes to compare summary statistics, like quantiles, for different years, countries, or regions, it is desirable to have an estimated distribution at a resolution of 1 year. Rizzi et al. (2015) obtained good results with the PCLM, while Rizzi et al. (2016) compared the PCLM to several other algorithms for the ungrouping of coarse data and found it to perform best.

6.2 Histograms and Scale Transformation

The top panel of Figure 6.3 shows a histogram of a large number of observations of the blood parameter RDW, representing the standardized width of the distribution of the size of red blood cells. It is based on the distribution of the mean corpuscular volume (MCV) of the cells: RDW = 100 * SD(MCV) / mean(MCV).

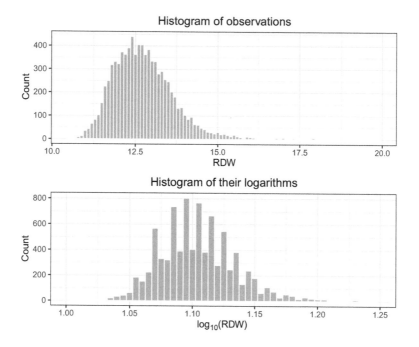

Figure 6.3 Top: histogram of RDW (scaled width of red blood cell distribution), using a linear scale. Bottom: histogram after taking logarithms (to base 10). The comb-shaped artefact is caused by rounding of the reported values to a resolution of 0.1. R code in f-rdw-hist.R

The distribution is skewed to the right, so a logarithmic transformation seems appropriate. This leads to the histogram in the bottom panel of the figure, which shows a surprising pattern of strong systematic variation in the counts. This is a consequence of the values of RDW being rounded to steps of 0.1.

It is no problem to smooth the histogram on the logarithmic scale, but as such would force us to choose a subjective value of λ. We cannot rely on AIC in this setting because it would undersmooth the comblike histogram. Recall the discussion of overdispersion in Section 3.6.

We use the PCLM to estimate a smooth density on the logarithmic scale, fitting it to the histogram on the linear scale. The grid runs from 1.0 to 1.3, with 151 steps of 0.002. We use an identity matrix (Whittaker basis) instead of a B-spline basis matrix, so $\gamma = e^\beta$. The elements of C are computed as follows: c_{ij} is the fraction of logarithmic interval j that overlaps with linear interval i. Using AIC to choose the penalty weight, we arrive at the results shown in Figure 6.4 (with $\log_{10}(\lambda) = 3.1$). The improvement is clear.

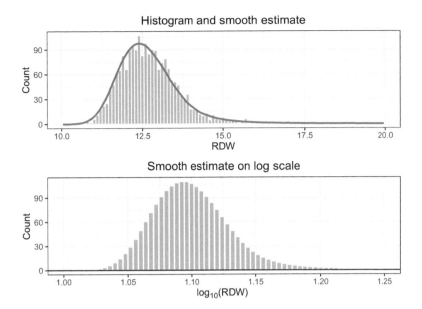

Figure 6.4 Top: histogram of RDW (scaled width of red blood cell distribution), using a linear scale, with the PCLM-based smooth distribution. Bottom: estimated smooth distribution on the logarithmic scale. R code in `f-rdw-pclm.R`

6.3 Individual Censoring

In the previous applications, we had a small number of given intervals and the counts of observations they contain. A more complicated situation arises when each raw observation has its own interval. This commonly can occur in screening situations, e.g., when the occurrence of an event lies between two visits at known times. Figure 6.5 (top panel) shows an example: interval censoring of incidence time of HIV infections of hemophilia patients. The data are published by De Gruttola and Lakatos (1989) and have been used by Braun et al. (2005) to propose kernel smoothing for interval censored observations.

Let γ be a discrete density on a fine grid, with midpoints u_j, for $j = 1 :
q$ and $\sum_j \gamma_j = 1$. For patient i, we know the start l_i and the end r_i of the interval. The composition matrix C has one row per patient, with $c_{ij} = 1$ if $l_i \leq u_j \leq r_i$. It follows that $\mu = C\gamma$ gives us the probabilities of the individual intervals for each patient. We optimize the log-likelihood, with a roughness penalty on $\log(\gamma)$. We also need the explicit constraint $\sum_j \gamma_j = 1$ to get a proper distribution. Figure 6.5 (bottom panel) displays the estimated smooth density. The HFS algorithm (Section 3.4) was used to tune λ.

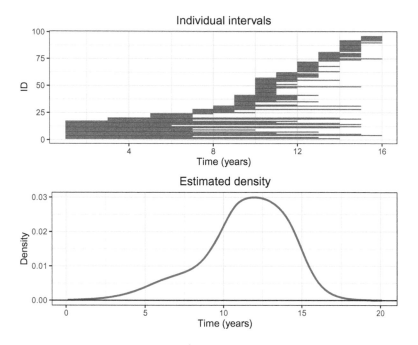

Figure 6.5 Top: individual intervals in which HIV infections occurred. Bottom: smooth estimate of the distribution, obtained with the penalized composite link model. Latent grid with 101 bins; identity matrix as basis. R code in f-dens-HIV.R

We skip the technical details here, which can be found in a technical report written by Jutta Gampe. See our website: https://psplines.bitbucket.io/ Support/NotesIC-EM-PCLM.pdf.

6.4 Latent Mixtures

The next example relates to a severely overdispersed discrete distribution. In the region surrounding Rotterdam in the Netherlands, the Rijnmond Environmental Agency registers approximately 20,000 total complaints annually from regional inhabitants regarding odors, dust, and noise, among other environmental annoyances. The daily number of odor complaints is highly variable, as can be seen from the distribution displayed in Figure 6.6, which covers the year 1988. The total for odor complaints is 5,370. Maximum likelihood estimation of a Poisson distribution yields a deviance of 2,382.0 (on 99 degrees of freedom),

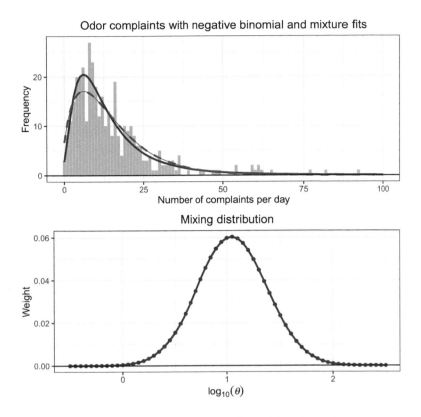

Figure 6.6 Top: distribution of daily number of complaints about odor annoyance (bars), with the estimated negative binomial distribution (broken red line) and the fit of the PCLM model (solid blue line). Bottom: the estimated mixing distributions. The dots indicate the grid points used for the model. R code in f-complaints2.R

whereas a negative binomial distribution fits much better with a deviance of 121.8 (on 98 degrees of freedom). Yet, there remains systematic lack of fit, most prominently found in the left tail.

A negative binomial distribution can be interpreted as a continuous mixture of Poisson distributions, of which the expected values (here indicated by θ) are drawn from a gamma distribution. Apparently for the complaint data, the gamma distribution does not create enough variation. Using the PCLM, we can estimate a smooth nonparametric latent distribution for θ. We use a linear grid for $\log_{10}(\theta)$, from -0.5 to 2.5 with steps of 0.05. The cubic B-spline basis has 10 segments.

With a second-order difference penalty and $\lambda \approx 50$, AIC attains its minimum at 101.4, which is a marked improvement compared to the negative binomial distribution. With $d = 3$, AIC shows a monotone decrease with increasing λ, approaching the value 98.2, implying that the mixing distribution of $\log(\theta)$ is a discrete approximation of the normal distribution. Figure 6.6 shows the complaint data distribution, overlaid by the optimal mixed distribution ($d = 3$, $\lambda = 10^6$, AIC $= 98.2$) and the negative binomial distribution. It also show the estimated distribution of $\log_{10}(\theta)$.

6.5 Notes and Details

The penalized CLM is proposed by Eilers (2007), and it was applied there to both the environmental complaint and the lead concentration data sets. Another application was the back-calculation of HIV infection rates from observed counts of cases and a known distribution of incubation times.

Surprisingly, neither the CLM nor its penalized version have received much attention in the literature. Eilers (2012) calls it the "neglected model." We hope that the examples in this chapter will demonstrate its utility again and help to make it more popular.

With a proper choice of C, $\mu = C\gamma$ covers many observational schemes. Camarda et al. (2008, 2017) use it in models for digit preference. There also the elements of C were estimated from the data. Lambert and Eilers (2009) present a Bayesian approach to estimate densities from grouped observations. As a physical example, de Rooi et al. (2014) present an application to diffraction scans in crystallography, where the contributions of X-rays at two different wavelengths have to be separated.

There is a rich literature on nonparametric maximum likelihood estimation of latent mixture distributions. Examples can be found in Aitkin et al. (2005) and Schlattmann (2009). The traditional approach assumes an unknown number of probability mass points, at unknown positions. It is straightforward, but generally slow to estimate these with the EM algorithm. A smooth mixing distribution makes more sense, both from a theoretical and a practical point of view. The environmental complaint data offers a case in point: it is highly unlikely that the expected number of complaints for a single day is drawn from a small set of mass points. In addition, a smooth latent distribution gives more sensible results in Bayesian estimates of θ for individual days. A similar application is the estimation of a frailty distribution in survival analysis, which can be found in Yavuz and Lambert (2016).

The PCLM has been applied to grouped data in two dimensions as well. Two-dimensional histograms with wide bins are modeled in Lambert (2011). The aggregation there is in rectangles. Ayma et al. (2016) consider a more complicated case, estimating smooth intensity surfaces from counts that are aggregated over spatial units (counties). These authors also implemented a mixed model approach with random effects on the aggregation scale to account for overdispersion.

Camarda et al. (2016) apply the PCLM to sums of curves in an application to age-dependent human mortality in individual years. There γ contains two stacked intensity curves. They both are positive, and their logarithms are modeled. The observed mortality is the sum of these intensities, multiplied by the exposure. In the same paper, this application has been extended to mortality tables, summing intensity surfaces. More on mortality tables can be found in Section 8.9.

7

Signal Regression

In previous chapters, our goal was to estimate a curve from noisy or distorted data. The data were close enough to the curve to provide strong information about it. Now we switch to problems, variants of multivariate calibration, for which this is not the case.

An example is estimation of the fat content of biscuit dough, using optical spectra, obtained with a near infrared (NIR) spectrometer. Fat can be measured in the laboratory, but that is time consuming. A spectrometer can be mounted on the machine that makes the dough, delivering a spectrum almost instantaneously. Each spectrum, say x, has 600 channels. We want a coefficient vector β, such that $x'\beta$ is a good estimate of y, the fat content. For this purpose, 40 samples of dough have been selected and analyzed in the lab, and their spectra have been measured. So we have a matrix X and a vector y to estimate β.

This is a singular regression problem, for which many solutions have been proposed in the literature. We propose to force β to be smooth and call it penalized signal regression (PSR). Using P-splines, the system of penalized least squares equations is reduced to the size of the basis, with great gains in computation speed.

With many more regressors than observations, a perfect fit to any vector y can be obtained. Of real interest is the external prediction performance of the model, and this is explored with cross-validation to find the optimal weight of the penalty. We also present generalized linear PSR, relying on AIC to optimize the penalty for classifying phonemes with audio spectra.

PSR can be extended to handle problems in which each x is not a vector, but a matrix, using tensor products P-splines. We combine excitation-emission fluorescence spectra and with sugar quality (ash content) to illustrate this model.

Standard (multidimensional) PSR assumes linearity, but we can borrow from single-index models, $E(y) = f(X\beta)$, and estimate β and $f(\cdot)$ from the data. We call this SISR (single-index signal regression).

7.1 A Chemical Calibration Problem

Like other regression problems, we have a response vector y and a matrix X, containing the regressors in its columns. What is special now is that each row of X is a (digitized) spectrum, time series, or other signal. Thus the columns have a natural order and consequently an indexing variable.

As a motivating example, consider the set of curves in Figure 7.1 (bottom panel). Each curve represents a spectrum, based on the strength of near infrared (NIR) light reflection by a sample of biscuit dough. These curves form the rows of X; they were obtained by taking first differences of observed spectra in the top panel. This preprocessing is done to remove the shifts that can be seen in

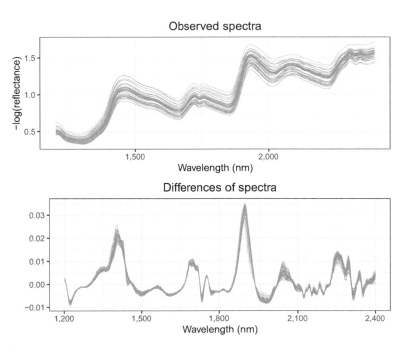

Figure 7.1 NIR spectra for the biscuit data, where each curve ($m = 39$) represents $p = 601$ NIR wavelengths (top), and the corresponding first differenced NIR spectra (bottom). R code in f-psr-biscuit.R

the original spectra, which are artefacts of the physical properties of the dough and not important to the regression.

For each dough sample, the amount of fat was determined in a laboratory. These values give a vector y. Obtaining them is a costly time-consuming process that involves physical transportation of samples. In contrast, a reflectance spectrum can be obtained on-site and quickly. A prediction model that gives a fast accurate, and inexpensive estimate of fat content can be of great value to a biscuit bakery. The advantages can be even greater because other dough properties, such as the amounts of sucrose, water, and flour, may have to be determine routinely too. The hope is that the same NIR spectra can be used for several properties by developing models based on the same X but different responses.

In the spirit of P-splines, we can impose smoothness directly on β by minimizing

$$S(\beta) = ||y - X\beta||^2 + \lambda||D\beta||^2, \tag{7.1}$$

where D is the usual difference matrix of order d, with tuning parameter λ. The resulting system of equations is

$$\hat{\beta} = (X'X + \lambda D'D)^{-1}X'y, \tag{7.2}$$

showing the familiar structure that we have seen many times before in this book.

Working directly with β can be potentially unattractive because the size of the system of equations in (7.2) grows with the instrument's resolution. In the example data, β has 600 elements, but modern high-resolution instruments can measure thousands of wavelengths. One practical solution is to write $\beta = B\alpha$, with B a B-spline basis, and then place a roughness penalty on α. This constraint on β is one choice to regularize estimation, and it is one that either assumes that the coefficients are smooth or the smoothing of the coefficients is non-detrimental to prediction. We emphasize that we are not smoothing the rows of X, but we rather smooth the coefficient vector β, in a way to "optimize" external prediction while using the unprocessed (differenced) signals.

We called this *penalized signal regression* (PSR) (Marx and Eilers, 1999). The penalized objective function becomes

$$S(\alpha) = ||y - XB\alpha||^2 + \lambda||D\alpha||^2, \tag{7.3}$$

resulting in the system of equations

$$(B'X'XB + \lambda D'D)\alpha = B'X'y.$$

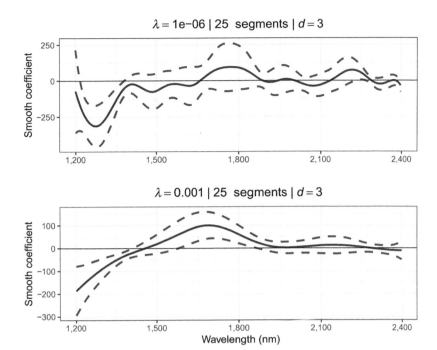

Figure 7.2 P-spline smooth coefficient vectors for biscuit data (including twice standard error bands) with tuning parameter $\lambda = 10^{-6}$ (top) and 0.001 (bottom) using 25 segments, and $d = 3$. R code in f-psrcoef.R

Introducing $U = XB$, we have the following explicit solution

$$\hat{\alpha} = (U'U + \lambda D'D)^{-1}U'y$$
$$\hat{\beta} = B\hat{\alpha}. \tag{7.4}$$

Figure 7.2 displays the smooth coefficient vector $\hat{\beta}$ for two values of λ. The optimal choice of λ can be made using cross-validation, e.g., LOOCV, as presented in Section 3.1. Figure 7.3 shows how the prediction error changes with λ, with a clear minimum.

To keep the presentation simple, we have not included an intercept term in the model thus far. Experience has shown that it is generally needed, changing the model to $\mu = \beta_0 + X\beta$ or, more conveniently, $\mu = \alpha_0 + U\alpha = U_\star\alpha_\star$, where $U_\star = [1 \mid U]$ and $\alpha_\star = (\alpha_0, \alpha')'$. We do not want α_0 to be penalized. This can be achieved by modifying the matrix D. As U is now augmented with a leading column of ones, we replace D in (7.4) by a matrix $D_\star$ having an extra column of zeros: $D_\star = [0 \mid D]$.

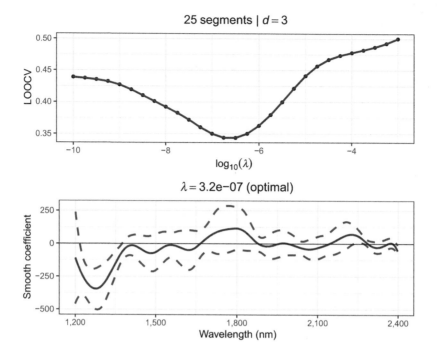

Figure 7.3 Tracking LOOCV as a function of $\log_{10}(\lambda)$ for the biscuit data (top), and the optimal smooth coefficient vector (with twice standard error bands) corresponding to minimum LOOCV (bottom). R code in f-psropt.R

Standard errors of $\hat{\alpha}_\star$ and $\hat{\beta}$ follow from equation (2.16):

$$\mathrm{cov}(\hat{\alpha}_\star) \approx \sigma^2 (U_\star' U_\star + \lambda D_\star' D_\star)^{-1} \quad \text{and}$$
$$\mathrm{cov}(\hat{\beta}) \approx \sigma^2 B \hat{V} B', \tag{7.5}$$

where $\hat{V}$ is the appropriate sub-matrix of $\mathrm{cov}(\hat{\alpha}_\star)$ that does not involve the intercept. The estimates of σ^2 and ED follow as

$$\hat{\sigma}^2 = \frac{||y - U_\star \hat{\alpha}_\star||^2}{m - \mathrm{ED}},$$

and

$$\mathrm{ED} = \mathrm{trace}((U_\star' U_\star + \lambda D_\star' D_\star)^{-1} U_\star' U_\star).$$

Figure 7.3 (top panel) shows for the biscuit data that the optimal tuning parameter is $\lambda \approx 3.2 \times 10^{-7}$, yielding an effective dimension of ED = 19.4.

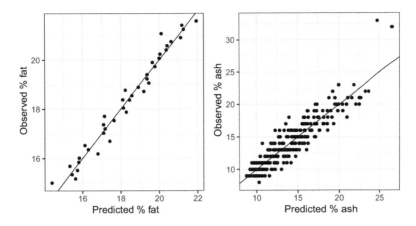

Figure 7.4 Externally predicted versus observed response for two different models percentage of fat (1D PSR, left), percentage of ash (2D PSR, right), using optimal λ based on LOOCV. R code in f-LOOCVpsr.R

We used 25 segments for the basis and a third-order penalty. The bottom portion of the same figure shows $\hat{\beta}$ with twice standard error bands. The graph suggests that the coefficients for wavelengths from 1,200 to 1,400 nm are "significant," but it is hardly meaningful to interpret the coefficient curve. We display the coefficients here mainly to illustrate the mechanics of P-spline estimation. There is very little information in the data to steer estimation of the high dimensional coefficients, and the influence of the penalty is strong. However, the prediction performance is very relevant; it can be judged from Figure 7.4 (left panel). We see that it is quite good, with correlations of 0.984 (left) and 0.914 (right). The right panel is further discussed in Section 7.3, and the apparent nonlinear features for prediction with larger values of ash are addressed in Section 7.4.

Notice that there is little (if any) preprocessing of the data, with the exception of using first differenced spectra. The PSR approach is completely transparent and avoids "black boxes" and algorithmic armor, as found in machine learning or even with PLS techniques. In full disclosure, initially there were $m = 40$ biscuits; however, observation #23 was discarded as an outlier, leaving $m = 39$. Also the original spectra had a wider range of 1,100 nm to 2,498 nm (in steps of 2 nm). The wavelengths at the ends were known to be less reliable for instrumental reasons. The biscuit data come from Osborne et al. (1984) and also appear in Stone and Brooks (1990).

7.2 Extensions to the Generalized Linear Model

Extending the PSR model into the GLM to accommodate non-normal response variables is nearly trivial. Estimation of $\alpha_\star = (\alpha_0, \alpha')'$ follows from the iterative scheme presented in (2.22), replacing B with $U_\star = (1 \mid U)$. Again some care has to be taken again to ensure an unpenalized intercept using the modified difference matrix $D_\star = [0 \mid D]$, of proper dimension. Upon convergence, we denote the estimated smooth coefficient vector as $\hat{\beta} = B\hat{\alpha}$.

Using the results found in (7.5), standard error bands can be constructed for β with

$$\mathrm{cov}(\hat{\alpha}_\star) \approx (U_\star' \hat{W} U_\star + \lambda D_\star' D_\star)^{-1} \quad \text{and}$$
$$\mathrm{cov}(\hat{\beta}) \approx B \hat{V} B', \tag{7.6}$$

where $\hat{V}$ is the proper sub-matrix of $\mathrm{cov}(\hat{\alpha}_\star)$.

To illustrate signal regression with a binary response, we consider the example of phoneme discrimination in speech records (Hastie et al., 1995, 2009). The two phonemes are *ao* (as in *water*) and *aa* (as in *dark*); they form the binary response y. Each record is 32 ms long, sampled at 16 kHz; a log-periodogram is computed from it, and the first 150 frequencies are selected (among 256). There are ($m = 1717$) rows of X (695 associated with $y = 1$). Other phonemes are also in the data set, such as *iy* (as in *she*). The classification problem between *aa-ao* is chosen, which is generally more difficult to discriminate than others, for example, *ao-iy*.

To give an impression of the data, Figure 7.5 shows an example log-periodogram for each phoneme. Although the log-periodograms are very rough, we do not try to smooth them. We rather force the coefficient vector to be smooth. The model of interest is

$$\mathrm{logit}(\pi) = \beta_0 + X\beta = \alpha_0 + XB\alpha = U_\star \alpha_\star = \eta, \tag{7.7}$$

where π is the probability of observing an *aa*.

Using 20 segments for the basis and a third-order penalty, the optimal value of $\lambda \approx 0.32$. Figure 7.6 (top) shows the AIC trace as a function of $\log_{10}(\lambda)$. The bottom panel displays $\hat{\beta}$ with twice standard error bands. Notice that these bands suggest that there appears to be little information beyond (approximately) the 75th frequency. The deviance is 1,289.6 (on approximately 1,695.0 residual degrees of freedom), with ED $= 21.9$; the percent correct classification is 83.5, using a basic cutoff probability of 50%.

Figure 7.7 shows the receiver operating characteristic (ROC) curve for the logit penalized signal regression associated with the phoneme classification

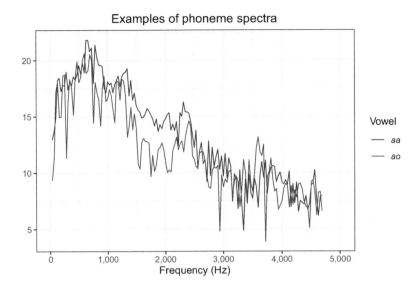

Figure 7.5 Typical log-periodograms for *aa-ao*. R code in f-vowelspec.R

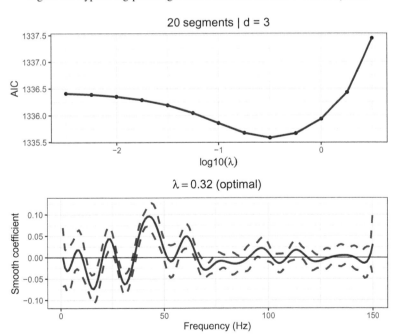

Figure 7.6 Tracking AIC as a function of $\log_{10}(\lambda)$ for the phoneme data (top), and the optimal smooth coefficient vector (with twice standard error bands) corresponding to minimum AIC (bottom). R code in f-vowelopt.R

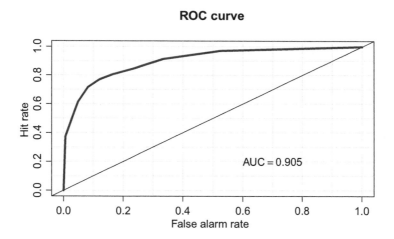

Figure 7.7 The receiver operating characteristic (ROC) curve for the logit penalized
signal regression for the *aa-ao* phoneme data, optimally tuned with AIC. R code
in f-vowel-roc.R

of *aa-ao*. The area under the curve (AUC) is 0.905, while the naïve rule is
0.405 (0.595) for *aa* (*ao*). As external prediction is paramount, data splitting
was also further explored using a 50–50 split, with the even (odd) indices
used for the train (test) sets, respectively. AIC on the training set was used to
optimize tuning. For both the test and external test sets, the ROC curves looked
very similar to Figure 7.7, each with an AUC of approximately 0.900.

7.3 Multidimensional Signal Regression

We next extend penalized signal regression into higher dimensions and consider
regressors that come in the form of a two-dimensional signal or image. We
term this method *multidimensional penalized signal regression*, or MPSR
(Marx and Eilers, 2005). To motivate the problem, we use the $m = 268$
observations, 3,997 regressor (in the form of a two-dimensional signal), and
two response variables (ash, color) sugar fluorescence data set that can be
found in Bro (1999). A detailed description of the data can be found at
www.models.kvl.dk/Sugar_Process. The image in Figure 7.8 displays the
regressors for the first observation of the data set. The corresponding response
for ash (expressed as a percentage) is $y = 10$. There are $571 \times 7 = 3,997$
regressors, along two indexing axes v with $p = 571$ emission channels (nm)
and $\check{v}$ with $\check{p} = 7$ excitation channels (nm). Ash content is a measure of
inorganic impurities in the refined sugar, so we aim to build a model

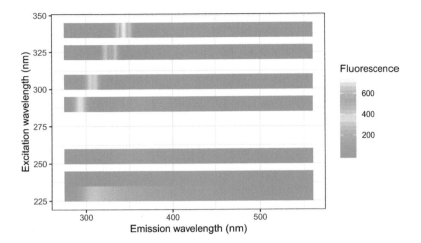

Figure 7.8 Two-dimensional regressor image of dimension 268 (emission) × 7 (excitation) wavelengths, associated with the first observation with ash = 10. R code in f-grid-sugar2D.R

that is useful for prediction of this quality measure, when given a new fluorescence image.

MPSR assumes a single overarching smooth coefficient surface. The coefficient surface weighs each signal and is usually chosen to optimize a prediction criterion, again using leave-one-out CV. Figure 7.9 displays the "optimal" estimated coefficient image for the sugar example with highly interactive features. Although no special treatment was given to the two-dimensional spectra for modeling (i.e., we used the entire spectra), we present the coefficient surface with a zeroed-out corner in Figure 7.9. This triangular region represents where the excitation wavelengths exceed those of the emission wavelengths, which is not possible due to a physical energy constraint.

Conceptually, the MPSR solution is straightforward. Using tools in Chapter 4, we express the coefficient surface through a rich tensor product B-spline basis, which is the first step in dimension reduction, and then further regularize smoothness using difference penalties on each row and each column of the tensor coefficients. We view such as sensible constraints that take into account the spatial structure of the regressors, while ensuring smoothness in the coefficient surface.

Given the ith image regressor matrix $X_i = [x_{ijk}]$ of dimension $p \times \check{p}$, signal regressor support matrix $(v, \check{v})$, and coefficient surface β_{jk}, we express the mean

$$\mu_i = \sum_{j=1}^{p} \sum_{k=1}^{\check{p}} x_{ijk} \beta_{jk}, \qquad (7.8)$$

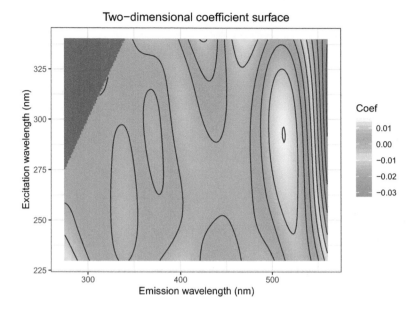

Figure 7.9 Optimal two-dimensional coefficient image surface using LOOCV, for response ash. R code in f-sugar-coef-image.R

where $i = 1 : m$; $j = 1 : p$; $k = 1 : \check{p}$. Using tensor product B-splines, (7.8) can be reexpressed as

$$\mu_i = \sum_{j=1}^{p} \sum_{k=1}^{\check{p}} x_{ijk} \sum_{r=1}^{n} \sum_{s=1}^{\check{n}} b_{jr} \check{b}_{ks} a_{rs}, \tag{7.9}$$

where $A = [a_{rs}]$ is the n by $\check{n}$ array of tensor product coefficients. The B-spline bases are denoted by $B = [b_{jr}]$ and $\check{B} = [b_{ks}]$ and have dimensions p by n and $\check{p}$ by $\check{n}$, respectively. The form of (7.9) is needed for computation. More explicitly,

$$\text{vec}\{\beta_{jk}\} = \mathcal{B}\alpha, \tag{7.10}$$

where $\alpha = \text{vec}(A)$ is the vectorization of the matrix of tensor product coefficients associated with the coefficient surface. The matrix $\mathcal{B} = B\Box\check{B} = (B \otimes 1'_{\check{p}}) \odot (1'_p \otimes \check{B})$ is of dimension $p\check{p}$ by $n\check{n}$, with the notation more fully explained in Section 4.4.

MPSR finds a practical solution to minimize

$$S = ||y - X\mathcal{B}\alpha||^2 = ||y - M\alpha||^2,$$

where X is the m by $p\breve{p}$ matrix of vectorized two-dimensional signals, and $M = X\mathcal{B}$ is m by $n\breve{n}$ with lower column dimension. As in Section 4.5, discrete roughness or difference penalties are imposed on α. Although we implement penalization on the vector form of coefficients $\alpha = \text{vec}(A)$, the motivation and mechanics of penalization is really executed on the array of coefficients in A, both on the rows and columns of A. The objective function is modified to minimize

$$
\begin{aligned}
S^* &= ||y - X\mathcal{B}\alpha||^2 + \lambda||DA||_F^2 + \breve{\lambda}||A\breve{D}'||_F^2 \\
&= ||y - M\alpha||^2 + \lambda\alpha' P\alpha + \breve{\lambda}\alpha'\breve{P}\alpha,
\end{aligned}
\tag{7.11}
$$

with $P = (\breve{I} \otimes D)'(\breve{I} \otimes D)$ and $\breve{P} = (\breve{D} \otimes I)'(\breve{D} \otimes I)$. If needed, the order of the difference penalty is allowed to vary across orientation, $(d, \breve{d})$. We see from the objective S^* that there are two separate tuning parameters to weigh the anisotropic penalty. The explicit solution for (7.11) follows almost trivially and is

$$
\hat{\alpha} = (M'M + \lambda P + \breve{\lambda}\breve{P})^{-1}M'y.
\tag{7.12}
$$

The predicted values are $\hat{y} = M\hat{\alpha}$. It follows naturally that the effective "hat" matrix is $H = [h_{ii'}] = M(M'M + \lambda P + \breve{\lambda}\breve{P})^{-1}M'$. We choose the penalty tuning parameters $(\lambda, \breve{\lambda})$ for reliable prediction. Leave-one-out CV calculations are exact and easily accessible now using (3.2) with the hat diagonals given above that are associated with the two-dimensional spectra fit. The optimal $(\lambda, \breve{\lambda})$ can be found using a search algorithm. For the sugar example, the optimal LOOCV=1.52, which can be interpreted as a standard deviation in units of percent ash. Prediction performance is further illustrated in Figure 7.4 (right panel), which provides a visualization of external prediction error.

The effective dimension of the estimated coefficient surface can be approximated by familiar formulas seen throughout this book

$$
\text{ED} = \text{trace}\,((M'M + \lambda P + \breve{\lambda}\breve{P})^{-1}M'M),
$$

and the error variance component estimated by

$$
\hat{\sigma}^2 = \frac{||y - \hat{y}||^2}{m - \text{ED}}.
$$

For given λ and $\breve{\lambda}$, standard error surfaces can be constructed using

$$
\text{cov}(\hat{\gamma}) = \hat{\sigma}^2(M'M + \lambda P + \breve{\lambda}\breve{P})^{-1}.
$$

A translation back to the variance of the estimated coefficient surface, $\hat{\beta} = \mathcal{B}\hat{\alpha}$, results in

$$\mathrm{cov}(\hat{\beta}) = \mathcal{B}\mathrm{cov}(\hat{\alpha})\mathcal{B}'. \tag{7.13}$$

Standard error surfaces can be constructed using the square root of diagonals of $\mathrm{cov}(\hat{\beta})$.

The model can be modified to include other factors or covariates, and the objective (7.11) could even have additional penalties if desired. In the sugar example, we also included an intercept term α_0. Thus the modified P-spline solution becomes

$$(\hat{\alpha}_0, \hat{\alpha}')' = (M'_\star M_\star + \lambda P_\star + \check{\lambda} \check{P}_\star)^{-1} M'_\star y,$$

with $M_\star = (1 \mid M)$, and $P_\star$ and $\check{P}_\star$, pads an extra first row and column of zeros to ensures an unpenalized intercept.

The sugar MPSR model used 250 cubic tensor products, with $n = 25$ along emission and $\check{n} = 10$ along excitation, and the optimal penalty parameters were $\lambda = 81,110$ and $\check{\lambda} = 52,275$, using third-order penalties on the rows and columns ($d = \check{d} = 3$). The effective dimension of the estimated surface is dramatically reduced to ED $= 36.9$, which can also be seen in Figure 7.9. Each regressor image was mean centered, but not scaled, and used an intercept term.

As with PSR, the MPSR model can be transplanted into the generalized linear model, accommodating, e.g., binomial or Poisson responses. With $h(\cdot)$ denoting the inverse link function, the mean response is now modeled using $\mu = h(X\mathcal{B}\alpha) = h(M\alpha)$. Estimation of α follows once again from the iterative scheme presented in (2.22), replacing B with M. Upon convergence, we denote the estimated smooth coefficient surface as $\mathcal{B}\hat{\alpha}$, which can be reshaped into a p by $\check{p}$ matrix. We choose optimal $(\lambda, \check{\lambda})$ by minimizing AIC $= \mathrm{dev}(y; \hat{\alpha}) + 2\,\mathrm{ED}$, with ED $= \mathrm{trace}((M'\hat{W}M + \lambda P + \check{\lambda}\check{P})^{-1} M'\hat{W}M)$.

7.4 Further Extensions

Extensions of the PSR model reach far beyond that of what has been presented in this chapter. One such modification is the exploration of more flexible PSR models through the estimation of an explicit, but unknown, link function, f. To start, consider that the implicit assumption of an identity link function to be slightly misspecified. To accommodate possible nonlinearities, the linear predictor is allowed to bend through smooth f,

$$\mu = f(X\beta) = f(U\alpha) = f(\eta)$$

(the intercept is suppressed to simplify notation). The resulting new objective function is

$$S_f(\alpha) = ||y - f(U\alpha)||^2 + \lambda||D\alpha|| + \check{\lambda}||\check{D}\theta||^2, \qquad (7.14)$$

where θ contains the standard P-spline coefficients to estimate f. We see that (7.14) essentially has one smooth function ($U\alpha$) embedded within another one (f). In fact, we can apply standard P-spline smoothing techniques from Chapter 2 to estimate f, smoothing the (η, y) data pairs. For fixed f, a Taylor series approximation (around starting values $\tilde{\alpha}$) is

$$f(U\alpha) \approx f(U\tilde{\alpha}) + \dot{f}(U\tilde{\alpha})U(\alpha - \tilde{\alpha}), \qquad (7.15)$$

where $\dot{f}$ denotes the derivative of f. Substituting (7.15) into (7.14), a modified objective function for α emerges, which replaces y with $y^\star = y - f(U\tilde{\alpha}) + \dot{f}(U\tilde{\alpha})U\tilde{\alpha}$ and replaces U with $U^\star = \text{diag}(\dot{f}(U\tilde{\alpha}))U$. Given the resulting new estimates of α from this modification, then the linear predictor $\eta = U\alpha$ can also be estimated, which can be further used to estimate f using standard P-splines on (η, y). Cycling between estimates of α and f is done until convergence. To ensure identifiability, normalization on α is needed. We refer to this method as *single-index signal regression*, or SISR (Eilers et al., 2009). Extensions of SISR into multidimensional signals uses $f(M\alpha)$ and is implemented in a similar way (Marx et al., 2011).

Other variations of PSR include varying coefficient ideas. For example, the PSR smooth coefficient vector is constructed over the index of the signal. However, it may be the case that there is another measured covariate t, e.g., temperature, such that $\hat{\beta}$ varies smoothly over t. In essence a two-dimensional surface is produced and then sliced at a particular level of the covariate t. With some of the technical details described below, such a varying coefficient PSR approach is the topic of Eilers and Marx (2003), where the problem is effectively solved using a modified tensor product basis (see Chapter 4) with $U = XB$ (for the signal) and $\check{B}$ (for the covariate dimension). For the ith observation, with signal x_{ik} ($k = 1 : p$) and covariate t_i, the varying signal coefficient construction stems from the following

$$\mu_i = \sum_{j=1}^{p} x_{ij} \sum_{r=1}^{n} \sum_{s=1}^{\check{n}} B_r(v_j)\check{B}_s(t_i)\alpha_{rs}$$

$$= \sum_{j=1}^{p} \sum_{r=1}^{n} \sum_{s=1}^{\check{n}} x_{ij}b_{jr}\check{b}_{is}\alpha_{rs}$$

$$= \sum_{r=1}^{n} \sum_{s=1}^{\check{n}} (\sum_{j=1}^{p} x_{ij} b_{jr}) \check{b}_{is} \alpha_{rs}$$

$$= \sum_{r=1}^{n} \sum_{s=1}^{\check{n}} u_{ir} \check{b}_{is} \alpha_{rs}. \tag{7.16}$$

In situations where the link function is unknown, but is to be explicitly and flexibly estimated using P-splines, SISR models are useful and have been presented in Eilers et al. (2009) (one-dimensional signals) and Marx et al. (2011) (for two-dimensional signals). Marx (2015) takes this type of varying coefficient PSR setting one step further by introducing f in a varying SISR model, termed VSISR. This model allows both varying signal coefficients in combination with a varying link function. Figure 7.10 provides the main deliverable for the VSISR model: two tensor product surfaces – one for the signal coefficients and the other for the link function – each sliced at a specific level of the covariate t, simultaneously producing both a smoothly varying

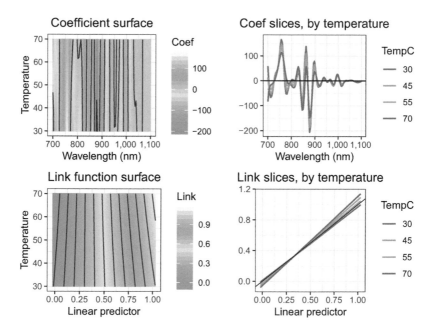

Figure 7.10 The coefficient surface (top, left) is sliced at specific levels of the covariate t, producing varying signal coefficients (top, right); The link function surface (bottom, left) is also sliced at specific levels of t, producing varying link functions (bottom, right). R code in f-VSISR.R

coefficient model and varying link model. The bottom left panel demonstrates the varying (across temperature) nonlinear adjustments for the linear predictor. There are four tuning parameters, associated with the rows and columns of each surface.

7.5 Notes and Details

We find that the broad framework of the PSR approach has much to offer: (a) The entire signal/image can be used as regressors, with little or no preprocessing. (b) The "$p > m$" problem is easily handled, providing a manageable system of equations, while dramatically reducing the nominal dimension in estimation. (c) The candidate coefficient curve/surface can be very general (nonadditive), allowing polynomial connections with strong penalization. (d) The approach is grounded in regression, thus CV and other diagnostics are quickly accessible. (e) It is easily transplanted to the generalized linear model (e.g., binary response) framework. (f) SISR extensions are tractable. (g) As future (spectroscopy) instruments improve resolution, the system of equations remains unchanged as n or $n\check{n}$, even while p or $p\check{p}$ becomes very large.

The area of signal regression or functional regression has generated enormous interest over the past quarter-century. The overview papers of Frank and Friedman (1993) and Morris (2015) serve as excellent "bookends" to the arch of developments. The discussion paper of Greven and Scheipl (2017) additionally provides a comprehensive framework for additive (mixed) models for functional responses and/or functional covariates. A textbook that serve as a bedrock for functional data analysis is Ramsay and Silverman (2003).

The initial work on P-spline signal regression can be found in Marx and Eilers (1999), which was then extended by the same authors to multidimensional signal regression in Marx and Eilers (2005). The use of a roughness penalty in multivariate calibration can be traced back to the discussion in Hastie and Tibshirani (1993) within Frank and Friedman (1993), where they presented signal regression using unpenalized B-splines.

As mentioned in Chapter 4, signal regression has been incorporated into additive structure models in Eilers and Marx (2002). Using P-spline tensor products, the varying coefficient model for signal regressors was first constructed within the work found in Eilers and Marx (2003). In situations where the link function is unknown, but is to be explicitly and flexibly estimated using P-splines, SISR models are useful and are presented in a variety of settings in Eilers et al. (2009), Marx et al. (2011), and Marx (2015).

When addressing functional regressors, a low dimensional linear combination method, such as partial least squares (PLS), is often a candidate approach. Aguilera et al. (2016) develop penalized versions of PLS for functional data, whereas Li and Marx (2008) use a hybrid of PLS and P-spline approaches to sharpen prediction. A nice P-spline application for functional classification for food quality can be found in Aguilera-Morillo and Aguilera (2015).

8

Special Subjects

In this chapter, we hope to give the impression that – with some imagination – nearly "anything is possible" using P-splines. We present a number of applications, some of which are nonstandard, using unusual modifications of P-splines. The main changes will be in the penalty, as it is the core element. But we also modify the basis, to handle circular data.

We emphasize that the B-spline basis matrix must be properly computed. The discrete penalty only works correctly when all knots – that define the basis – are truly equidistant. Some B-spline implementations introduce repeated knots at the boundaries of the domain and thus are not appropriate for P-splines.

Introducing a number of variations of the difference penalty, we adapt P-splines to special characteristics of the data, like periodic, circular, and piecewise-constant behavior. With specialized, asymmetric, and adaptive penalties, we can further impose shape constraints, e.g., flat asymptotes, monotonicity, or a unimodal shape. This is a very flexible tool because different shape constraints can be combined, or even be selectively applied to parts of the data.

Some complex signals consist of two or more components with different characteristics. We show how to separate them using a model with multiple components and "tailored" penalties.

Thus far, we have been using a constant λ. When the smoothness of the data trend varies strongly along x, the result may be disappointing. Making λ a function of x can solve this problem. We describe two approaches: using a simple parametric function for $\lambda(x)$ and true adaptive penalization, modeling a nonconstant variance in a mixed model with P-splines.

Finally, we present an important application for classic P-splines that is found in survival analysis and smoothing (and extrapolation) of mortality tables.

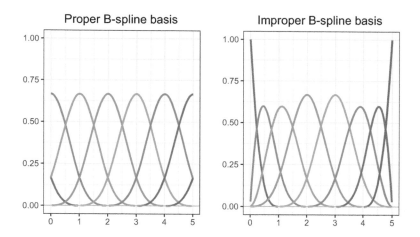

Figure 8.1 Two B-spline bases. Left: the proper basis for P-splines, with all B-splines of equal shape, but shifted horizontally. Right: a basis with multiple knots at the boundaries, which is unsuitable for P-splines. R code in f-bad-base.R

8.1 The Proper B-spline Basis

The B-spline basis is the workhorse of P-splines, and it is critical to set it up properly. The difference penalty requires a B-spline basis matrix as shown in the left panel of Figure 8.1. Appendix C.1 gives the technical details for its construction, but the main point is that all B-splines must have the same shape and be evenly spaced. At the boundaries, we find some "incomplete" splines, of which not all segments are used. When we use the algorithm in Appendix C.1, we get the required basis matrix.

The right panel of Figure 8.1 shows an unsuitable B-spline basis matrix. It has multiple knots at both ends, leading to splines at the boundary that look as if they were squeezed up against a wall. When multiple knots are combined with a difference penalty, undesirable results occur. Wand and Ormerod (2008) claim failures of P-splines in support of their O-splines, but in fact they used the wrong basis, i.e., the one that is presented in the right panel of Figure 8.1. See Eilers et al. (2015) for details.

8.2 Harmonic Smoothing

In Section 2.4, we discussed automatic interpolation and extrapolation. With a second-order difference penalty, the interpolated coefficients follow a cubic polynomial, while extrapolated coefficients form a linear sequence. These results follows from the difference equation

$$\breve{\alpha}_{j-2} - 4\breve{\alpha}_{j-1} + 6\breve{\alpha}_j - 4\breve{\alpha}_{j+1} + \breve{\alpha}_{j+2} = 0, \tag{8.1}$$

implied by the penalty term $\sum_j (\breve{\alpha}_{j-1} - 2\breve{\alpha}_j + \breve{\alpha}_{j+1})^2$ which follows from $\lambda \breve{D}' \breve{D} \breve{\alpha} = 0$, where $\breve{D}$ and $\breve{\alpha}$ contain the rows of D and α with the missing data.

When we change the penalty to $\sum_j (\alpha_{j-1} - 2\psi\alpha_j + \alpha_{j+1})^2$, the difference equation changes from (8.1) to

$$\breve{\alpha}_{j-2} - 4\psi\breve{\alpha}_{j-1} + 6\psi^2\breve{\alpha}_j - 4\psi\breve{\alpha}_{j+1} + \breve{\alpha}_{j+2} = 0. \tag{8.2}$$

This homogeneous difference equation has repeated complex roots. One can show that the general solution is

$$\breve{\alpha}_j = (c_1 + c_2 j)\cos(2j\pi/p) + (c_3 + c_4 j)\sin(2j\pi/p). \tag{8.3}$$

This is the sum of a sine and a cosine, each with a linearly changing amplitude. If the period is p, then we have $\psi = \cos(2\pi/p)$. We call this a harmonic penalty.

For extrapolation we have a similar situation as in Section 2.4 (near (2.9)), where it was shown that extrapolation with the standard penalty is linear, not cubic (as for interpolation). For the harmonic penalty one can show that extrapolation of the coefficients leads to a sum of a sine and a cosine with period p. Their amplitudes have the values to connect properly to the coefficients of supported B-splines.

The local curve fit $B\breve{\alpha}$ is not exactly a (co)sine function, but rather a piecewise cubic approximation, which is quite close if we use many B-splines. The period of the fitted curve is p/h, where h is the distance between the knots that is equal to the distance between the peaks of neighboring B-splines.

Figure 8.2 shows the magnitude (minus the logarithm of the brightness) of a variable star. The observations are intermittent, sometimes leaving large gaps. Harmonic smoothing interpolates these gaps in a more realistic way than what we would get with the standard penalty. Note that this is only a proof of concept. An eyeball estimate of the period, approximately 110 days, was used to determine ψ. A more sophisticated analysis would involve formal estimation of the period.

It is interesting to take a look at the equivalent kernels for a Whittaker smoother with harmonic penalty; see Figure 8.3. The period is determined by ψ, and the decay rate is set by the penalty parameter λ: a larger value of λ gives a slower decay, but the decay rate also depends on ψ.

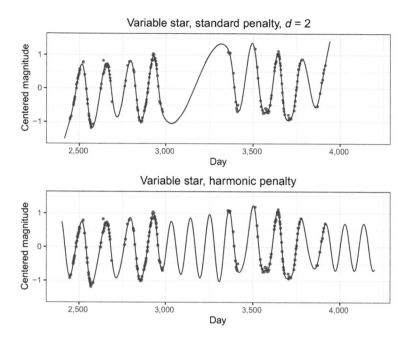

Figure 8.2 Smoothing the magnitude of a variable star with missing observations. Top: using standard P-splines with 100 B-spline segments and a second-order penalty, $\lambda = 0.1$. Bottom: using a harmonic penalty, assuming a period of 100 days. R code in f-varstar.R

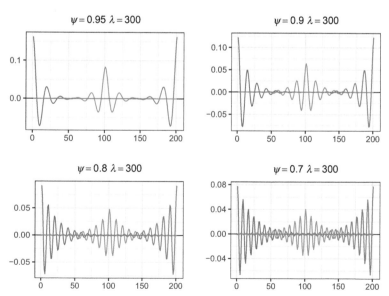

Figure 8.3 Equivalent kernels of a Whittaker smoother with harmonic penalty. Columns 1, 101, and 201 of the hat matrix. R code in f-eqkern-harm.R

8.3 Circular Smoothing

In some applications x has a circular domain. Examples are compass directions or times within days. In such cases, the fitted curve on the left side of the domain should connect smoothly to its other end. This will not generally happen when using the standard B-spline basis and the standard difference penalty.

To get the required circular result, both the basis and penalty have to be changed. The number of basis functions is in fact reduced, and instead of shifting them on the real line, they are rotated on a circle. This is illustrated in Figure 8.4 for cubic B-splines. In the left panel, the lowest three splines properly connect at the boundaries. Our package JOPS contains a function cbase to compute a circular B-spline basis of any desired degree.

We illustrate this distinction between standard and circular smoothing in Figure 8.5. To get the desired fit, as shown in the lower panel, the penalty can be modified in two ways. The first option is to introduce additional differences, connecting left and right ends. With first-order differences one extra term, $\lambda(\alpha_1 - \alpha_n)^2$, is added, and with second-order differences two extra terms are needed: $\lambda(\alpha_1 - 2\alpha_n + \alpha_{n-1})^2$ and $\lambda(\alpha_2 - 2\alpha_1 + \alpha_n)^2$. We call this a circular penalty.

A disadvantage of this penalty is that for large λ the fit tends toward a horizontal line, even for second-order differences. It is more attractive to modify

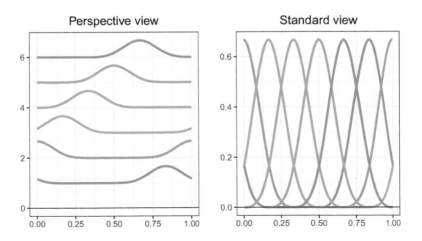

Figure 8.4 Illustration of a circular B-spline basis. Left: each spline shifted vertically by one unit, for visual separation. All splines are identical, but rotated by multiples of the same distance. Right: the same basis without shifts. Only the colors show which B-splines are connected. R code in f-cbase.R

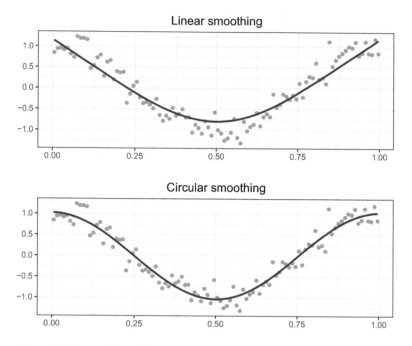

Figure 8.5 Smoothing with a standard (cubic) B-spline basis (top) and with a circular basis (bottom). R code in f-periodic.R

the harmonic penalty (see the previous section) with extra terms $\lambda(\alpha_1 - 2\psi\alpha_n + \alpha_{n-1})^2$ and $\lambda(\alpha_2 - 2\psi\alpha_1 + \alpha_n)^2$, where $\psi = \cos(2\pi/n)$, with n the number of segments (which is equal to the number of B-splines for a circular basis). The JOPS package contains a function cdiff to construct the proper penalty matrix. With this penalty, a large λ pushes the fitted curve toward a cosine-shaped curve with one period on the domain of x. In fact, it is a sum of a sine and a cosine, and their amplitudes are automatically estimated to give the best fit to the data.

The circular basis and penalty are also convenient for smoothing histograms of circular data. Let the histogram counts be contained in the vector y. Using a circular basis B with the matrix that forms circular differences D, we model the expected values as $\mu = \exp(B\alpha + \gamma)$ and solve the penalized likelihood equations, as with standard histogram smoothing. Note that there is an unpenalized intercept parameter γ in the linear predictor. This term is needed to achieve $\sum_i y_i = \sum_i \mu_i$ because $D\alpha \neq 0$ with circular differences (which does equal to zero for the standard differences). To estimate α and γ,

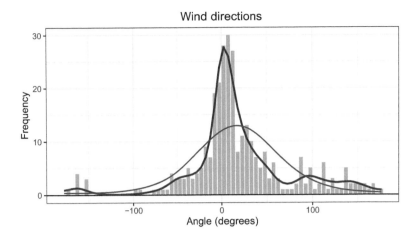

Figure 8.6 Smoothing a histogram of wind directions with a circular basis and a circular harmonic penalty. The blue line is based on minimum AIC ($\lambda = 10^{-1.1}$). The thinner red line ($\lambda = 10^6$) illustrates the von Mises limit. R code in f-circular-wind.R

we extend B with a column of ones to get $\breve{B}$, and D with a column of zeros, to get $\breve{D}$ and solve the penalized likelihood equations $\breve{B}'(y - \mu) = \lambda \breve{D}' \breve{D} \breve{\alpha}$, where $\breve{\alpha} = [\alpha' \mid \gamma]'$ and $\mu = \exp(\breve{B} \breve{\alpha})$.

An interesting property of circular histogram smoothing is that the von Mises distribution is approached for large λ. The equation for the von Mises distribution (on the domain 0 to 2π) is

$$f(x) = \exp(\kappa \cos(x - \mu))/2\pi I_0(\kappa), \tag{8.4}$$

showing that the logarithm of the density is a cosine with proper amplitude and phase. Here $I_0(\kappa)$ is the modified Bessel function of order zero.

This is analogous to getting a (discretized) normal distribution as the limit, when fitting a linear histogram with P-splines using Poisson count responses, a log link function, and a third-order penalty, as presented in Section 2.12.1.

Figure 8.6 shows an example for wind directions. The data are available as wind in the package circular. We converted from radians to degrees and rotated the scale to run from -180 to 180 degrees. The thick line uses $\lambda = 10^{-1.1}$, as chosen by minimizing AIC. The thin line corresponds to $\lambda = 10^6$, illustrating the limiting distribution.

8.4 Signal Separation with Penalties

For a given penalty matrix D: if $D\alpha = 0$, then α lies in the null space of D. We saw this to be the case when α is constant or a linear sequence with D being the matrix that forms second-order differences (see Section 2.8). In general, when the rows of D define a linear difference equation, any sequence that obeys this equation will lie in the null space. We can also use this fact to our advantage to separate components within signals.

The principle is to model an observed signal as a sum of two components and give each component its own difference penalty. An example is a sum of a smooth trend and a harmonic signal. The standard penalty with second-order differences is applied to the trend component and a harmonic penalty (see Section 8.3) to the second one.

An application is shown in Figure 8.7, where we see a short section of an ECG (electrocardiogram) that is severely disturbed by a 60-Hz signal coming from the electric power system. The data were obtained from the FANTASIA

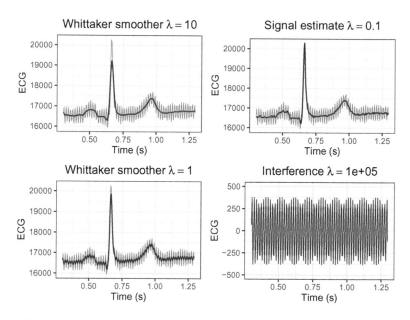

Figure 8.7 Disturbance removal in a small section of an ECG by separating two signals using different penalties. Panels in left column: data (gray) and results of Whittaker smoothing (blue) with two different λs. Top-right: data (gray) and extracted ECG (blue). Lower-right: extracted 60-Hz disturbance. R code in f-fit-hum.R

database at Physionet (https://physionet.org/). A longer (60 s) section is available in the JOPS package. The objective function is

$$S = ||y - v - s||^2 + \lambda_1 ||Dv||^2 + \lambda_2 \sum_i (s_i - 2\psi s_{i-1} + s_{i-2})^2. \qquad (8.5)$$

Here v is the ECG signal, and s is the 60-Hz disturbance. The sampling frequency is 250 Hz, hence the time step between observations is $\Delta t = 4$ ms. With $\psi = \cos(60 \times \Delta t) = 0.125581$, a 60 Hz (co)sine wave lies in the null space of the second penalty. A high value of λ_2 will force s to pick up this sine wave. On the other hand, λ_1 should be relatively small, to ensure that v identifies the "trend," which is the undistorted ECG signal.

The panels in Figure 8.7 show the results obtained with the identity matrix as basis, for two values of the penalty parameter λ. If $\lambda = 10$, the disturbance is reduced strongly, but the peak in the ECG signal is heavily distorted. For $\lambda = 1$, the disturbance is reduced, but still present. We find that the model with two components does a much better job: the second component completely absorbs the disturbance, while the first component shows the clean ECG. The other component is displayed separately in the lower right panel. In the figure, it is a visual artefact that the sine wave does not appear to have a constant amplitude, which is due to the relatively low sampling frequency: on average $250/60 = 4.167$ samples per period.

To fit the model, the basis matrix is $B = [I \mid I]$, with I denoting the m identity matrix, where m is the number of observations. If $\theta' = [v' \mid s']$, the objective function is

$$S = ||y - B\theta||^2 + \lambda_1 ||Dv||^2 + \lambda_2 ||Cs||^2, \qquad (8.6)$$

with D as the standard and C as the harmonic differencing matrix. The system of equations to solve is

$$\begin{bmatrix} I + \lambda_1 D'D & 0 \\ 0 & I + \lambda_2 C'C \end{bmatrix} \begin{bmatrix} \hat{v} \\ \hat{s} \end{bmatrix} = \begin{bmatrix} y \\ y \end{bmatrix}. \qquad (8.7)$$

Here the values of λ_1 and λ_2 were chosen subjectively. Note that the choice of the latter is not critical: values from 10^3 to 10^6 were tried and found to give essentially identical results.

It is remarkable that two completely different time series can be estimated, while only one is observed. This is another example of the power of penalties. Because the two penalty matrices have different null spaces, no collinearity issues occur in the system (8.7) leading to identifiability of the separate signals. The effective dimensions of the two components do differ notably, with 175.5 for the ECG signal and 2.01 for the interference. It may come as a surprise

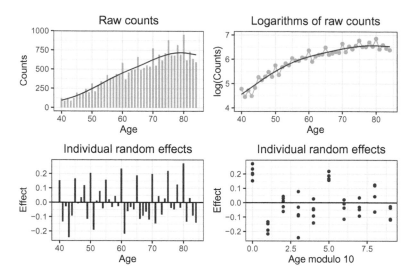

Figure 8.8 Counts of male deaths in Greece, in 1960, versus age, fitted by a model with a smooth trend plus individual random effects. Top left: raw counts and the trend. Top right: logarithms of raw counts and fitted trend. Bottom left: the individual random effects versus age. Bottom right: the individual random effects versus age modulo 10, to emphasize the repeating pattern of digit preference. R code in `f-Greece-PRIDE.R`

that the latter signal, with much variation, has a very low effective dimension. However, that variation is completely systematic: the estimate almost perfectly obeys a second-order difference equation.

Note also that here we have a variant of an additive model with two components. Instead of two independent variables and similar penalty matrices, we have only one independent variable and two penalties with different structures. This scheme can be extended to more components. An example is the separation of multiple (co)sines with different (known) frequencies.

For a second example, we return to the death counts from Greece. In Section 3.6, we saw that – due to strong overdispersion – generalized linear smoothing with an assumed Poisson distribution did not work well. Quasi-likelihood (QL) provided a solution. Despite QL being an effective estimation method, it does not represent any proper underlying distribution.

Perperoglou and Eilers (2010) propose the use of individual random effects for overdispersion. The model specifies $E(y) = \mu = \exp(\eta) = \exp(B\alpha + u)$ and $y \sim \text{Pois}(\mu)$, where $B\alpha$ is the familiar sum of B-splines and u is an unstructured vector. The penalized deviance is defined as

$$Q = 2 \sum_i y_i \log(y_i/\mu_i) + \lambda ||D\alpha||^2 + \kappa ||u||^2. \qquad (8.8)$$

We have a roughness penalty on α and also have a (ridge) penalty on the size of u. The penalized likelihood equations are

$$\begin{bmatrix} B'WB + \lambda D'D & B'W \\ WB & W + \kappa I \end{bmatrix} \begin{bmatrix} \alpha \\ u \end{bmatrix} = \begin{bmatrix} B'Wy \\ Wy \end{bmatrix}, \tag{8.9}$$

with $W = \text{diag}(\mu)$. This is a generalized additive model with a Poisson distributed response.

The matrix in the lower-right corner of the matrix in (8.9) is diagonal with dimension m. The system of equations is extremely sparse. This is a property that can be exploited for efficient computation with large data sets. Perperoglou and Eilers (2010) provide R code.

In the lower-right panel of Figure 8.8, the random effects are plotted against the last digit of the age. We see that ages with end digits 0 and 5 occur frequently, while those ending on 1 and 9 are observed less often. This is a typical pattern caused by digit preference, the human tendency to round uncertain or estimated numbers to comfortable and pleasing values.

The next step in an analysis of these data could be to reduce the number of random effects to 10, one for each possible end digit. The goal of this section is to show possibilities for data splitting with tailored penalties, so we will not pursue this further. A proper analysis could additionally take into account the transition of counts that are occurring: the higher observed counts for the ages having an end digit of 0 or 5 must come from neighboring ages with their own end digits. Such an analysis, using the composite link model is presented by Camarda et al. (2008).

8.5 Double Penalties

As we have seen in Figure 8.2, interpolation or extrapolation using the standard second-order penalty is less flamboyant than what we get with the harmonic penalty. Sometimes we strive for even tighter results. A first-order penalty gives linear interpolation. However, we can obtain a balance between linear and cubic interpolation by combining the two penalties, as shown in Figure 8.9.

Eilers and Goeman (2004) propose a double penalty having the form

$$\text{Pen} = \lambda \sum_j (\Delta^2 \alpha_j)^2 + \gamma \sqrt{\lambda} \sum_j (\Delta \alpha_j)^2. \tag{8.10}$$

It changes the equivalent kernels, although not dramatically. Figure 8.10 shows selected columns of the hat matrix of the Whittaker smoother for different values of γ (a similar plot for the standard Whitaker smoother was presented

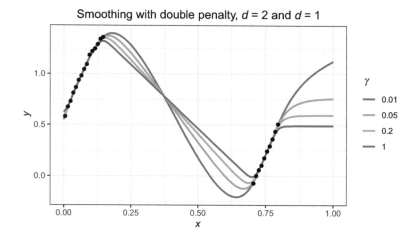

Figure 8.9 Combining first- and second-order penalties to get tight interpolation and extrapolation (100 cubic B-spline segments, $\lambda = 1$). R code in f-double-pen.R

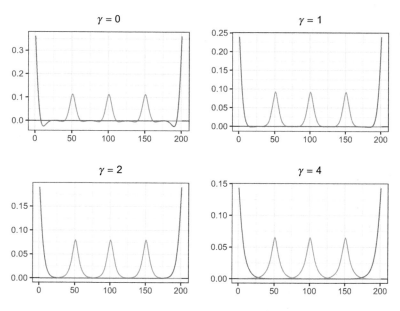

Figure 8.10 Illustration of equivalent kernels for the double penalty that combines first and second differences $\lambda = 100$. The differently colored curves show the values in rows 1, 51, 101, 151, and 201 of the 201 by 201 hat matrix of the Whittaker smoother with the double penalty. R code in f-eqkern-2pen.R

in Figure 2.17). The most interesting consequence is that the minima of the negative sidelobes are not negative if $\gamma \geq 1.8$.

This is useful when we want to guarantee that smoothing of nonnegative data leads to nonnegative curve fits. P-splines with only a second-order difference penalty can violate this demand. Eilers and Goeman (2004) use this idea for "quick and dirty" smoothing of counts in a histogram, where negative results are unwelcome. In the case of a two-dimensional histogram, smoothing of the columns, followed by smoothing of rows (or the other way around), such an approach is fast and practical. Note that all columns can be smoothed in one operation to get the two-dimensional means in M because:

$$(B'B + P)A = B'Y, \quad M = BA, \tag{8.11}$$

where A is a matrix in which column k contains the B-spline coefficients for the smooth columns of Y. The same operation is applied to M' to smooth the rows. Xiao et al. (2013) presented variations and extensions of this idea and called it the sandwich smoother. Note that B can be the identity matrix, so that effectively the Whittaker smoother is applied to each column (and row) of Y.

A disadvantage is that this simple approach cannot handle general weights, which makes it unsuitable for generalized linear smoothing or automatic interpolation of missing data. But when the data allow its use, computation can be extremely fast, especially when sparse matrices are used for B and P.

8.6 Piecewise Constant Smoothing

Recall Figure 5.2, which showed a large basis and the sum of absolute values of second-order differences. There we found a piecewise linear fit to our data that had sharp bends in some places. If we use first-order differences, we get a piecewise constant fit. This is useful for some applications. Smoothing of copy number variations in (tumor) DNA is one of them. First we will work with simulated data, and then switch over to a real data illustration.

Figure 8.11 shows a series of 400 simulated observations. To smooth them, we choose the objective function $||y - B\alpha||^2 + \lambda||D\alpha||^1$, which has a LASSO-like penalty on the differences of α. Tibshirani et al. (2005) call this the fused lasso (and included a sum of absolute values penalty on α). Eilers and de Menezes (2005) propose median smoothing with the objective function $||y - B\alpha||^1 + \lambda||D\alpha||^1$. The fit to the data is measured as the sum of absolute values of residuals. Generalizations to quantiles are straightforward: introduce asymmetric weights and use (penalized) quantile regression (refer to Chapter 5 for details).

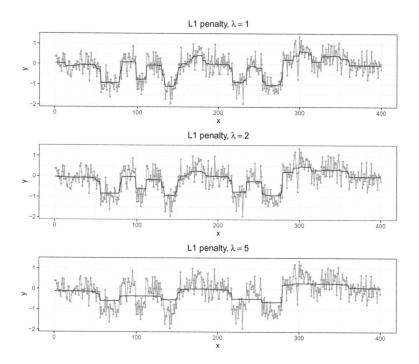

Figure 8.11 Smoothing of simulated data with the sum of absolute values of differences in the penalty, for different values of λ, as indicated in the titles of the panels. R code in f-cgh-L1.R

With the sum of squares of the residuals as the measure of fit, the result of smoothing is shown in Figure 8.11. The simulation assumed a piecewise constant data series, with uncorrelated normal errors. The effect of the smoothing is not overwhelming: there is a bias toward zero (0), which is very pronounced when λ is large, and the steps are not really crisp.

Rippe et al. (2012b) propose to use $||y - B\alpha||^2 + \lambda||D\alpha||^0$, where $||u||^0 = \sum_j |u_j|^0$. Effectively, the penalty now is on the number of nonzero absolute differences. Theoretically, this zero-norm penalty is awkward: the objective function is non-convex, so it is very difficult to locate its global minimum. Also, we do not have pleasant analytic expressions as found with quadratic penalties. In practice, however, it is easy to get good results. In Section 5.1, we showed how to translate a sum of absolute values of residuals into a weighted sum of squares. The trick is to use the fact that in general $|u| = u^2/|u|$. In a similar way, we can use the equivalence $|\alpha_j|^0 = \alpha_j^2/\alpha_j^2$. Of course, α is not known, but repeated use of $|\alpha_j|^0 \approx \alpha_j^2/\tilde{\alpha}_j^2$ resolves this issue, where $\tilde{\alpha}$ is the current approximation to α. To avoid instabilities when elements of $\tilde{\alpha}$ get very

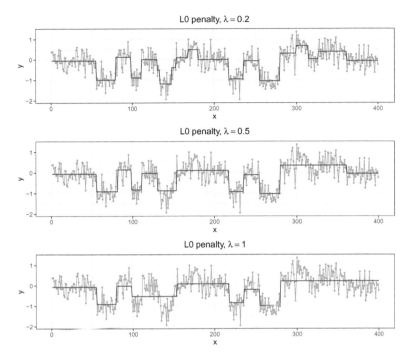

Figure 8.12 Smoothing simulated data with the L_0 norm of the absolute values of differences in the penalty, for different values of λ, as indicated in the titles of the panels. R code in `f-cgh-L0.R`

close to zero, we include a small shift $\delta = 0.001$, so the iterations are: minimize $||y - B\alpha||^2 + \lambda(D\alpha)'VD\alpha$, with V diagonal, $v_{jj} = 1/(\tilde{\phi}_j^2 + \delta^2)$, and $\phi = D\alpha$.

Figure 8.12 shows results for three values of λ. The jumps now appear crisper for any value of λ; only the number of segments decreases with increasing λ. The identity matrix was used as the basis. Using sparse matrices, computation takes only a fraction of a second, and convergence is relatively quick: about 20 iterations are needed to reduce the maximum of the change in α to 0.001. To start the iterations, $V = I$ is chosen.

A real data application of piecewise constant smoothing is next presented for the analysis of copy number variations in (tumor) DNA. In healthy cells, human chromosomes (except for the sex chromosomes) always occur in pairs. In tumors, sections of chromosomes can be missing (so-called deletions), or they can occur more than two times (so-called amplifications). As a result, copy numbers can deviate locally from the normal value of two. There are several techniques to measure copy numbers, and one of them is comparative genomic hybridization (CGH). Unfortunately, CGH gives rather noisy results,

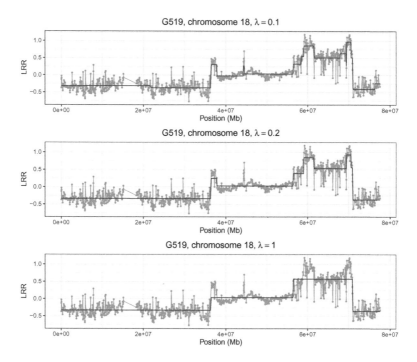

Figure 8.13 A section of chromosome 18 of data set G519. Smoothing with the
sum of absolute values of differences in the penalty, for different values of λ, as
indicated in the titles of the panels. R code in f-cgh-G519.R

as is illustrated by Figure 8.13. The full data are available in the Bioconductor
package Vega as G519. Here, only a section of chromosome 18 is shown. The
smoother does a reasonable job, in that it finds crisp segments, but it is difficult
to judge just how realistic they are. The pattern of the noise is not stable, with
little variation in the middle of the graphs and strong (negative) spikes toward
the right. Rippe et al. (2012b) present extensive simulations.

8.7 Shape Constraints

In Section 8.5, we obtained positive equivalent kernels with the Whittaker
smoother by combining first- and second-order differences in the penalty.
We now look at very flexible approach to shape constraints, using explicit
(asymmetric) penalties to achieve a variety of results. Some examples of shape
constraints include a locally horizontal slope, a sign restriction, a monotonically

increasing (decreasing) trend, or a convex (concave) shape. These constraints can be combined in various ways, and they can even be applied selectively on chosen parts of the domain.

Recall that B-splines are positive everywhere. If $\mu = B\alpha$ describes the fit of a model to data, then properties of α translate directly to μ. If all elements of α are positive, then μ must be positive everywhere. If the elements of α decrease monotonically, this will also be true of μ. In fact, a (discrete) shape property of the coefficients guarantees the same (continuous) shape property for the fitted curve. This illustrates once again that the coefficients form the parametric skeleton of a B-spline fit.

Constraints on the coefficients may actually be stricter than needed. A simple example illustrates this point. Consider a cubic B-spline basis matrix B with, say, 21 columns. Let the coefficient vector be such that $\alpha_j = 1$ for all j, except for $j = 11$. If $\alpha_{11} = 0$, the minimum of $B\alpha$ is $\frac{1}{3}$. The maximum of a cubic B-spline is $\frac{2}{3}$, so when $\alpha_{11} = -0.5$, the minimum is 0. This example is of limited practical relevance because the vector α is far from smooth. When $\alpha_{11} = \alpha_{12} = 0$, the minimum of $B\alpha$ is approximately 0.0425. We see that a globally positive curve fit can be obtained with some negative elements in α, for some data sets. Even though such a curve may fit somewhat better, we are willing to pay a (small) price to have a simple algorithm with guaranteed results.

Figure 8.14 shows a plot of heights of 500 Dutch boys against their age; it is a random sample from the data set boys7482 in the package AGD. The maximum

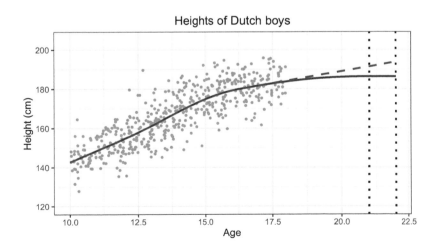

Figure 8.14 Smoothing with a penalty on the slope, which is forced to be zero beyond age 20, using an additional penalty. R code in f-zero-slope.R

age in the data is 20 years, but for a more dramatic effect it is set to 18 in the sample. The curve is extrapolated to age 22. Without special measures, we get a linear trend with quite a large slope at the ages above 18. This is unrealistic because height growth generally stops before age 20. With an extra penalty, the slope can be forced to be zero for ages from 21 to 22, leading to a more realistic curve. In Section 2.5, we showed how to compute derivatives of a P-spline fit $\hat{\mu} = B\hat{\alpha}$:

$$\frac{d}{dt}\sum_j B_j(t;p)\alpha_j = \sum_j (p-1)B_j(t;p-1)\Delta\alpha_j/h, \qquad (8.12)$$

where h is the distance between two knots, and p is the degree of the B-splines. If $\tilde{B}$ contains the B-spline of degree $p-1$, we can write

$$\frac{d}{dt}B\alpha = \tilde{B}(D_1\alpha)/h, \qquad (8.13)$$

where D_1 is the matrix that forms first differences: $D_1\alpha = \Delta\alpha$. In our example, we compute $\tilde{B}$ for $21 \le x \le 22$, on a grid with small steps (0.2). We then add the extra penalty $\kappa||\tilde{B}D_1\alpha||^2$, with κ a large number, e.g., 10^8, which gives the desired shape, as is shown in Figure 8.14.

The matrix $\tilde{B}$ can be extended to cover multiple subdomains of x. Eilers (2017) presents an example: the relationship between temperature and the amount of gas delivered by a distribution station. At very low temperatures the curve is flat because the capacity of the station is limited. At high temperatures no gas is needed for heating, leading to a flat curve too.

In other applications, we might want μ to increase monotonically. Our familiar objective function can be extended to

$$S = ||y - B\alpha||^2 + \lambda||D\alpha||^2 + \kappa\alpha'D_1'VD_1\alpha. \qquad (8.14)$$

The first two terms are the P-spline pair. In the third term, D_1 is the matrix that forms first differences of α, $V = \text{diag}(v)$ with $v_j = I(\alpha_{j+1} \le \alpha_j)$, and κ is set to a large number, say 10^8. The notation does not reflect it, but v is not given a priori, but computed iteratively. Given V, $\hat{\alpha}$ is computed as

$$\hat{\alpha} = (B'B + \lambda D'D + \kappa V)^{-1}B'y, \qquad (8.15)$$

and a new v follows trivially for a given α. Simple iterative updating of V and α in turn works surprisingly well in practice, but we have no proof of convergence.

Other constraints can be implemented by taking the signs of $\Delta_d\alpha$ to determine the elements of v: e.g., with $d=2$, one can enforce convexity or concavity. With $d = 0$, one can enforce sign constraints. Multiple constraints

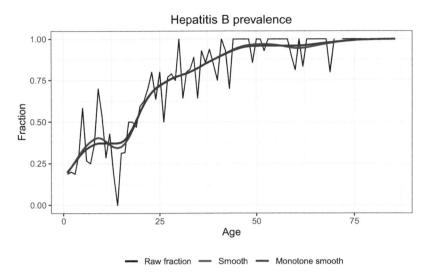

Figure 8.15 Generalized linear smoothing of the prevalence of hepatitis B in a sample of Bulgarian males. The raw fractions are shown by the thin black curve. The red curve shows the unconstrained trend. The blue curve is constrained, by an asymmetric penalty, to have a nonnegative slope everywhere. R code in f-hepatitis-mon.R

can be combined by adding specific penalties together, e.g., to generate a monotonically increasing convex fit. With $v_j = u_j I(\alpha_j \leq 0)$ and with a pre-specified pattern of zeros and ones in u, a selective shape constraint can be realized, which is only active where $u = 1$.

Because the monotonicity constraint works on the B-spline coefficients, it also works in a generalized linear setting. An example is shown in Figure 8.15. Small samples of Bulgarian males of ages from 0 to 80 were tested for hepatitis B antibodies (Keiding, 1991). The raw fraction of positive cases is shown, as well as a smooth fit (red curve), using a binomial log-likelihood and a second-order penalty. The curve shows a decrease around two ages, 15 and 60. This is undesirable, as it is known that traces of an infection by hepatitis B never leave the body. Therefore the prevalence cannot decrease with age, and it makes sense to estimate a monotone nondecreasing trend. This can be achieved with the asymmetric heavy penalty on negative differences of the linear predictor, giving the blue curve.

Asymmetric penalties also work in two dimensions, as has been shown by Bollaerts et al. (2006). There are no new principles involved. There is a matrix of coefficients, and we apply the asymmetric penalty to the rows and to the columns of this matrix. The resulting algorithm is very efficient because the

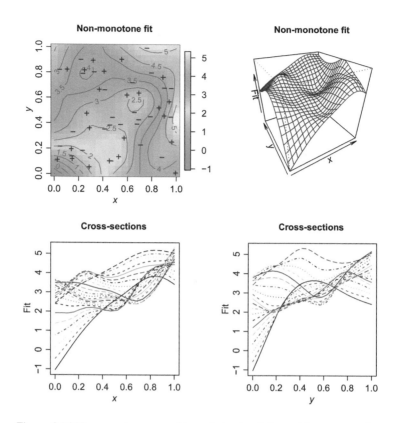

Figure 8.16 Non-monotone smoothing of simulated data with tensor product P-splines. Upper-left panel: positions of the data points and the signs of their residuals, indicated with − and + symbols. Contour lines of the fitted surface are shown in blue. Upper-right panel: perspective view of the fitted surface. Bottom panels: cross-sections of the fitted surface in two directions, emphasizing the non-monotonic behavior. R code in f-non-monotone-2d.R

sparseness of the spline bases and the penalties can be exploited. Figure 8.16 is based on 50 simulated data points: $z_i = 4(x_i + y_i - x_i y_i) + \epsilon_i$, with x and y drawn from a uniform distribution between 0 and 1 and ϵ from the standard normal distribution. It is clear that we do not get a monotone increasing fit, unless the extra penalty is implemented. Figure 8.17 shows the penalties in action.

This simulation is the one that has been used by Liao and Meyer (2019), so as to compare their package cgam to scam. The latter package was written by Pya and Wood (2015). Figure 1 in the paper by Liao and Meyer (2019) shows that scam gave an incorrect estimate of the surface. Our own simulations showed this to be the case consistently, also when we simulated (many) more data points.

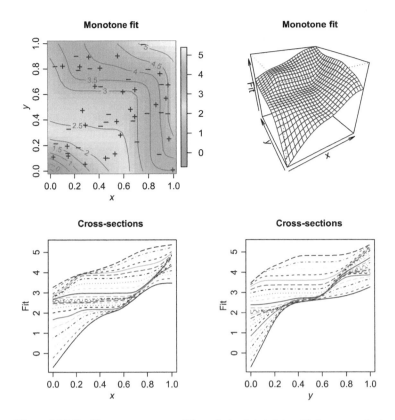

Figure 8.17 Double monotone smoothing of simulated data with tensor product P-splines and automatic tuning of the (isotropic) roughness penalty with the HFS algorithm. Upper-left panel: positions of the data points and the signs of their residuals, indicated with − and + symbols. Contour lines of the fitted surface are shown in blue. Upper-right panel: perspective view of the fitted surface. Bottom panels: cross-sections of the fitted surface in two directions, emphasizing the monotonic behavior. R code in `f-monotone-2d-mix.R`

Both `cgam` to `scam` are slow, as a test on a PC with an Intel I3-3220 CPU showed. With 50 data points `cgam` is the clear winner, taking only 0.6 seconds, while `scam` needs 8 seconds. Yet with 2,000 data points, these times are 47 and 27 seconds, and `scam` wins. Apparently the computing time of `cgam` increases quadratically with the size of the data set. In contrast, the monotone P-spline fit takes only 0.3 seconds for 2,000 data points. This holds for one value of λ. It can be updated automatically with the Harville–Fellner–Schall (HFS) algorithm. Only a few extra iterations (compared to monotone fitting) are needed to get convergence.

This example illustrates (again) that, with proper penalties, we do not have to worry when the number of basis functions is (much) larger than the number of observations. The cubic B-spline bases use 20 segments for x and y, leading to $23^2 = 529$ tensor products. Although there are only 50 observations, no problems occur. The effective model dimension is 12.3.

Eilers (2005) shows how to fit a positive unimodal curve by modeling its logarithm and forcing it to be concave. A log-concave density can be estimated by combining histogram smoothing with an adaptive penalty on the second differences of the spline coefficients (Eilers and Borgdorff, 2007). The log-concave shape is an advantage when estimating a mixture of nonparametric densities. This idea has been extended to two dimensions by Rippe et al. (2012a) for genotype estimation in massive data sets of single nucleotide polymorphisms (SNPs).

8.8 Variable and Adaptive Penalties

In the previous section, we used a penalty based on $D'VD$, with $V = \text{diag}(v)$ and v based on the signs of differences of coefficients to achieve monotone smoothing. This was an example of a weighted penalty. When we construct v in an intelligent way, there are many more examples. One such example is the case with $v_j = \lambda \exp(\gamma j/n)$, with n as the length of α. When γ is positive (negative), the weight of the penalty increases (decreases) toward the right boundary of the domain of x. A typical application is the smoothing of a "chirp" or swept sine, i.e., a sine wave with decreasing frequency and variable amplitude as shown in Figure 8.18. The amount of smoothing can be optimized using cross-validation, searching on a two-dimensional grid for γ and $\log(\lambda)$. It is clear that the variable penalty does good work here. When the penalty weights are constant ($\gamma = 0$), the fitted curve is too wiggly at the right end, while it also misses the changes at the left end.

Exponentially increasing (or decreasing) weights in the penalty are a simple device. They can be effective, as we have seen. In the present application, visual inspection of the data makes them plausible beforehand. It is convenient to have an automatic procedure that adapts the weights in the penalty to the data under study. There are several possibilities: Wood (2017) presents theory and R software for adaptive splines in the package mgcv. Rodríguez-Álvarez et al. (2019) describe a similar model and the package SOPexamples, using P-splines.

One example in the paper by Rodríguez-Álvarez et al. (2019) is the smoothing of an X-ray diffraction scan. In Section 5.4, the data were used

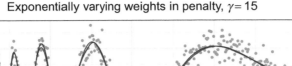

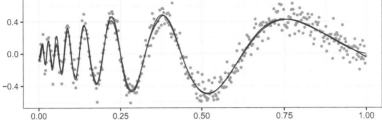

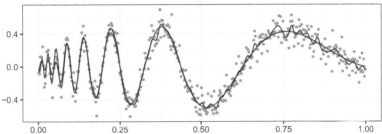

Figure 8.18 Smoothing with a variable penalty. The data were simulated by adding noise with a normal distribution to a "swept sine" with decreasing frequency and variable amplitude, depicted by the red line in both panels. The identity matrix was used as the basis. The blue line in the lower panel shows the output of standard P-splines. In the upper panel, variable weights were used according to $v_i = \lambda \exp(\gamma i)$. Both γ and the smoothing parameter λ were selected from a grid by cross-validation. R code in `f-swept-sine.R`

to illustrate baseline estimation. Because the signal has sharp peaks with very smooth (almost flat) sections between them, it is a serious challenge to adaptive smoothers. The penalty should be light in the peaks, but quite heavy elsewhere. Figure 8.19 shows the data and the fit obtained with the package `SOPexamples`. The function `mgcv` gives essentially the same result, but it is much slower: it takes a little over 1,000 seconds, whereas `SOPexamples` only need 5 seconds.

The X-ray scan consists of 2,000 photon counts, so a Poisson model was specified. The smooth curve used 200 B-splines segments, while $\lambda(x)$ used 80 segments. Figure 8.19 presents the data, the smooth fit, and the residuals. The latter shows very little structure. Such is not the case in Figure 8.20, where λ is constant (and tuned with a variant of Harville's algorithm in a mixed model setting). Pronounced ripples are also visible in the flat parts and the top of the left peak has clearly been missed.

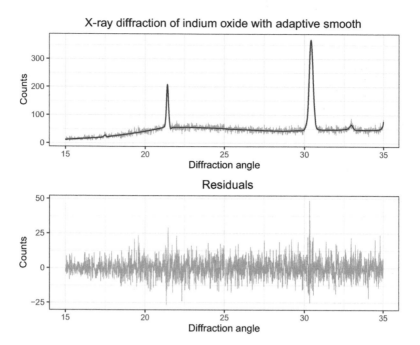

Figure 8.19 Adaptive smoothing of an X-ray diffractometry scan of indium oxide with the package SOPexamples. Top: data and fit; bottom: residuals. R code in f-indox-adapt.R

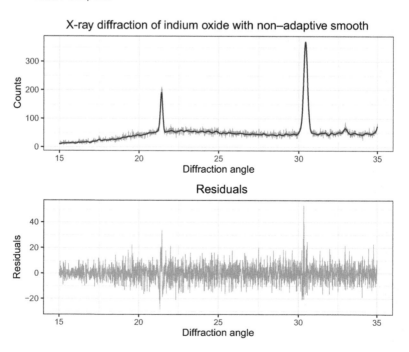

Figure 8.20 Nonadaptive smoothing of an X-ray diffractometry scan of indium oxide with the package SOPexamples. Top: data and fit; bottom: residuals. R code in f-indox-constant.R

8.9 Survival Analysis and Mortality Modeling

An elegant approach to survival analysis divides the time axis into many bins, then counts the number of events in each bin, forming the vector y, while counting the number of persons at risk in each bin, forming the vector r. This sometimes called the life table approach. Indexing the intervals by j, a generalized linear model with a Poisson response allows estimation of the hazard curve: $\mu_j = E(y_j) = r_j \exp(h_j)$, where the log-hazard h_j can be a parametric function, e.g., a polynomial (Efron, 1988) or constructed from B-splines (Eilers, 1998).

Covariates can be introduced with the familiar proportional hazard scheme. We keep track of the individuals, indexed by i, and construct a matrix Y, with $y_{ij} = 1$ if the event for individual i occurred in interval j. All other y_{ij} are set to zero. Similarly, we construct the exposure matrix R, with $r_{ij} = 1$ if individual i is at risk in interval j. Note that for censored individuals, the rows of Y contain only zeros.

Let x_{il} be the value of covariate l for individual i. The model is

$$\mu_{ij} = r_{ij}h_{ij} = r_{ij} \exp(\sum_k b_{jk}\alpha_k + \sum_l x_{il}\gamma_l), \qquad (8.16)$$

where b_{jk} represents the value of kth B-spline in interval j. Note that an explicit estimate of the (logarithm of the) baseline hazard is obtained, in contrast to the familiar Cox model, where it is swept under the carpet with partial likelihood. van Houwelingen and Eilers (2000) extend the model with time-varying effects of the covariates, along the lines of the varying coefficient model (see Section 4.2). Lambert and Eilers (2005) present a Bayesian version of this model.

The model presented in (8.16) is general enough to handle repeated events, as the matrix Y can have multiple ones per row, while R keeps track of the intervals in which the individuals were at risk. After an event, they can remain at risk, in contrast to non-repeatable events.

Figure 8.21 illustrates survival modeling with P-splines, using the ovarian cancer data set in the package CoxRidge. The original source is Verweij and van Houwelingen (1993). To tune λ, we use the HFS algorithm. Starting from $\lambda = 100$, six iterations were sufficient to reduce the size of the updates of h to less than 10^{-4}.

Mortality modeling goes along the same lines, using counts of persons exposed in r, and counts of persons dying in y, in age intervals usually 1 year wide. It is more challenging to model two-dimensional mortality tables that are based on intervals for age and calendar year. Currie et al. (2004) describe how to use tensor product P-splines for this purpose. Currie et al. (2006) and Eilers

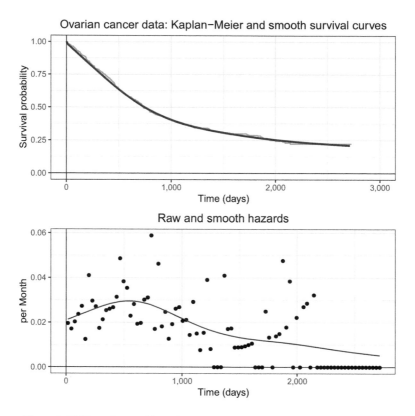

Figure 8.21 Hazard smoothing with P-splines for the ovarian cancer data. Top: smooth survival curve compared to Kaplan–Meier. Bottom: raw and smooth hazard functions; λ optimized with the HFS algorithm. R code in f-surv-OVA.R

et al. (2006) show how to use the array algorithm (see Appendix D) for efficient smoothing of life tables.

A special aspect of mortality modeling is extrapolation, usually to future years, which is of crucial importance for many actuarial calculations. In principle one can use one-dimensional fitting and extrapolation, separately for each year, but there is no guarantee that the predicted curves for different ages will not cross. Having penalties in both the age and time directions generally prevents this unpleasant feature.

A somewhat disturbing effect of double penalties is that estimated values for observed cells in the life table will change when the extrapolation span is changed. Currie (2019) presents such an illustration and a discussion. It appears that the effect is relatively small, but that it increases when the forecasting horizon moves farther away.

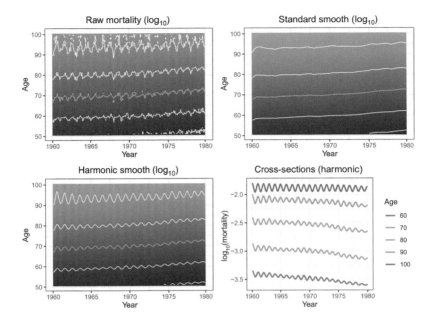

Figure 8.22 Life table smoothing with monthly data on cardiovascular deaths of women in the United States, using tensor products P-splines. The penalty on age is the standard one, using second-order differences; the one on time is harmonic with period 1 year. The distance between the contour levels in the images is 0.5, and the green contour is at level −3. R code in f-mortality.R

Camarda (2012) presents P-spline tools for life tables, which are available in the package MortalitySmooth. The paper and the documentation of the package present many examples.

As a nonstandard illustration, we smooth a table of monthly mortality of women in the United States, caused by cardiovascular diseases. The upper-left panel of Figure 8.22 shows the raw mortality for ages 51 to 100, for each month in 1961 to 1979. The penalty along age uses second-order differences, while the penalty in the time direction is harmonic, with a period of 1 year. This penalty emphasizes seasonal patterns, as can be seen in the lower-left panel of Figure 8.22. Cross-sections of the surface (lower-right panel) show that the amplitude of relative seasonal variation increases with age and decreases over time, at a faster rate for younger ages. For comparison, the smooth with standard penalties is also presented.

Eilers et al. (2008) use a model with three two-dimensional components: an overall trend, a modulated sine function and a modulated cosine function. The modulation is done by smooth functions of time and age. This is a two-dimensional variant of the varying-coefficient model (VCM) that was introduced in Section 4.2. The (co)sine functions have a period of 1 year. Marx et al. (2010) keep the modulation idea, but models the seasonal pattern by 12 parameters, estimated from the data. Currie et al. (2006) put the data into a table with dimensions age, year, and month and model it with three-dimensional tensor-products. All these models have specific coefficients to handle seasonal effects. That is not the case in the model in Figure 8.22. There the penalty emphasizes a seasonal pattern.

8.10 Notes and Details

The penalty is the key element of P-splines, and the B-splines play a subordinate role. Due to the complete separation of the degree of the splines and the order of the discrete penalty, we are free to choose the penalty in any way we like. Creative use of this freedom leads to interesting and useful applications, of which several examples were presented in this chapter. More illustrations can be found in Eilers (2017), which presents uncommon penalties to solve common problems.

P-splines with a circular, double, or harmonic penalty are discrete equivalents to the L-splines of Welham et al. (2006). They study continuous penalties based on differential operators, where we use difference operators. Our difference penalties are not approximations to continuous penalties.

In Appendix E we show how to write P-splines as a "random" model, dropping the fixed part of a mixed model. Then we can work directly with the basis matrix and the penalty matrix. The variations of basis and penalty fit into this scheme seamlessly.

At the end of Chapter 2 and in Appendix B, we remarked that the discrete penalty is not meant to be an approximation to a continuous penalty (like the integral of the squared second derivative of the curve). It is a separate entity, with its own interpretation. The applications in this chapter and others prove that there is no need at all for a continuous penalty.

Appendix A P-splines for the Impatient

If you start with P-splines from scratch, you might be a bit overwhelmed by the choices that should be made: number and degree of the B-splines, their domain, the order of the penalty, and the value of the smoothing parameter. In this appendix we work through them systematically and indicate sensible default values for most of them. The functions in the JOPS package use these defaults.

There exist myths about P-splines that linger on, although we have shown them to be incorrect on several occasions. In Section A.2 we comment on them (again).

A.1 P-splines starter

The domain. This is the region of the x-axis on which the B-splines are defined. Often the minimum and maximum of x can be chosen as left and right boundaries (the default choice). In other cases, one can round them to pleasant numbers. Take Figure 2.12 as an example. The range of x is 0.060 to 19.964, and the domain was chosen to run from 0 to 20. It can do no harm to choose the domain (much) wider than the range of x. In Figure 8.14 the range of x is 10.034 to 17.973. The left boundary of the domain is set to 10 and the right boundary to 22. Extrapolation occurs automatically.

The domain should be wide enough to include all observed x. If this is not the case, the function bbase (that computes a B-spline basis matrix) automatically extends the domain to $\min(x)$ at the left and $\max(x)$ at the right. It also produces a warning if this happens.

The degree of the B-splines. The default choice is 3, giving cubic B-splines that consist of smoothly joining cubic polynomial segments. In practice there is seldom a need for another value.

The number of B-splines The default choice is 10, but more is a safe bet. For some data a very flexible curve may be needed, and 10 B-splines might not be enough. It is *impossible* to have too many B-splines because the penalty removes any singularities.

The order of the penalty. The default choice is 2. Generally it strikes a good balance between smoothness of the fit and closeness to the data. In special cases a third-order penalty is advisable. An example is density estimation (see Section 3.3).

The smoothing parameter. This is λ, the key element of P-splines, and there is no default choice. If your data are well behaved, a good value can be determined automatically with one of the methods described in Chapter 3, but there is no guarantee that they will always give a meaningful result. Smooth trends with serially correlated errors can lead to surprises, i.e., much less smoothing than expected. See Section 3.6.

It always is a good strategy to explore a range of values for λ and judge the results visually. Such a range should be large and use a linear grid of values for $\log_{10}(\lambda)$.

In most cases, two basis matrices are computed: one for fitting and the other for plotting a fitted curve on a nice grid. It is crucial that domain, degree, and number of the B-splines in the second matrix are equal to those in the first.

A.2 Popular myths about P-splines

The difference penalty approximates a derivative penalty. This is not true. For a derivative penalty to work, a piecewise-continuous curve fit of high enough degree is needed. Otherwise the derivative vanishes, and the penalty cannot do its work. With a continuous penalty, the order of the penalty and the degree of the B-splines are strongly coupled. A difference penalty on the coefficients of the B-splines does not have this problem. Any degree of the B-splines can be combined with any order of the penalty.

The knots of B-splines should be quantiles of the abscissae. This is only true when no penalty is being used, as otherwise some B-splines may have no support. Always use a penalty because it eliminates the effects of no support, in addition to smoothing. Evenly spaced knots are a natural and easy choice.

You should use less B-splines than observations. This is another manifestation of the "no support" myth. It is not true. The number of B-splines should only be larger than the order of the penalty. This myth is responsible for the fact that you cannot always compute a rich B-spline basis in R, if you use the bs() function in the spline package. This function simply refuses to do the computation. Our function bbase() does not have this problem.

It is a good idea to optimize the number of knots. It is not. It means a lot of work, with minimal rewards. Rules of thumb, like that of Ruppert (2002), have no value.

The smoothing spline is sacred. It is not. Unfortunately, it has been glorified, with the unpleasant consequence that the continuous penalty became the standard. See the first item in this list.

O'Sullivan splines are better. This claim of Wand and Ormerod (2008) is wrong. They use a wrong B-spline basis, with multiple knots at the ends. See Eilers et al. (2015). O'Sullivan's penalty is based on the integral of a squared (higher) derivative of the fitted curve, so it has the drawbacks that were mentioned in the first item of this list.

Appendix B P-splines and Competitors

Here we present a systematic summary of P-spline properties and compare them to their most popular competitors. To make comparisons easy, in the next section, we present a "consumer score card" (Table B.1), which is similar to the one that we presented in our original paper (Eilers and Marx, 1996).

B.1 P-splines Summary

- P-splines combine (many evenly spaced) B-splines with a discrete roughness penalty on their coefficients.
- The B-splines all have the same shape and are evenly spaced; optimal knot placement is not an issue.
- Thanks to the penalty, the number of B-splines can be chosen freely. It is not possible to have too many B-splines.
- B-splines of any degree can be computed quickly and easily. In many cases linear B-splines work well. They are extremely easy to compute (see Appendix C.1). With many knots, they give a pleasing piecewise linear fit.
- A B-spline basis matrix is intrinsically sparse. Our software can compute very large B-splines bases in a sparse matrix format efficiently. The penalty matrix is also sparse. Using sparse matrix software, data series with millions of observations can be smoothed in a fraction of a second.
- A P-spline model is *parametric*. The B-spline coefficients are the parameters. They are close to the local function values; see Figure 1.1. They have a direct and clear interpretation. This is not the case for most parametric models. For linear P-splines, the fitted curve is obtained by connecting the dots that represent the coefficients.
- The penalty is the key element. Usually it is based on (higher-order) differences of the coefficients. Its order can be chosen freely, independent of the degree of the B-splines. More general difference equations can be used in special cases, as for periodic or circular data.

Table B.1. *A comparison of smoothers on many properties (the symbols have the following meaning: − poor, + good)*

Aspect	KS	LR	SS	RSF	RSA	TPF	PS
Fitting speed	−	−	−	+	+	+	+
Optimization speed	−	−	−	−	−	+	+
Boundary effects	−	+	+	+	+	+	+
Sparse designs	−	−	+	+	+	−	+
Non-normal data	+	+	+	+	+	+	+
Implementation	+	+	+	+	−	+	+
Parametric limit	−	+	+	−	−	+	+
Special limits	−	−	+	−	−	−	+
Density broadening	−	+	+	+	+	−	+
Adaptive	+	+	+	−	+	+	+
Compact result	−	−	−	+	+	+	+
Moments conservation	−	+	+	+	+	+	+
Easy standard errors	+	+	−	+	+	+	+
Signal regression	−	−	+	+	+	+	+
Additive models	−	−	−	+	+	+	+
Multidimensional	+	+	+	+	+	−	+
Anisotropic	+	+	−	+	+	−	+
Mixed model	−	−	+	+	+	+	+
Effective dimension	−	−	+	+	+	+	+

- The discrete penalty is *not* an approximation to a continuous one. The popular integrated squared second derivative, i.e., the one we know from smoothing splines or O'Sullivan (1986), demands a curve fit that consists of polynomial pieces of degree 3 or higher; otherwise the penalty disappears.
- P-splines are based on (penalized) regression, so non-normal data can be handled with ease, adapting the generalized linear model framework.
- Numerous extensions are easy to implement, such as additive and varying coefficient models, quantile and expectile smoothing, signal regression, and the composite link model, among others.
- P-splines can be interpreted and analyzed as mixed models. Penalty parameters become ratios of variances. Fast algorithms can estimate multiple penalty parameters with ease.
- Bayesian P-splines can be realized easily, using Markov chains or Laplace approximation. Either framework computes tuning parameters automatically.
- The effective dimension of a P-spline model is well defined and easy to compute. It is useful for quantifying model complexity, cross-validation, and the computation of AIC.

- Tensor products of B-spline bases and extended penalties generalize P-splines for multidimensional smoothing. Large data sets can be handled straightforwardly. Data on huge grids (1,000 by 1,000 cells, or larger) are no problem because array algorithms make the computations highly efficient and fast.

B.2 Consumer Score Card

In Table B.1, we display our score card, comparing P-splines to several of their most popular competitors. In the subsections that follow, we discuss the most salient (dis)advantages of each smoother, with a few references. The abbreviations in the column headers have the following meanings:

KS: kernel smoother
LR: local regression
SS: smoothing splines
RSF: regression splines with fixed knots
RSA: regression splines with adaptive knots
TPF: truncated power functions
PS: P-splines.

The rows indicate properties of the vanilla smoothers. Their meaning follows.

Fitting speed Can the smoother be fitted quickly?
Optimization speed Can the amount of smoothing be optimized efficiently?
Boundary effects Does the smoother show artefacts at the boundaries of the data domain?
Sparse designs Can large data sets that require a large amount of memory be efficiently and precisely fit with a sparse representation of the smoother?
Non-normal data Can non-normal data be smoothed in the style of generalized linear models?
Implementation Is it easy to implement the smoother in a small number of lines of R code, using standard functions and matrix operations?
Parametric limit Can we get a meaningful parametric limit if the amount of smoothing is made (very) large?
Special limits Can the smoother be modified to get special limits?
Density broadening For density estimation, can we have its variance independent of the amount of smoothing?
Adaptive Can the smoother accommodate a varying tuning parameter that allows the amount of smoothness to change along the domain?
Compact result Can the smoother be summarized (and reconstructed) from a small set of parameters?
Moments conservation Are moments (up to a certain order) of the smooth identical to those of the raw data?

Easy standard errors Can standard error bands be easily constructed?
Signal regression Can the smoother be used for (efficient) signal regression?
Additive models Is the smoother a convenient building block for additive models?
Multidimensional Can the smoother be extended higher dimensions?
Anisotropic Can the multidimensional smoother have different amounts of smoothing
          for each dimension?
Mixed model Can the smoother be written as a mixed model?
Effective dimension Are (partial) effective model dimensions well defined?

B.2.1 Kernel Smoothers

In one dimension, the key component of a kernel smoother (Wand and Jones, 1995)
is a weighted moving average, where the weights follow a Gaussian or similar shape.
The amount of smoothing is tuned by the width of the kernel. It is charmingly simple
to explain and to implement, and it is popular for theoretical work because weighted
averaging allows easy asymptotic analysis.

A straightforward implementation of a kernel smoother is inefficient for large data
sets. This can be improved by first collecting counts and averages in narrow bins and
working with these summaries. The result of kernel smoothing cannot be summarized
in a compact way: the fitted curve is the summary.

Kernel smoothers can deal well with non-normal data. An example is density
estimation from a histogram, where the moving average is a natural and effective
tool. Unless special measures are taken, the kernel smoother suffers from boundary
effects, meaning that the estimate density extends beyond the domain of the observations,
leading to bias. If there is a natural boundary, as in the case of nonnegative observations,
this is plainly wrong. Kernel density estimates generally have larger variance than the
observations.

Other properties of kernel smoothers include:

- The kernel smoother can be used in additive models, but only in combination with
  backfitting. The same is true for semi-parametric models. Kernels are unsuitable for
  signal regression.
- The computations for kernel smoothing have a small footprint; no large matrices are
  involved.
- The parametric limit for heavy smoothing is a constant, which is not very
  interesting. Interpolation is limited to gaps that are not wider than the width of the
  kernel and extrapolation is infeasible.
- The simplicity of kernels can be attractive for multidimensional smoothing,
  computing weighted averages over moving rectangular domains. The width of the
  kernel can be different for each dimension, allowing anisotropic smoothing.
- To tune the amount of smoothing, brute force is needed. There is no "hat" matrix to
  streamline the calculations. There is no obvious connection to either mixed models.
- The width of the kernel can be made to vary with the position of its midpoint,
  offering a mechanism for adaptive smoothing, based on prior assumptions about the
  data.

B.2.2 Local Regression

Local regression (Fan and Gijbels, 1996; Loader, 1999) is similar to kernel smoothing. Weighted (linear) regression lines are computed in a moving window, and the value of the line at the centers of the windows gives the smooth result. Most comments on the kernel smoother apply to local regression. Interpolation and extrapolation are different; the local parametric model allows it.

B.2.3 Smoothing Splines

The wish to replace Whittaker's discrete smoother by a continuous equivalent stimulated Schoenberg (1964) to develop the smoothing spline. The objective function (Wang, 2011) is

$$Q = \sum_{i=1}^{n} \{y_i - \hat{f}(x_i)\}^2 + \lambda \int \hat{f}''(x)^2 \, dx, \qquad (B.1)$$

which is a sum of a measure of fit and a roughness penalty, with tuning parameter λ. The smooth $\hat{f}$ is chosen to minimize Q. The solution to this optimization problem is a curve through the pairs $(x_i, \hat{\mu}_i)$, which consists of piecewise-cubic segments, smoothly joining at the xs. To find the solution, a banded linear system has to be solved, which can be done very efficiently with sparse matrices. Using sparse matrices, the computation time can be made proportional to the number of observations.

Some colleagues are convinced that the integral of the square of the second derivative is more natural than the sum of squares of second differences of B-spline coefficients. We do not share this opinion. In practice, it has a number of disadvantages.

Other properties of smoothing splines include:

- There are no explicit coefficients: the fitted values at the observations define the curve.
- There are no boundary problems, and the limit for strong smoothing is a linear function. Interpolation uses cubic segments.
- Without special treatment, the smoothing spline chokes on data in which, for each x, multiple ys can occur. A solution is to replace those observations by their average and apply weights proportional to their number. See also Appendix C.3.
- By replacing the sum of squares in (B.1) with a proper likelihood, non-normal data can be handled well – provided that the roughness penalty works on the linear predictor. When fitting a density to a histogram in this way, variance inflation cannot be avoided. To resolve this, the third-order derivative should be used in the penalty, leading to quintic splines. This is rare in theory and practice.
- Smoothing splines are not attractive for additive or semi-parametric models because the number of parameters is equal to the number of observations. Only backfitting is practical.

Note that the splines presented in O'Sullivan (1986) are not discussed here, as they are introduced in Chapter 1 and more explicitly within the final Notes and Details section of Chapter 2.

B.2.4 Regression Splines

Hastie and Tibshirani (1990) provide a nice overview of regression splines and other smoothers. Regression splines do not use a penalty to tune smoothness of the fitted curve. Instead one tries to optimize the number and positions of B-spline knots. In principle this is a powerful approach because it can adapt the splines – locally and globally – to the data. Unfortunately it also leads to a difficult nonlinear optimization problem.

Regression splines have no boundary problems. Interpolation can be handled by proper choice of the knots. In principle extrapolation is feasible, by placing knots outside the domain of the data. Assuming that cubic B-splines are being used, the polynomial limit is a cubic function. To get a linear limit, one has to switch to linear B-splines. See Kooperberg and Stone (1991) for applications to density estimation.

B.2.5 Truncated Power Functions

The typical truncated power function (TPF) model (Ruppert et al., 2003) uses global polynomial basis functions (X) in combination with truncated power functions (F). For a given degree p, column j of F is given by

$$f_{ij} = (x_i - t_j)^p I(x_i > t_j), \tag{B.2}$$

$I(u)$ is the indicator function; it is 1 when $u \geq 0$, and 0 when $u < 0$. The vector t contains the knots. The model for $E(y) = \mu$ is given by

$$\mu_i = \sum_{k=0}^{p} \beta_k x_i^k + \sum_{j=1}^{n-1} b_j f_{ij}, \tag{B.3}$$

or in matrix notation

$$\mu = X\beta + Fb, \tag{B.4}$$

where X is an m by $p + 1$ matrix with x_i^0 to x_i^p in columns 1 to $p + 1$ of row i. The TPF objective is to minimize

$$Q_F = ||y - X\beta - Fb||^2 + \kappa ||b||^2, \tag{B.5}$$

in which we recognize a ridge penalty on b. Minimization of Q_F leads to the system of equations

$$\begin{bmatrix} X'X & X'F \\ F'X & F'F + \kappa I \end{bmatrix} \begin{bmatrix} \beta \\ b \end{bmatrix} = \begin{bmatrix} X'y \\ F'y \end{bmatrix}. \tag{B.6}$$

For the knots, quantiles of the observed xs are used. This choice probably was inspired by misguided ideas about the support of the basis functions, especially when there are gaps in the data. Without a penalty this is important, but when using a penalty it becomes irrelevant (Eilers and Marx, 2010).

Truncated power functions have been promoted, sometimes aggressively, by many authors. We have, very explicitly, pointed out their many shortcomings (Eilers and Marx, 2010). In fact, the only advantage of TPF is their straightforward connection to mixed models, which has some pedagogical value.

For $p = 1$, the fitted curve is piecewise-linear. In principle it can be improved by using truncated quadratic or cubic functions, but the numerical condition of the equations becomes very poor.

We know of no successful extension of true TPF to two or more dimensions. One likely reason is that the problems with the numerical condition dramatically get out of hand. Radial basis functions have been proposed, combined with a sophisticated scheme for placing their centers. Anisotropy is impossible because ridge penalties have no sense of direction.

Appendix C Computational Details

C.1 Construction of B-splines

There are several ways to compute a B-spline basis matrix, and de Boor (2001) and Dierckx (1993) serve as excellent standard references. The recursive algorithms of de Boor are most often cited. In our view, they are not easy to follow, and they do not lend themselves well to vectorized and sparse matrix operation.

In theory, one can work from first principles, i.e., by explicitly computing the parameters of the polynomial segments. Take quadratic splines as an example: there are 9 (3 by 3) coefficients, 8 constraints (on values and derivatives), and the condition that at every x all B-splines sum to 1. This is not an attractive line of attack.

However, linear B-splines are an exception. As we saw in Figure 2.16, there is one rising and one falling linear segment between any pair of adjacent knots. Only a few lines of code are needed to compute a linear basis, as shown in the following display.

```
# Computation of a linear B-spline basis for given x

# Specify domain and number of segments
xl = 0; xr = 1; nseg = 50

# Compute the basis
n = nseg + 1
B = matrix(0, m, n)
dx = (xr - xl) / nseg
for (i in 1:m) {
  k = floor((x[i] - xl) / dx)
  u = (x[i] - k * dx) / dx
  B[i, k + 1:2] = c(1 - u, u)
}
```

The P-spline fit is piecewise linear, which is sufficient in many applications, especially if the number of segments is high. Using a sparse matrix package, like spam, is attractive because one can specify values for rows, columns, and element values as vectors when filling the matrix, while avoiding programming loops.

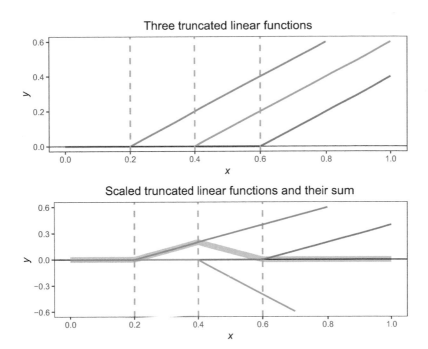

Figure C.1 Construction of a linear B-spline using second-order differences of truncated linear functions. Upper panel: the truncated linear functions. Lower panel: the same functions, scaled by 1, −2, and 1, using the same colors, as well as their sum (in gray). The vertical broken lines indicate the knots where truncation takes place. R code in f-truncl.R

Another easy and instructive approach uses differences of truncated power functions (TPF). A TPF of degree p is defined as $f(x \mid t, p) = (x - t)_+^p = (x - t)^p I(x > t)$, with $I(\cdot)$ the indicator function. Figure C.1 (upper panel) shows three truncated linear functions, say $f_1(x)$, $f_2(x)$, and $f_3(x)$. The lower panel shows $f_1(x)$, $-2f_2(x)$, and $f_3(x)$, using the same colors as in the upper panel. Their sum, $f_1(x) - 2f_2(x) + f_3(x)$, gives one linear B-spline, represented by the thick gray curve. If we would have a fourth linear function, $f_4(x)$, truncated at $x = 0.8$, then $f_2(x) - 2f_3(x) + f_4(x)$ would also form a linear B-spline, but shifted by 0.2 (one knot distance) to the right. Using this recipe, a whole B-spline basis matrix can be computed from $n + 2$ truncated linear functions. Expressed in R: B = c * T %*% t(diff(diag(n + 2), diff = 2)). Here T is a matrix with the truncated linear functions in $n+2$ columns. The constant c is needed to correct for the distance between the knots (h) and to make each row of B sum to 1. Its value is $(-1)^{p+1}/(h^p p!)$.

Figure C.2 illustrates the recipe for using truncated quadratic functions to construct quadratic B-splines, this time using third-order differences. Note that we compute differences of columns of a matrix with TPF. In our package JOPS, we use this recipe to compute B-splines.

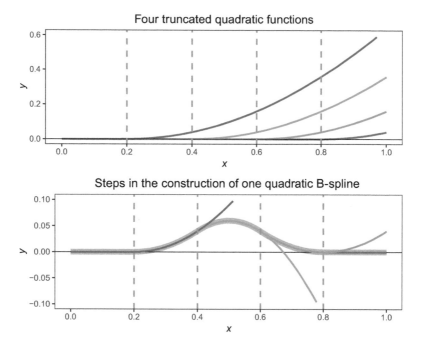

Figure C.2 Construction of a quadratic B-spline using third-order differences of truncated quadratic functions. Upper panel: the truncated quadratic functions. Lower panel: the same functions, scaled by 1, −3, 3, and −1, using the same colors, as well as their sum (in gray). The vertical broken lines indicate the knots where truncation takes place. R code in `f-trunc2.R`

For the quadratic B-spline in Figure C.2, the four terms $f_1(x) - 3f_2(x) + 3f_3(x) - f_4(x)$ sum to 0 to the right of the fourth knot. However, far away from that fourth knot, these terms can have large values. In principle, there is a danger of rounding errors. In practice, there is no reason to be worried, due to the high precision of modern floating point arithmetic (Eilers and Marx, 2010). However, we can avoid the issue completely because we know that the B-spline is exactly zero beyond the fourth knot, so we simply insert zeros there. This reasoning applies to all B-splines in the basis matrix.

In some applications a large basis is needed. An example is artefact removal in X-ray diffraction scans, using thousands of B-splines (de Rooi et al., 2014). Another example comes from computing a long series on a grid from irregularly sampled observations. In this case, it is attractive to use sparse matrix algorithms because in any row of the basis matrix only four elements are non-zero. Everything is fine once the basis is constructed, but prior to this, the matrix with truncated power functions is far from sparse, wasting a lot of memory and computation.

The even spacing of the knots provides an elegant solution. Consider the values in row i of B, relating to x_i. With cubic splines, only four elements are non-zero, say in columns k to $k + 3$. If we subtract one knot distance from x_i, the same numerical values will be found, but occurring in columns $k - 1$ up to $k + 2$. In general, if we shift x_i by t knot distances, the B-spline evaluations will move t columns, but do not change their values. Using this fact, we subtract the proper number of knot distances from each x such that a pseudo x near the left boundary of the domain is obtained. For this pseudo x, the values of the B-splines are calculated and shifted back to their proper columns.

To summarize a B-spline basis, it is sufficient to report the domain, the number of segments, and the degree of the splines. This allows computation of the basis matrix for arbitrary positions on the domain. If the coefficients are reported too, the fitted curve can be computed at arbitrary resolution, at any time.

C.2 Fast Cross-Validation

The following derivation is an extension of Hyndman (2014). The penalized least squares equations are

$$(B'B + P)\hat{\alpha} = B'y, \quad \text{with} \quad P = \lambda D'D.$$

Leaving out observation i changes the system to

$$(B'B - b_i b_i' + P)\tilde{\alpha} = B'y - b_i y_i,$$

where b_i' indicates row i of B. The solution is

$$\tilde{\alpha} = (B'B - b_i b_i' + P)^{-1}(B'y - b_i y_i). \tag{C.1}$$

The matrix to be inverted is a rank one modification of $(B'B + P)$, and the famous Sherman–Morrison–Woodbury formula gives us an explicit expression for its inverse:

$$(B'B - b_i b_i' + P)^{-1} = (B'B + P)^{-1} + \frac{(B'B + P)^{-1} b_i b_i' (B'B + P)^{-1}}{1 - b_i' (B'B + P)^{-1} b_i}. \tag{C.2}$$

As $b_i'(B'B + P)^{-1} b_i = h_{ii}$, with $H = B(B'B + P)^{-1}B'$, the hat matrix, we find

$$\tilde{\alpha} = \left[(B'B + P)^{-1} + \frac{(B'B + P)^{-1} b_i b_i' (B'B + P)^{-1}}{1 - h_{ii}} \right] (B'y - b_i y_i). \tag{C.3}$$

When we expand the product we get four terms, which can be simplified:

$$(B'B + P)^{-1} B'y = \hat{\alpha}$$

$$-(B'B + P)^{-1} b_i y_i = -\frac{(B'B + P)^{-1}}{1 - h_{ii}} b_i (1 - h_{ii}) y_i$$

$$\frac{(B'B + P)^{-1} b_i b_i' (B'B + P)^{-1}}{1 - h_{ii}} B'y = \frac{(B'B + P)^{-1} b_i}{1 - h_{ii}} b_i' \hat{\alpha}$$

$$-\frac{(B'B + P)^{-1} b_i b_i' (B'B + P)^{-1}}{1 - h_{ii}} b_i y_i = -\frac{(B'B + P)^{-1} b_i}{1 - h_{ii}} h_{ii} y_i. \tag{C.4}$$

Combining terms, we obtain

$$\tilde{\alpha} = \hat{\alpha} - \frac{(B'B + P)^{-1}b_i}{1 - h_{ii}} \left[y_i(1 - h_{ii}) - b_i'\hat{\alpha} + h_{ii}y_i \right]. \tag{C.5}$$

We are interested in $\hat{\mu}_{-i} = b_i'\tilde{\alpha}$, the predicted value when observation i is left out. We find

$$\hat{\mu}_{-i} = b_i'\hat{\alpha} - \frac{b_i'(B'B + P)^{-1}b_i}{1 - h_{ii}}(y_i - b_i'\hat{\alpha}) = \hat{\mu}_i - h_{ii}(y_i - \hat{\mu}_i)/(1 - h_{ii}), \tag{C.6}$$

and finally

$$y_i - \hat{\mu}_{-i} = (y_i - \hat{\mu}_i)/(1 - h_{ii})$$
$$e_{-i} = e_i/(1 - h_{ii}). \tag{C.7}$$

C.3 Artificial Grids for Large Data

Suppose we want to compute a trend in a scatterplot with one million observations. To do so, we can construct a B-spline basis matrix B with one million rows and, say, 20 columns and compute its inner product, which involves heavy computation and requires a large amount of computer memory when B is a full matrix. A sparse basis is much more efficient. An even more efficient approach is to allocate the observations to a grid of, say, 100 bins, based on x. In each bin we count the number of observations, giving a vector w, and we compute their sums, giving the vector s. A varying coefficient model (Section 4.2) that fits s with $\text{diag}(w)B\alpha$ gives us the desired trend.

After filling the bins, the amount of computation is independent of the number of observations. The same gain can be obtained for the computation of the sum of squares of residuals, if we also collect sums of squares of y in another vector, say v.

A more formal description introduces an m by n indicator array, R, such that $r_{ij} = 1$ if observation i falls into bin j. All other r_{ij} in row i are zero. Let $\mu = RB\alpha$, with B a suitable B-spline basis, defined on a grid with positions from 1 to n. We form the objective function

$$S = ||y - RB\alpha||^2 + \lambda||D\alpha||^2. \tag{C.8}$$

The penalized normal equations are

$$(B'R'RB + \lambda D'D)\hat{\alpha} = B'R'y \quad \text{or} \quad (B'WB + \lambda D'D)\hat{\alpha} = B's, \tag{C.9}$$

because $R'y = s$ and $R'R = W = \text{diag}(w)$.

Although the definition for the sum of squares of residuals is $\sum_i(y_i - \hat{\mu}_i)^2$, it is inefficient to use this form for computation with many observations. Let $\hat{g} = B\hat{\alpha}$, then we get the same result using

$$\sum_i y_i^2 - 2\sum_j(\hat{g}_js_j) + \sum_j(w_j\hat{g}_j^2) = \sum_j(v_j - 2\hat{g}_js_j + w_j\hat{g}_j^2),$$

which effectively is a sum over all bins of the squares of the residuals in each bin.

The vectors s and w can be computed quickly, needing very little memory. The binning introduces a small rounding error, which can be mitigated by increasing the number of bins to, say, 200 or 500 if this is a concern. When the number of bins is 100, there is no need to invoke a B-spline basis: B can be replaced by the identity matrix, in the style of the Whittaker smoother.

Sparse matrices come in handy here. If we use the package *spam*, the counts and sums in bins can be computed automatically. The function *spam* requires three vectors to specify a sparse matrix: the row indices, the column indices, and the values of the corresponding elements. If the same pair of row and column indices occurs multiple times, the sum of all elements with these indices is stored in the corresponding cell of the sparse matrix. To get w, the second and third input vector are set to all ones, and to get s, the third vector is replaced by y.

The binning scheme can also be used in two (or more) dimensions in combination with the array algorithm (see Appendix D). The array method is so fast that binning on a fine grid is even attractive for a few thousand observations.

Appendix D Array Algorithms

Consider smoothing matrix $Y = [y_{ij}]$, with weights in the matrix $W = [w_{ij}]$, using tensor product B-splines and (initially) without a penalty (see Section 4.3). The array of fitted values is $M = [\mu_{ij}]$, expressed as $M = B A \breve{B}'$, where $A = [\alpha_{kl}]$ is the matrix that contains the coefficients for the tensor products. Equivalently, $\mu_{ij} = \sum_k \sum_l b_{ik} \breve{b}_{jl} a_{kl}$. To estimate A by least squares, we minimize

$$S = \sum_i \sum_j w_{ij} (y_{ij} - \sum_k \sum_l b_{ik} \breve{b}_{jl} a_{kl})^2. \tag{D.1}$$

To use a standard regression routine here, like `lsfit()` in R, we have to turn the matrices Y and W into vectors and the four-dimensional array (with elements $b_{ik} \breve{b}_{jl}$) into a matrix. In principle, this is not difficult to do, but we quickly run into problems with both (memory) space and (computation) time. An example will clarify this.

Suppose Y and W each have 1,000 rows and 1,000 columns. As also pointed out in Section 4.7, this is not an extravagant size when working with images. Suppose we have 20 B-splines in both B and $\breve{B}$. The equivalent vectors for Y and W each have one million elements and pose no problems. However, the matrix equivalent of $b_{ik} \breve{b}_{jl}$ is the Kronecker product $\breve{B} \otimes B$, having one million rows and 400 columns, using 3.2 Gb of memory. The computation of inner products is taxing, while a large memory is needed to store results.

Expressed in the original terms, the normal equations for the least squares solution are

$$\sum_{k'} \sum_{l'} s_{klk'l'} \hat{\alpha}_{j'k'} = \sum_i \sum_j w_{ij} b_{ik} \breve{b}_{jl} y_{ij}, \tag{D.2}$$

or

$$\sum_{k'} \sum_{l'} (\sum_i \sum_j w_{ij} b_{ik} \breve{b}_{jl} b_{ik'} \breve{b}_{jl'}) \hat{\alpha}_{j'k'} = \sum_i \sum_j w_{ij} b_{ik} \breve{b}_{jl} y_{ij}, \tag{D.3}$$

for all combinations of l and k.

This system is not necessarily very large, here with 400 (20 times 20) equations and 400 unknowns, so this is not an obstacle. However, the computation of the elements $\sum_i \sum_j w_{ij} b_{ik} \breve{b}_{jl} b_{ik'} \breve{b}_{jl'}$ of the system matrix is formidable, when following the obvious path. We obtain the terms in the right-hand side efficiently, in matrix form as $B'(W \odot Y) \breve{B}$, where $\odot$ indicates element by element multiplication.

174

Consider the matrix with elements $b_{ik}b_{ik'}$ for all k and k'. We can write it as $\mathcal{B} = B \square B$, the "box product" of B with itself. The name comes from the LaTeX code, \Box, for the symbol $\square$. The rows of $\mathcal{B}$ are Kronecker products of the rows of B. The matrix $\mathcal{B}$ has 1,000 rows and 400 columns, an unproblematic size. Analogously, we can define $\breve{\mathcal{B}} = \breve{B} \square \breve{B}$. Now it can be shown that the matrix product $\mathcal{B}'W\breve{\mathcal{B}}$ contains all the elements of the array S, but that they are not in the required positions (Eilers et al., 2006). If B has n columns, and $\breve{B}$ has $\breve{n}$ columns, S has $n\breve{n}$ rows and columns. But $\mathcal{B}'W\breve{\mathcal{B}}$ has n^2 rows and $\breve{n}^2$ columns. However, it is easy to shuffle its elements into the right places of a matrix of the right size, to get S, as the following fragment of code shows.

```
# Forming and solving the normal equations with the array
    algorithm
# B1, B2 are basis matrices for first and second dimension
# Computation of penalty matrix P not shown
# Data matrix in Y, weights in W
T1 = rowtens(B1)
T2 = rowtens(B2)
Q = t(T1) %*% W %*% T2
n1 = ncol(B1)
n2 = ncol(B2)
dim(Q) = c(n1, n1, n2, n2)
Q = aperm(Q, c(1, 3, 2, 4))
dim(Q) = c(n1 * n2, n1 * n2)
r = t(B1) %*% (W * Y) %*% B2
dim(r) = c(n1 * n2, 1)
A = solve(Q + P, r) # P is penalty matrix
dim(A) = c(n1, n2)
Mu = B1 %*% A %*% t(B2)
```

Currie et al. (2006) coin the names generalized linear array model (GLAM) and array algorithm. They also show how to extend the algorithm to higher dimensions.

Note that the array algorithm is only a fast way to compute the required inner products for the normal equations, which do not change. The computations for the effective dimension (once the penalties have been added) and standard errors do not change. However, there is an elegant shortcut for the trace of the equivalent hat matrix. Currie et al. (2006) present this equivalence for the general case of multiple dimensions. For two dimensions, the code is simplified to the following fragment. In the resulting matrix H, $h_{ij} = \partial \hat{y}_{ij} / \partial y_{ij}$.

```
# Efficient computation of the diagonal of the hat matrix
# Continuation of the previous code fragment
G = solve(Q + P)
dim(G) = c(n1, n2, n1, n2)
G = aperm(G, c(1, 3, 2, 4))
dim(G) = c(n1 * n1, n2 * n2)
H = W * (T1 %*% G %*% t(T2))
```

Appendix E Mixed Model Equations

E.1 Mixed Model Basics

Consider the following mixed model:

$$y = X\beta + Zc + \epsilon \quad \text{with} \quad c \sim \mathcal{N}(0, \tau^2 I_{n-d}), \quad \epsilon \sim \mathcal{N}(0, \sigma^2 I_m). \qquad \text{(E.1)}$$

Both σ and τ are unknown and have to be estimated from the data, as are β and c. Hard-boiled frequentists say that c is *predicted*, not estimated, because they maintain that estimation only applies to fixed parameters. We will not need this distinction.

We can write P-splines as a mixed model by constructing proper X and Z matrices of the form $X = B\breve{X}$ and $Z = B\breve{Z}$. Let $\breve{X} = [\breve{x}_{jk}]$ $(n \times d)$ with $\breve{x}_{jk} = j^{k-1}$. We have that $D\breve{X} = 0$, showing that the columns of X lie in the null space of D. Let $\breve{Z} = D'(DD')^{-1}$, and let $\alpha = \breve{X}\beta + \breve{Z}c$. We then find that

$$D\alpha = D\breve{X}\beta + DD'(DD')^{-1}c = 0 + c. \qquad \text{(E.2)}$$

Thus, $X = B\breve{X}$ and $Z = B\breve{Z}$ give us a possible pair of component matrices for the mixed model (Eilers, 1999).

An alternative choice is to use the singular value decomposition $D = USV'$ and take $Z = BVS^{-1}$ (Currie et al., 2006). Note that also, in this case, the order of the differences determines both X and Z.

Another alternative is to use truncated power functions, as advocated by Ruppert et al. (2003). Their equivalence to P-splines is discussed in detail by Eilers and Marx (2010). The implied order of the penalty is determined by the degree of the truncated power functions.

Why is the transformation to a mixed model attractive? A psychological reason is that many statisticians are reluctant to accept penalties, but once they learn about the equivalent mixed model, they feel that they are in trusted territory. A technical reason is that variance estimation takes the place of searching for optimal tuning via cross-validation or Akaike's information criterion (AIC). A relatively simple but effective algorithm for variance estimation will be presented below, an extension and simplification of work by Harville (1977).

Conditional on σ and τ, the kernel of the log-likelihood is

$$L = -\frac{||y - X\beta - Zc||^2}{2\sigma^2} - \frac{||c||^2}{2\tau^2}, \tag{E.3}$$

or, with $\lambda = \sigma^2/\tau^2$

$$-2\sigma^2 L = ||y - X\beta - Zc||^2 + \lambda||c||^2. \tag{E.4}$$

Here we recognize a penalized least squares objective function, with a penalty on the size (the squared norm) of c.

A slight drawback of these mixed model representations is that because $c = D\alpha$, the coefficients c themselves no longer have the elegant interpretation that α presents (see Figures 2.15 and 2.16). Even if α itself is smooth, c will show a noisy pattern. However, it is straightforward to compute $\alpha = \breve{X}\beta + \breve{Z}c$ for presentation.

For given σ and τ, with $\lambda = \sigma^2/\tau^2$, the parameter vectors β and c are estimated by solving the system

$$\begin{bmatrix} X'X & X'Z \\ Z'X & Z'Z + \lambda I \end{bmatrix} \begin{bmatrix} \beta \\ c \end{bmatrix} = \begin{bmatrix} X'y \\ Z'y \end{bmatrix}. \tag{E.5}$$

These are the so-called Henderson equations (Henderson, 1975). To get at the variances, more work is needed. A crucial matrix is

$$K = \begin{bmatrix} K_{11} & K_{12} \\ K_{21} & K_{22} \end{bmatrix} = \begin{bmatrix} X'X & X'Z \\ Z'X & Z'Z + \lambda I \end{bmatrix}^{-1} \begin{bmatrix} X'X & X'Z \\ Z'X & Z'Z \end{bmatrix}. \tag{E.6}$$

We will find that

$$\tau^2 = \frac{||c||^2}{\rho} \quad \text{and} \quad \sigma^2 = \frac{||y - X\hat{\beta} - Z\hat{c}||^2}{(m - d - \rho)}, \tag{E.7}$$

with $\rho = \text{trace}(K_{22})$ for the effective dimension of c, and m denoting the number of observations. Note that ρ is not the effective model dimension (ED); in fact ED $= \rho + d$, where d comes from the fixed component of the model (the number of columns of X).

These equations suggest an iterative algorithm, updating σ and τ and the effective dimension in turn. In Appendix E.2, it is shown that this is a simplification of an algorithm by Harville (1977). We introduced it as the HFS algorithm in Section 3.4. Practice has shown that it is a reliable and relatively quick scheme that is simple to implement. We have been using it in many places in this book.

The algorithm also works directly for mixed models with multiple random effects, making it suitable for additive models (see Section 4.1).

The mixed model has fixed and random effects. We can simplify it to a pure random effects model by eliminating the fixed effects and working directly with the B-splines and their coefficients. This approach is proposed by Pawitan (2001) and streamlined by Lee et al. (2006). Through (E.2), we find that, with $Z = BD'(DD')^{-1}$, we have $c = D\alpha$, yielding

$$\hat{\tau}^2 = ||D\hat{\alpha}||^2/(\text{ED} - d) \quad \text{and} \quad \hat{\sigma}^2 = ||y - B\hat{\alpha}||^2/(m - \text{ED}). \tag{E.8}$$

The effective model dimension, ED, is obtained from

$$K = (B'B + \lambda D'D)^{-1}B'B \quad \text{with} \quad \text{ED} = \text{trace}(K). \tag{E.9}$$

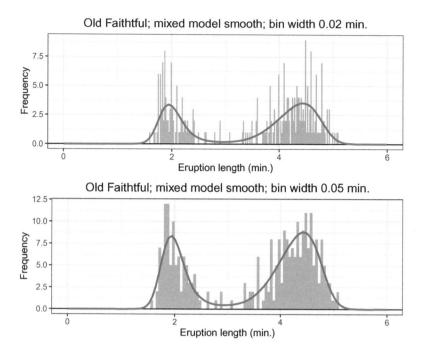

Figure E.1 Automatic smoothing of the histogram of eruption times of Old Faithful, using the pure random effects model, for two bin sizes. R code in f-geyser-mixmod.R

This suggest similar iterative formulas as for the "standard" mixed model (see Section 3.4). As expected, the results are identical. The fixed effects do not appear in the equations, but they are estimated implicitly. This explains why d occurs in the equation for $\hat{\tau}^2$ in (E.8). Our website, in the section on supporting material, contains the script Harvile-extended.R that compares lme(), Harville and the simplified HFS algorithm. See Appendix G.

The simplifications also apply to generalized linear models. A beautiful illustration is density estimation with penalized Poisson regression, as presented in Section 2.12.1. The idea is to apply the random effects model and variance estimation to the linear predictor. A consequence of the assumed Poisson distribution is that $\sigma^2 = 1$, and thus only τ has to be estimated using

$$\tilde{\tau}^2 = ||D\tilde{\alpha}||^2/(\tilde{\mathrm{ED}} - d) \quad \text{with} \quad \tilde{\mathrm{ED}} = \mathrm{trace}((B'WB + \lambda D'D)^{-1}B'WB). \quad (E.10)$$

Figure E.1 shows results for the Old Faithful geyser, using two bin widths and starting from $\tilde{\lambda} = 1$. The results are similar to those in Figure 3.3, which were obtained with AIC minimization. Here we see stronger somewhat smoothing, especially in the right peak. Convergence is fast: after 10 iterations the relative changes in the λ estimates are less than 1 in 10^4. On the other hand, an AIC profile has the advantage that it shows how pronounced a minimum is and if there are multiple local optima.

Like AIC or cross-validation, the random effects model can go astray when the data are overdispersed. If we apply it to the Old Faithful eruption times with digit preference (Section 3.6), the result is almost identical to that in Figure 3.13.

It can also happen that the data indicate very strong smoothing. In such a case, τ tends toward a very small value, and the iterations will stop because of numerical problems (a near singular system of equations). A simple solution is to use a threshold with a (very) low value and stop when $\tilde{\tau}$ passes it. Another solution is to always add a small number to $\|D\alpha\|^2$.

E.2 Harville's Algorithm

Consider a generalization of the mixed model that we presented in Section E.1, defined by

$$y = X\beta + Zc + \epsilon \quad \text{with} \quad c \sim \mathcal{N}(0, G) \quad \text{and} \quad \epsilon \sim \mathcal{N}(0, R). \tag{E.11}$$

It follows that $y \sim \mathcal{N}(X\beta, R + ZGZ')$. This is the so-called marginal formulation of the model: the random component c is translated into a covariance structure between the observations. Only β remains visible, the (fixed) parameters of the model.

The deviance, which is minus two times the log-likelihood, is

$$\mathcal{D} = \log|V| + (y - X\beta)'V^{-1}(y - X\beta), \tag{E.12}$$

with $V = R + ZGZ'$. If R and G are known, the maximum likelihood estimates of β and c follow from the so-called Henderson equations:

$$\begin{bmatrix} X'R^{-1}X & X'R^{-1}Z \\ Z'R^{-1}X & Z'R^{-1}Z + G^{-1} \end{bmatrix} \begin{bmatrix} \hat{\beta} \\ \hat{c} \end{bmatrix} = \begin{bmatrix} X'R^{-1}y \\ Z'R^{-1}y \end{bmatrix}. \tag{E.13}$$

Henderson assumes that G is a block-diagonal matrix with block j equal to $\tau^2 I_j$, with I_j, an identity matrix with q_j rows. The Henderson equations are of little use if the variances σ^2 and τ_j^2 are unknown. Harville (1977) shows how to estimate them using an iterative algorithm. He defined

$$S = R^{-1} - R^{-1}X(X'R^{-1}X)^{-1}X'R^{-1}, \tag{E.14}$$

and

$$T = I - (I + Z'SZG)^{-1}. \tag{E.15}$$

In general, there will be r sets of random parameters, having lengths $q_1 \ldots q_j \ldots q_r$. Hence Z consists of r blocks, with block Z_j having m rows and q_j columns. Then T has a block structure, with T_{jk} having q_j rows and q_k columns.

We indicate current estimates with a tilde, as in $\tilde{c}$. As Harville showed, an updated estimate of τ_j^2, associated with random component c_j, is

$$\hat{\tau}_j^2 = \frac{\tilde{c}_j'\tilde{c}_j}{q_j - \text{trace}(\tilde{T}_{jj})}. \tag{E.16}$$

In (E.16), we recognize a sum of squares divided by an effective dimension, $\rho_j = q_j - \text{trace}(\tilde{T}_{jj})$. An updated estimate of σ^2 is obtained in a similar way, from

$$\hat{\sigma}^2 = \frac{\|y - X\tilde{\beta} - Z\tilde{c}\|^2}{m - \text{trace}(\tilde{T})}. \tag{E.17}$$

These are remarkable results, which predate Schall (1991) and Fellner (1986) (who cites Harville's 1977 paper).

A disadvantage of Harville's algorithm is that S, an m by m matrix, must be computed to get T. With many observations this is undesirable. There are ways to streamline the computation of $Z'SZ$ because S is the inverse of a matrix update by an outer product, so the Sherman–Morrison–Woodbury formula applies. It is more attractive to get rid of S completely. It occurs because Harville explicitly eliminates the contribution of the fixed effects in X to (E.13). This is a persistent tradition in the mixed model folklore that is followed almost without exemption, but unnecessarily complicates matters, as we will show now.

Define F as

$$F = \begin{bmatrix} F_{11} & F_{12} \\ F_{21} & F_{22} \end{bmatrix} = \begin{bmatrix} X'R^{-1}X & X'R^{-1}Z \\ Z'R^{-1}X & Z'R^{-1}Z + G^{-1} \end{bmatrix}^{-1} \begin{bmatrix} X'R^{-1}X & X'R^{-1}Z \\ Z'R^{-1}X & Z'R^{-1}Z \end{bmatrix}. \tag{E.18}$$

Multiplying both sides of this equation by the inverse of the first matrix in the right-hand side, we obtain

$$X'R^{-1}XF_{12} + X'R^{-1}ZF_{22} = X'R^{-1}Z,$$
$$Z'R^{-1}XF_{12} + (Z'R^{-1}Z + G^{-1})F_{22} = Z'R^{-1}Z. \tag{E.19}$$

From the first line above, it follows that $F_{12} = (X'R^{-1}X)^{-1}(X'R^{-1}Z - X'R^{-1}ZF_{22})$. By further substituting the second line above and rearranging terms, we arrive at

$$(Z'R^{-1}Z + G^{-1} - Z'R^{-1}X(X'R^{-1}X)^{-1}X'R^{-1}Z)F_{22}$$
$$= Z'R^{-1}Z - Z'R^{-1}X(X'R^{-1}X)^{-1}X'R^{-1}Z, \tag{E.20}$$

which can be written as

$$(G^{-1} + Z'SZ)F_{22} = Z'SZ.$$

An obvious identity is

$$(G^{-1} + Z'SZ)F_{22} = Z'SZ = Z'SZ + G^{-1} - G^{-1}.$$

Multiplying by $(G^{-1} + Z'SZ)^{-1}$, we get

$$F_{22} = I - (G^{-1} + Z'SZ)^{-1}G^{-1} = I - (I + Z'SZG)^{-1}. \tag{E.21}$$

Comparing (E.21) to (E.15), we see that $F_{22} = T$. Hence we get T almost for free as the sub-matrix F_{22}. This means that $\rho_1 = \text{trace}(F_{22})$, the effective dimension of the random effects.

With r random components, the computation of F does not change. It has $(r + 1)^2$ blocks, and we find that $\rho_j = \text{trace}(F_{j+1,j+1})$ for the jth partial effective dimension.

From the estimates of β and c, it follows that $\hat{y} = X\hat{\beta} + Z\hat{c}$. The residuals are $y - \hat{y}$. Harville uses

$$\hat{\sigma}^2 = \frac{(y - \hat{y})'(y - \hat{y})}{m - q_0}, \tag{E.22}$$

with q_0 the length of β. An alternative expression is

$$\hat{\sigma}^2 = \frac{(y - \hat{y})'(y - \hat{y})}{m - \sum_{j=0}^{r} \rho_j}. \tag{E.23}$$

Here $q_0 + \sum_{j=1}^{r} \rho_j$ can be interpreted as the effective model dimension. In (E.23), we again recognize a sum of squares divided by an effective dimension, which is not the case for (E.22). Our numerical results show that these equations give different values during the iterations, becoming equal at convergence. We prefer (E.23) because of its familiar interpretation.

The bottom line is that we get attractive simplifications: the partial effective dimensions follow from the diagonal of F, as defined in (E.18). They are divided into the sums of squares of the elements of the corresponding random effects, as in (E.16) to get updated variances. The variance of the errors is updated with (E.23).

E.3 Connections to the Hat Matrix

From $\hat{y} = X\hat{\beta} + Z\hat{c}$, it follows that

$$\hat{y} = Hy = [X \ Z] \begin{bmatrix} X'R^{-1}X & X'R^{-1}Z \\ Z'R^{-1}X & Z'R^{-1}Z + G^{-1} \end{bmatrix}^{-1} [X \ Z]'y. \tag{E.24}$$

This defines the so-called hat matrix H. Its trace is equal to that of the trace of F in (E.18). This result follows from the fact that cyclic permutation does not change the trace of a matrix product. Moving $[X \ Z]$, to make it the last factor in the chain, gives F. Let

$$Q = \begin{bmatrix} X'R^{-1}X & X'R^{-1}Z \\ Z'R^{-1}X & Z'R^{-1}Z + G^{-1} \end{bmatrix}^{-1}. \tag{E.25}$$

Thus

$$H = [X \ Z]Q \begin{bmatrix} X' \\ Z' \end{bmatrix} = [XQ \ ZQ] \begin{bmatrix} X' \\ Z' \end{bmatrix} = XQX' + ZQZ'. \tag{E.26}$$

Now we have written H as a sum of partial hat matrices, and $\text{trace}(H) = \text{trace}(XQX') + \text{trace}(ZQZ')$. This decomposition extends straightforwardly to multiple random effects, and we find that $H = XQX' + \sum_{j=1}^{r} Z_j QZ_j'$. The traces of these components of the hat matrix are equal to the corresponding partial effective dimensions: $\text{trace}(Z_j QZ_j') = \rho_j$.

Appendix F   Standard Errors in Detail

Consider the P-spline model $y = B\alpha + \epsilon$, with only random effects α having the precision matrix $P/\tau^2 = D'D/\tau^2$, and independent ϵ with variance σ^2. Minus two times the log-likelihood of α or the deviance (apart from a constant) is

$$\text{dev} = m \log(2\pi\sigma^2) + ||y - B\alpha||^2/\sigma^2 + (n - d)\log(2\pi\sigma^2) + \alpha' P\alpha/\tau^2, \quad \text{(F.1)}$$

where d is the order of the differences formed by D. Purists would not use the term *likelihood* here because α does not contain fixed parameters. Lee et al. (2017), in their chapter 9, call it an h-likelihood. For fixed σ and τ, the first and second terms are constant, and we have

$$\text{dev} = ||y - B\alpha||^2/\sigma^2 + \alpha' P\alpha/\tau^2 + k_1. \quad \text{(F.2)}$$

Expanding the first term in (F.2) gives

$$\text{dev} = y'y/\sigma^2 - 2y'B\alpha/\sigma^2 + \alpha' B'B\alpha/\sigma^2 + \alpha' P\alpha/\tau^2 + k_1. \quad \text{(F.3)}$$

The first term in (F.3) is a constant, so

$$\text{dev} = -2y'B\alpha/\sigma^2 + \alpha' B'B\alpha/\sigma^2 + \alpha' P\alpha/\tau^2 + k_2.$$

Because $(B'B/\sigma^2 + P/\tau^2)\hat{\alpha} = B'y/\sigma^2$, we can rewrite the first term to get

$$\text{dev} = -2\alpha'(B'B/\sigma^2 + P/\tau^2)\alpha + \alpha' B'B\alpha/\sigma^2 + \alpha' P\alpha/\tau^2 + k_2.$$

If we add $\hat{\alpha}'(B'B/\sigma^2 + P/\tau^2)\hat{\alpha}$ and subtract it from k_2, we can complete the square to get the bottom line,

$$\text{dev} = (\alpha - \hat{\alpha})'(B'B/\sigma^2 + P/\tau^2)(\alpha - \hat{\alpha}) + k_3. \quad \text{(F.4)}$$

Here we recognize the deviance of a normal density with expected value $\hat{\alpha}$ and covariance matrix $(B'B/\sigma^2 + P/\tau^2)^{-1}$, motivating the "Bayesian" covariance matrix for $\hat{\alpha}$.

An alternative approach starts from

$$\hat{\alpha} = (B'B + \lambda D'D)^{-1}B'(B\alpha + \epsilon) = Q(B\alpha + \epsilon). \quad \text{(F.5)}$$

There is a bias term $QB\alpha$ and a random term $Q\epsilon$. The latter has covariance

$$\sigma^2(QQ') = \sigma^2(B'B + \lambda D'D)^{-1}B'B(B'B + \lambda D'D)^{-1},$$

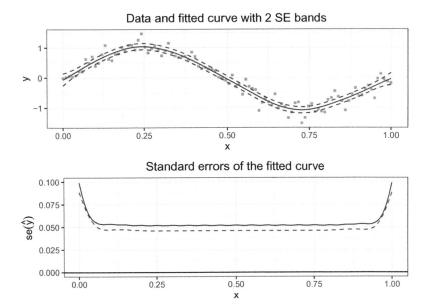

Figure F.1 Standard error estimates for a P-spline fit. Top: simulated data, optimized fit (20 cubic segments, second-order penalty), trend plus and minus two times the Bayesian estimate (broken lines). Bottom: Bayesian estimate (blue line) and sandwich estimate (red, broken line). R code in f-covariance.R

which is called the sandwich estimator.

Figure F.1 shows simulated data and the P-spline fit (optimized with the HFS algorithm). The differences between the two standard error curves are small. The Bayesian estimate is more conservative.

With a moderate number of B-splines in the basis, the computational costs of both covariance matrices are not very different. This is not true when we use the Whittaker smoother for a long data series. The Bayesian covariance matrix of $\hat{\mu}$ is $\hat{\sigma}^2(I + \lambda D'D)^{-1} = \hat{\sigma}^2 H$, and we only need its diagonal. As mentioned in Section 2.10, an efficient algorithm is available. Its computation time grows linearly with the number of observations. The sandwich estimator is $\hat{\sigma}^2 H^2$ and is expensive to compute.

Appendix G   The Website

This book is accompanied by a website, `https://psplines.bitbucket.io`, which offers the following:

- All the figures in the book.
- The R source files that can be used to reproduce all figures in the book. We have done our best to make the code user friendly and very readable, using comments and the `formatR` package.
- A document for each graph, showing the graph, its caption in the book, and the complete R code. The last two pages of this appendix show an example of such a document (Figure G.1, taken from Chapter 1, Figure 1.1).
- All the R code files in one ZIP archive.
- The code for the package `JOPS` (Joys of P-splines), and the package itself. It contains supporting functions and some additional data sets that are not available in existing packages.
- A P-splines "playground," which consists of a few interactive programs to explore changes in the number and degree of the B-splines, as well as the order and the weight of the penalty.
- Additional programs and documents.

With this website we have several goals:

- To hide many practical details, which would otherwise clutter the main text of this book. It is boring and potentially incomplete to sum them up for every graph or to have fragments of R code in many places.
- To make all details accessible and our results reproducible.
- To offer a resource for better understanding and gaining confidence with P-splines. We encourage users to play with parameter settings and to explore how they influence results.
- To offer teaching materials for courses on smoothing. We hope that one day every such course will give P-splines a central position.

- To lower the threshold for new users to embrace P-splines. Playing with our programs will make it clear exactly what the pros and cons are.
- To offer readers a good starting point and template for analyzing their own data. It is easier to modify an existing program, in small steps, than starting from scratch.
- To challenge readers to improve our code, by making programs more efficient, better organized, and more general.
- To stimulate research on P-splines, leading to more applications, new theoretical results, and better smoothing tools.
- To stimulate discussions with our readers. Our email addresses are on the website. We will be happy to get feedback and to respond to questions.

In summary, we want to share the joys of P-splines with our readers.

Show the essence of P-splines

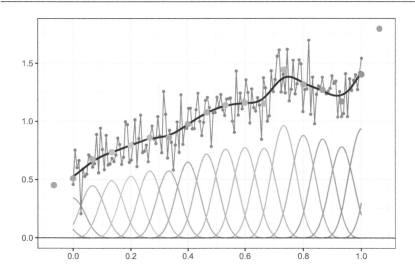

Figure G.1 The core idea of P-splines: a sum of B-spline basis functions, with gradually changing heights. The connected gray dots show simulated data. The blue curve shows the P-spline fit, and the large dots the B-spline coefficients (they have the same colors as the splines). The horizontal locations of these dots correspond to the knots, where the polynomial segments of the B-spline join. R code in f-ps-show.R

```
# Show the essence of P-splines
# A graph in the book 'Practical Smoothing. The Joys of P-splines'
# Paul Eilers and Brian Marx, 2019

library(ggplot2)
library(gridExtra)
library(colorspace)
library(JOPS)

# Simulate data
n = 150
set.seed(2016)
x = seq(0, 1, length = n)
y = 0.3 + sin(1.2 * x + 0.3) + rnorm(n) * 0.15
Data = data.frame(x, y, id = as.factor(15))

# Make a matrix containing the B-spline basis
ndx = 15
deg = 3
B = bbase(x, 0, 1, nseg = ndx, bdeg = deg)
nb = ncol(B)

# A basis for plotting the fit on the grid xg
ng = 500
xg = seq(0, 1, length = ng)
Bg = bbase(xg, 0, 1, nseg = ndx, bdeg = deg)

# Positions of the peaks of the B-splines
dk = 1/ndx
xa = (1:(ndx + deg)) * dk - (deg + 1) * dk/2

# Estimate the coefficients and compute the fit on the grid
D = diff(diag(nb), diff = 2)
lambda = 0.1
a = solve(t(B) %*% B + lambda * t(D) %*% D, t(B) %*% y)
z = Bg %*% a

# Make a natrix with B-splines scaled by coefficients
Bsc = Bg %*% diag(c(a))

# Create data frames for ggplot
Zf = data.frame(x = xg, y = z, id = as.factor(1))
C = data.frame(x = xa, y = a, id = as.factor(1))
Bf = data.frame(x = rep(xg, nb), y = as.vector(Bsc),
    id = as.factor(rep(1:nb, each = ng)))
Bf$y[abs(Bf$y) < 1e-04] = NA
Bf = na.omit(Bf)

# Build the graph
pal = rainbow_hcl(nb, c = 80, l = 80, start = 10, end = 350)
plt = ggplot(Bf, aes(x = x, y = y, group = id, colour = id)) +
  geom_line( size = 0.7) +
  geom_hline(yintercept = 0, size = 0.3) +
  geom_line(data = Data, color = I("grey60")) +
```

```
    geom_point(data = Data, color = I("grey60"), size = 0.9) +
    geom_line(data = Zf, size = 1, color = I('blue')) +
    geom_point(data = C, color = pal, size = 2.5) +
    xlab("") + ylab("") +
    JOPS_theme() +
    theme(legend.position = "none") +
    scale_x_continuous(breaks = seq(0, 1, by = 0.2)) +
    scale_color_manual(values = pal)

# Show the graphs on the screen
set_window(height = 4)
grid.arrange(plt, ncol = 1, nrow = 1)

# Save PDF version
save_PDF('f-ps-show')
```

References

Aguilera, A. M., Aguilera-Morillo, M. C., and Preda, C. 2016. Penalized versions of functional PLS regression. *Chemometrics and Intelligent Laboratory Systems*, **154**(May 15), 80–92.

Aguilera-Morillo, M. C., and Aguilera, A. M. 2015. P-spline estimation of functional classification methods for improving the quality in the food industry. *Communications in Statistics – Simulation and Computation*, **44**(10, SI), 2513–2534.

Aitkin, M., Francis, B., and Hinde, J. 2005. *Statistical Modelling in GLIM 4*. 2nd ed. Oxford Statistical Science Series, Oxford, UK.

Akaike, H. 1974. A new look at the statistical model identification. *IEEE Transactions on Automatic Control*, **19**(6), 716–723.

Ayma, D., Durbán, M., Lee, D.-J., and Eilers, P. H. C. 2016. Penalized composite link models for aggregated spatial count data: A mixed model approach. *Spatial Statistics*, **17**, 179–198.

Azzalini, A., and Bowman, A. W. 1990. A look at some data on the Old Faithful geyser. *Journal of the Royal Statistical Society, Series C*, **39**, 357–365.

Basford, K. E., Mclachlan, G. J., and York, M. G. 1977. Modelling the distribution of stamp paper thickness via finite normal mixtures: The 1872 Hidalgo stamp issue of Mexico revisited. *Journal of Applied Statistics*, **24**, 169–180.

Bollaerts, K., Eilers, P. H. C., and Aerts, M. 2006. Quantile regression with monotonicity restrictions using P-splines and the L_1-norm. *Statistical Modelling*, **6**, 189–207.

Braun, J., Duchesne, T., and Stafford, J. E. 2005. Local likelihood density estimation for interval censored data. *The Canadian Journal of Statistics*, **33**, 39–60.

Bro, R. 1999. Exploratory study of sugar production using fluorescence spectroscopy and multi-way analysis. *Chemometrics and Intelligent Laboratory Systems*, **46**, 133–147.

Camarda, C. G. 2012. Mortalitysmooth: An R package for smoothing Poisson counts with P-splines. *Journal of Statistical Software*, **50**, 1–24.

Camarda, C. G., Eilers, P. H. C., and Gampe, J. 2008. Modelling general patterns of digit preference. *Statistical Modelling*, **8**, 385–401.

Camarda, C. G., Eilers, P. H. C., and Gampe, J. 2016. Sums of smooth exponentials to decompose complex series of counts. *Statistical Modelling*, **16**(4), 279–296.

Camarda, C. G., Eilers, P. H. C., and Gampe, J. 2017. Modelling trends in digit preference patterns. *Journal of the Royal Statistical Society, Series C*, **66**(5), 893–918.

Claeskens, G., Krivobokova, T., and Opsomer, J. D. 2009. Asymptotic properties of penalized spline estimators. *Biometrika*, **96**, 529–544.

Currie, I. D. 2019. *Forecasting with penalty functions – Part III*. www.longevitas.co.uk/site/informationmatrix/forecastingwithpenaltyfunctionspart3.html.

Currie, I. D., and Durbán, M. 2002. Flexible smoothing with P-splines: A unified approach. *Statistical Modelling*, **2**, 333–349.

Currie, I. D., Durbán, M., and Eilers, P. H. C. 2004. Smoothing and forecasting mortality rates. *Statistical Modelling*, **4**, 279–298.

Currie, I. D., Durbán, M., and Eilers, P. H. C. 2006. Generalized linear array models with applications to multidimensional smoothing. *Journal of the Royal Statistical Society, Series B*, **68**, 259–280.

de Boor, C. 2001. *A Practical Guide to Splines, rev. ed.* New York: Springer-Verlag.

De Gruttola, V., and Lakatos, S. W. 1989. Analysis of doubly censored survival data, with applications to AIDS. *Biometrics*, **45**, 1–11.

de Rooi, J. J., Devos, O., Sliwa, M., Ruckebusch, C., and Eilers, P. H. C. 2013. Mixture models for two-dimensional baseline correction, applied to artifact elimination in time-resolved spectroscopy. *Analytica Chimica Acta*, **771**(Apr 10), 7–13.

dc Rooi, J. J., and Eilers, P. H. C. 2012. Mixture models for baseline estimation. *Chemometrics and Intelligent Laboratory Systems*, **117**(SI), 56–60.

de Rooi, J. J., van der Pers, N. M., Hendrikx, R. W. A., Delhez, R., Böttger, A. J., and Eilers, P. H. C. 2014. Smoothing of X-ray diffraction data and $K\alpha_2$ elimination using penalized likelihood and the composite link model. *Journal of Applied Crystallography*, **47**, 852–860.

Dierckx, P. 1993. *Curve and Surface Fitting with Splines*. Oxford: Clarendon Press.

Dobson, A. J., and Barnett, A. G. 2018. *An Introduction to Generalized Linear Models*, 4th ed. Boca Raton, FL: CRC Press.

Efron, B. 1988. Logistic regression, survival analysis, and the Kaplan–Meier curve. *Journal of the American Statistical Association*, **83**, 414–425.

Eilers, P. H. C. 1998. Hazard smoothing with B-splines. In: Marx, B. D., and Friedl, H. (eds.), *Proceedings of the 13th International Workshop on Statistical Modeling*, pp. 200–207. Baton Rouge: Louisiana State University.

Eilers, P. H. C. 1999. Discussion on: The analysis of designed experiments and longitudinal data by using smoothing splines. *Journal of the Royal Statistical Society, Series C*, **48**, 307–308.

Eilers, P. H. C. 2003. A perfect smoother. *Analytical Chemistry*, **75**, 3631–3636.

Eilers, P. H. C. 2005. Unimodal smoothing. *Journal of Chemometrics*, **19**, 317–328.

Eilers, P. H. C. 2007. Ill-posed problems with counts, the composite link model and penalized likelihood. *Statistical Modelling*, **7**, 239–254.

Eilers, P. H. C. 2012. Composite link, the neglected model. In: Komarek, A., and Nagy, S. (eds.), *Proceedings of the 27th International Workshop on Statistical Modelling*, pp. 11–22. Prague: Tribun EU.

Eilers, P. H. C. 2017. Uncommon penalties for common problems. *Journal of Chemometrics*, **31**(4, SI), 2878.

Eilers, P. H. C., and Borgdorff, M. W. 2007. Non-parametric log-concave mixtures. *Computational Statistics & Data Analysis*, **51**, 5444–5451.

Eilers, P. H. C., Currie, I. D., and Durbán, M. 2006. Fast and compact smoothing on large multidimensional grids. *Computational Statistics & Data Analysis*, **50**, 61–76.

Eilers, P. H. C., and de Menezes, R. X. 2005. Quantile smoothing of array CGH data. *Bioinformatics*, **21**, 1146–1153.

Eilers, P. H. C., Gampe, J., Marx, B. D., and Rau, R. 2008. Modulation models for seasonal time series and incidence tables. *Statistics in Medicine*, **27**, 3430–3441.

Eilers, P. H. C., and Goeman, J. J. 2004. Enhancing scatterplots with smoothed densities. *Bioinformatics*, **20**, 623–628.

Eilers, P. H. C., Li, B., and Marx, B. D. 2009. Multivariate calibration with single-index signal regression. *Chemometrics and Intelligent Laboratory Systems*, **96**, 196–202.

Eilers, P. H. C., and Marx, B. D. 1992. Generalized linear models with P-splines. In: L. Fahrmeir et al. (eds.), *Advances in GLIM and Statistical Modelling*. New York: Springer.

Eilers, P. H. C., and Marx, B. D. 1996. Flexible smoothing using B-splines and penalties (with comments and rejoinder). *Statistical Science*, **11**, 89–121.

Eilers, P. H. C., and Marx, B. D. 2002. Generalized linear additive smooth structures. *Journal of Computational and Graphical Statistics*, **11**, 758–783.

Eilers, P. H. C., and Marx, B. D. 2003. Multivariate calibration with temperature interaction using two-dimensional penalized signal regression. *Chemometrics and Intelligent Laboratory Systems*, **66**, 159–174.

Eilers, P. H. C., and Marx, B. D. 2010. Splines, knots and penalties. *Wiley Interdisciplinary Reviews: Computational Statistics*, **2**, 637–653.

Eilers, P. H. C., Marx, B. D., and Durbán, M. 2015. Twenty years of P-splines. *SORT-Statistics and Operations Research Transactions*, **39**(2), 149–186.

Fahrmeir, L., Kneib, T., and Lang, S. 2004. Penalized structured additive regression for space-time data: A Bayesian perspective. *Statistica Sinica*, **14**, 731–761.

Fahrmeir, L., and Tutz, G. 2001. *Multivariate Statistical Modelling Based on Generalized Linear Models*, 2nd ed. New York: Springer.

Fan, J., and Gijbels, I. 1996. *Local Polynomial Modelling and Its Applications*. London: Chapman and Hall.

Fellner, W. H. 1986. Robust estimation of variance components. *Technometrics*, **28**(1), 51–60.

Frank, I. E., and Friedman, J. H. 1993. A statistical view of some chemometric regression tools. *Technometrics*, **35**, 109–148.

Frasso, G., and Eilers, P. H. C. 2015. L- and V-curves for optimal smoothing. *Statistical Modelling*, **15**, 91–111.

Gentle, J. E. 2009. *Computational Statistics*. New York: Springer.

Gressani, O., and Lambert, P. 2018. Fast Bayesian inference using Laplace approximations in a flexible promotion time cure model based on P-splines. *Computational Statistics and Data Analysis*, **124**, 151–167.

Greven, S., and Scheipl, F. 2017. A general framework for functional regression modelling. *Statistical Modelling*, **17**, 1–35.

Hall, P., and Opsomer, J. D. 2005. Theory for penalised spline regression. *Biometrika*, **92**(1), 105–118.

Hansen, P. C. 1992. Analysis of discrete ill-posed problems by means of the L-curve. *SIAM Review*, **34**(4), 561–580.

Härdle, W. 1992. *Applied Nonparametric Regression*. Cambridge: Cambridge University Press.

Harville, D. A. 1977. Maximum likelihood approaches to variance component estimation and to related problems. *Journal of the American Statistical Association*, **72**, 320–338.

Hasselblad, V., Stead, A. G., and Galke, W. 1980. Analysis of coarsely grouped data from the lognormal distribution. *Journal of the American Statistical Association*, **75**, 771–778.

Hastie, T. J., Buja, A., and Tibshirani, R. J. 1995. Penalized discriminant analysis. *The Annals of Statistics*, **23**, 73–102.

Hastie, T. J., and Tibshirani, R. J. 1990. *Generalized Additive Models*. London: Chapman and Hall.

Hastie, T. J., and Tibshirani, R. J. 1993. Varying-coefficient models. *Journal of the Royal Statistical Society, Series B*, **55**, 757–796.

Hastie, T. J., Tibshirani, R. J., and Friedman, J. H. 2009. *Elements of Statistical Learning: Data Mining, Inference and Prediction*. 2nd ed. New York: Springer.

Henderson, C. R. 1975. Best linear unbiased estimation and prediction under a selection model. *Biometrics*, **31**, 423–447.

Hutchinson, M. F., and de Hoog, F. R. 1986. Smoothing noisy data with spline functions. *Numerische Mathematik*, **50**(3), 311–319.

Hyndman, R. 2014. *Fast computation of cross-validation in linear models*. https://robjhyndman.com/hyndsight/loocv-linear-models/.

Jarrow, R., Ruppert, D., and Yu, Y. 2004. Estimating the interest rate term structure of corporate debt with a semiparametric penalized spline model. *Journal of the American Statistical Association*, **99**, 57–66.

Jullion, A., and Lambert, P. 2007. Robust specification of the roughness penalty prior distribution in spatially adaptive Bayesian P-splines models. *Computational Statistics & Data Analysis*, **51**, 2542–2558.

Kauermann, G., Krivobokova, T., and Fahrmeir, L. 2009. Some asymptotic results on generalized penalized spline smoothing. *Journal of the Royal Statistical Society, Series B*, **71**, 487–503.

Kauermann, G., Krivobokova, T., and Semmler, W. 2011. Filtering time series with penalized splines. *Studies in Nonlinear Dynamic & Econometrics*, **15**, 1–26.

Keiding, N. 1991. Age-specific incidence and prevalence – a statistical perspective. *Journal of the Royal Statistical Society, Series A*, **154**, 371–412.

Kneib, T. 2013. Beyond mean regression. *Statistical Modelling*, **13**, 275–303.

Koenker, R. 2005. *Quantile Regression*. Cambridge: Cambridge University Press.

Koenker, R., and Bassett, G. 1978. Regression quantiles. *Econometrica*, **46**, 33–50.

Kooperberg, C., and Stone, C. J. 1991. A study of logspline density estimation. *Computational Statistics and Data Analysis*, **12**, 327–348.

Lambert, P. 2011. Smooth semiparametric and nonparametric Bayesian estimation of bivariate densities from bivariate histogram data. *Computational Statistics & Data Analysis*, **55**, 429–445.

Lambert, P., and Eilers, P. H. C. 2005. Bayesian proportional hazards model with time-varying regression coefficients: A penalized Poisson regression approach. *Statistics in Medicine*, **24**, 3977–3989.

Lambert, P., and Eilers, P. H. C. 2009. Bayesian density estimation from grouped continuous data. *Computational Statistics & Data Analysis*, **53**, 1388–1399.

Lang, S., Adebayo, S. B., Fahrmeir, L., and Steiner, W. J. 2003. Bayesian geoadditive seemingly unrelated regression. *Computational Statistics*, **18**, 263–292.

Lee, D.-J., and Durbán, M. 2009. Smooth-CAR mixed models for spatial count data. *Computational Statistics & Data Analysis*, **53**, 2968–2979.

Lee, D.-J., Durbán, M., and Eilers, P. H. C. 2013. Efficient two-dimensional smoothing with P-spline ANOVA mixed models and nested bases. *Computational Statistics & Data Analysis*, **61**, 22–37.

Lee, Y., Nelder, J. A., and Pawitan, Y. 2006. *Generalized Linear Models with Random Effects*. Boca Raton, FL: CRC Press.

Lee, Y., Nelder, J. A., and Pawitan, Y. 2017. *Generalized Linear Models with Random Effects*, 2nd ed. Boca Raton, FL: CRC Press.

Li, B., and Marx, B. D. 2008. Sharpening P-spline signal regression. *Statistical Modelling*, **8**, 367–383.

Li, Y., and Ruppert, D. 2008. On the asymptotics of penalized splines. *Biometrika*, **95**, 415–436.

Liao, X., and Meyer, M. C. 2019. cgam: An R package for the constrained generalized additive model. *Journal of Statistical Software*, **89**, Issue 5, 1–24.

Loader, C. 1999. *Local Regression and Likelihood*. New York: Springer.

Marx, B. D. 2010. P-spline varying coefficient models for complex data. In: Tutz, G., and Kneib, T. (eds.), *Statistical Modelling and Regression Structures*, pp. 19–43 New York: Springer.

Marx, B. D. 2015. Varying-coefficient single-index signal regression. *Chemometrics and Intelligent Laboratory Systems*, **143**, 111–121.

Marx, B. D., and Eilers, P. H. C. 1998. Direct generalized additive modeling with penalized likelihood. *Computational Statistics and Data Analysis*, **28**, 193–209.

Marx, B. D., and Eilers, P. H. C. 1999. Generalized linear regression on sampled signals and curves: A P-spline approach. *Technometrics*, **41**, 1–13.

Marx, B. D., and Eilers, P. H. C. 2005. Multidimensional penalized signal regression. *Technometrics*, **47**, 13–22.

Marx, B. D., Eilers, P. H. C., Gampe, J., and Rau, R. 2010. Bilinear modulation models for seasonal tables of counts. *Statistics and Computing*, **20**, 191–202.

Marx, B. D., Eilers, P. H. C., and Li, B. 2011. Multidimensional single-index signal regression. *Chemometrics and Intelligent Laboratory Systems*, **109**, 120–130.

McCullagh, P., and Nelder, J. A. 1989. *Generalized Linear Models*, 2nd ed. London: Chapman and Hall.

Morris, J. S. 2015. Functional regression. *Annual Review of Statistics and Its Application*, **2**, 321–359.

Newey, W., and Powell, J. L. 1987. Asymmetric least squares estimation and testing. *Econometrica*, **55**, 819–647.

Osborne, B. G., Fearn, T., Miller, A. R., and Douglas, S. 1984. Applications of near infrared reflectance spectroscopy to the compositional analysis of biscuits and biscuit dough. *Journal of Scientific Food Agriculture*, **35**, 99–105.

O'Sullivan, F. 1986. A statistical perspective on ill-posed inverse problems (with discussion). *Statistical Science*, **1**, 505–527.

Pandit, S. M., and Wu, S. M. 1993. *Time Series and System Analysis with Applications*. Malabar, FL: Krieger.

Pawitan, Y. 2001. *In All Likelihood*. Oxford: Oxford University Press.

Perperoglou, A., and Eilers, P. H. C. 2010. Penalized regression with individual deviance effects. *Computational Statistics*, **25**, 341–361.

Portnoy, S., and Koenker, R. 1997. The Gaussian hare and the Laplacian tortoise: Computability of squared-error versus absolute-error estimators. *Statistical Science*, **12**(4), 279–300.

Pya, N., and Wood, S. N. 2015. Shape constrained additive models. *Statistics and Computing*, **25**, 543–559.

Ramsay, J. O., and Silverman, B. W. 2003. *Functional Data Analysis*, 2nd ed. New York: Springer.

Rigby, R. A., and Stasinopoulos, M.D. 2005. Generalized additive models for location, scale and shape. *Journal of the Royal Computational Statistics & Applied Statistics*, **54**, 507–544.

Rigby, R. A., Stasinopoulos, M.D., Heller, G. Z., and De Bastiani, F. 2019. *Distributions for Modeling Location, Scale, and Shape: Using GAMLSS in R*. Boca Raton, FL: CRC Press.

Rippe, R. C. A., Meulman, J. J., and Eilers, P. H. C. 2012a. Reliable single chip genotyping with semi-parametric log-concave mixtures. *PLoS ONE*, **7**(10): e46267.

Rippe, R. C. A., Meulman, J. J., and Eilers, P. H. C. 2012b. Visualization of genomic changes by segmented smoothing using an l_0 penalty. *PLoS ONE*, **7**(6): e38230.

Rizzi, S., Gampe, J., and Eilers, P. H. C. 2015. Efficient estimation of smooth distributions from coarsely grouped data. *American Journal of Epidemiology*, **182**, 138–147.

Rizzi, S., Thinggaard, M., Engholm, G., Christensen, N., Johannesen, T. B., Vaupel, J. W., and Lindahl-Jacobsen, R. 2016. Comparison of non-parametric methods for ungrouping coarsely aggregated data. *BMC Medical Research Methodology*, **16**(May 23).

Rodríguez-Alvarez, M. X., Boer, M. P., van Eeuwijk, F. A., and Eilers, P. H. C. 2018. Correcting for spatial heterogeneity in plant breeding experiments with P-splines. *Spatial Statistics*, **23**, 52–71.

Rodríguez-Álvarez, M. X., Durbán, M., Lee, D.-J., and Eilers, P. H. C. 2019. On the estimation of variance parameters in non-standard generalised linear mixed models: Application to penalised smoothing. *Statistics and Computing*, **29**(June), 483–500.

Rodríguez-Alvarez, M. X., Lee, D.-J., Kneib, T., Durbán, M., and Eilers, P. H. C. 2015. Fast smoothing parameter separation in multidimensional generalized P-splines: The SAP algorithm. *Statistics and Computing*, **25**, 941–957.

Rue, H., Martino, S., and Chopin, N. 2009. Approximate Bayesian inference for latent Gaussian models using integrated nested Laplace approximations (with discussion). *Journal of the Royal Statistical Society, Series B*, **71**, 319–392.

Ruppert, D. 2002. Selecting the number of knots for penalized splines. *Journal of Computational and Graphical Statistics*, **11**, 735–757.

Ruppert, D., and Carroll, R. J. 2000. Spatially-adaptive penalties for spline fitting. *Australian & New Zealand Journal of Statistics*, **42**(2), 205–223.

Ruppert, D., Wand, M. P., and Carroll, R. J. 2003. *Semiparametric Regression*. Cambridge: Cambridge University Press.

Schall, R. 1991. Estimation in generalized linear models with random effects. *Biometrika*, **78**, 719–727.

Schimek, M. G. 2009. Semiparametric penalized generalized additive models for environmental research and epidemiology. *Environmetrics*, **20**, 699–717.

Schlattmann, P. 2009. *Medical Applications of Finite Mixture Models*. Berlin: Springer-Verlag.

Schlossmacher, E. J. 1973. An iterative technique for absolute deviations curve fitting. *Journal of the American Statistical Association*, **68**(344), 857–859.

Schnabel, S. K., and Eilers, P. H. C. 2009. Optimal expectile smoothing. *Computational Statistics & Data Analysis*, **53**, 4168–4177.

Schnabel, S. K., and Eilers, P. H. C. 2013a. A location-scale model for non-crossing expectile curves. *Stat*, **2**(1), 171–183.

Schnabel, S. K., and Eilers, P. H. C. 2013b. Simultaneous estimation of quantile curves using quantile sheets. *ASTA – Advances in Statistical Analysis*, **97**, 77–87.

Schoenberg, I. J. 1964. Spline functions and the problem of graduation. *Proceedings of the American Mathematical Society*, **52**, 947–950.

Seber, G. A. F., and Lee, A. J. 2003. *Linear Regression Analysis*, 2nd ed. Hoboken, NJ: Wiley.

Selvin, S. 2019. *The Joy of Statistics: A Treasury of Elementary Statistical Tools and their Applications*. Oxford: Oxford University Press.

Silverman, B. W. 1986. *Density Estimation for Statistics and Data Analysis*. London: Chapman and Hall.

Stasinopoulos, M.D., and Rigby, R. A. 2007. Generalized additive models for location scale and shape (GAMLSS) in R. *Journal of Statistical Software*, **23**.

Stasinopoulos, M.D., Rigby, R. A., Heller, G. Z., Voudouris, V., and De Bastiani, F. 2017. *Flexible Regression and Smoothing*. Boca Raton, FL: Taylor & Francis Ltd.

Stone, M., and Brooks, R. J. 1990. Continuum regression: Cross-validated sequentially constructed prediction embracing ordinary least squares, partial least squares and principal component regression. *Journal of the Royal Statistical Society, Series B*, **52**, 237–269.

Thompson, R., and Baker, R. J. 1981. Composite link functions in generalized linear models. *Applied Statistics*, **30**, 125–131.

Tibshirani, R. J., Saunders, M., Rosset, S., Zhu, J., and Knight, K. 2005. Sparsity and smoothness via the fused lasso. *Journal of the Royal Statistical Society, Series B*, **67**, 9.

Umlauf, N., Adler, D., Kneib, T., Lang, S., and Zeileis, A. 2015. Structured additive regression models: An R interface to BayesX. *Journal of Statistical Software*, **63**(21), 1–46.

van Buuren, S. 2007. Worm plot to diagnose fit in quantile regression. *Statistical Modelling*, **7**(4), 363–376.

van Houwelingen, J. C., and Eilers, P. H. C. 2000. Non-proportional hazards models in survival analysis. In: Bethlehem, J. G. and van der Heijden, P. G. M.

(eds.), *COMPSTAT Proceedings in Computational Statistics 14th Symposium*, pp. 151–160. New York: Springer.

Velazco, J. G., Rodríguez-Alvarez, X. M., Boer, M. P., Jordan, D. R., Eilers, P. H. C., Malosetti, M., and van Eeuwijk, F. A. 2017. Modelling spatial trends in sorghum breeding field trials using a two-dimensional P-spline mixed model. *Theoretical and Applied Genetics*, **130**, 1375–1392.

Verbeek, S., Eilers, P. H. C., Lawrence, K., Hennekam, R. C. M., and Versteegh, F. G. A. 2011. Growth charts for children with Ellis–van Creveld syndrome. *European Journal of Pediatrics*, **170**, 207–211.

Verweij, P. J. M., and van Houwelingen, H. C. 1993. Cross-validation in survival analysis. *Statistics in Medicine*, **12**, 2305–2314.

Waltrup, L. S., Sobotka, F., Kneib, T., and Kauermann, G. 2015. Expectile and quantile regression – David and Goliath? *Statistical Modelling*, **15**(5), 433–456.

Wand, M. P., and Jones, M. C. 1995. *Kernel Smoothing*. London: Chapman and Hall.

Wand, M. P., and Ormerod, J. T. 2008. On semiparametric regression with O'Sullivan penalized splines. *Australian & New Zealand Journal of Statistics*, **50**, 179–198.

Wang, Y. 2011. *Smoothing Splines: Methods and Applications*. Boca Raton, FL: CRC Press.

Wang, Y., Yue, Y. R., and Faraway, J. J. 2018. *Bayesian Regression Modeling with INLA*. Boca Raton, FL: CRC Press.

Welham, S. J., Cullis, B. R., Kenward, M. G., and Thompson, R. 2006. The analysis of longitudinal data using mixed model L-splines. *Biometrics*, **62**, 392–401.

Whittaker, E. T. 1923. On a new method of graduation. *Proceedings of the Edinburgh Mathematical Society*, **41**, 63–75.

Wood, S. N. 2017. *Generalized Additive Models: An Introduction with R*, 2nd ed. Boca Raton, FL: CRC Press.

Wood, S. N., and Fasiolo, M. 2017. A generalized Fellner-Schall method for smoothing parameter optimization with application to Tweedie location, scale and shape models. *Biometrics*, **73**, 1071–1081.

Xiao, L., Li, Y., and Ruppert, D. 2013. Fast bivariate P-splines: The sandwich smoother. *Journal of the Royal Statistical Society, Series B*, **75**, 577–599.

Yavuz, A, C., and Lambert, P. 2016. Semi-parametric frailty model for clustered interval-censored data. *Statistical Modelling*, **16**, 360–391.

Ye, J. 1998. On measuring and correcting the effects of data mining and model selection. *Journal of the American Statistical Association*, **93**, 120–131.

Yu, Y., and Ruppert, D. 2002. Penalized spline estimation for partially linear single-index models. *Journal of the American Statistical Association*, **97**, 1042–1054.

Index